Routing
first-step

Bill Parkhurst

Cisco Press

800 East 96th Street

Indianapolis, IN 46240

Routing
first-step

Bill Parkhurst

Copyright© 2005 Cisco Systems, Inc.

Published by:
Cisco Press
800 East 96th Street
Indianapolis, IN 46240 USA

Printed in the United States of America   1 2 3 4 5 6 7 8 9 0

First Printing   September 2004

Library of Congress Cataloging-in-Publication Number: 2003116566

ISBN: 1587201224

Warning and Disclaimer

This book is designed to provide information about routing. Every effort has been made to make this book as complete and as accurate as possible, but no warranty or fitness is implied.

The information is provided on an "as is" basis. The author, Cisco Press, and Cisco Systems, Inc., shall have neither liability nor responsibility to any person or entity with respect to any loss or damages arising from the information contained in this book or from the use of the discs or programs that may accompany it.

The opinions expressed in this book belong to the author and are not necessarily those of Cisco Systems, Inc.

Publisher
John Wait

Editor-in-Chief
John Kane

Cisco Representative
Anthony Wolfenden

**Cisco Press
Program Manager**
Nannette M. Noble

Production Manager
Patrick Kanouse

Development Editor
Dayna Isley

Senior Project Editor
San Dee Phillips

Copy Editor
Laura Williams

Technical Editors
Mark Gallo
Tyler Hodges
Kevin Turek

Editorial Assistant
Tammi Barnett

**Book and
Cover Designer**
Louisa Adair

Composition
Mark Shirar

Indexer
Tim Wright

Proofreader
Karen A. Gill

iii

Trademark Acknowledgments

All terms mentioned in this book that are known to be trademarks or service marks have been appropriately capitalized. Cisco Press or Cisco Systems, Inc., cannot attest to the accuracy of this information. Use of a term in this book should not be regarded as affecting the validity of any trademark or service mark.

Corporate and Government Sales

Cisco Press offers excellent discounts on this book when ordered in quantity for bulk purchases or special sales.

For more information please contact: U.S. Corporate and Government Sales 1-800-382-3419 corpsales@pearsontechgroup.com

For sales outside the U.S. please contact: International Sales international@pearsoned.com

Feedback Information

At Cisco Press, our goal is to create in-depth technical books of the highest quality and value. Each book is crafted with care and precision, undergoing rigorous development that involves the unique expertise of members from the professional technical community.

Readers' feedback is a natural continuation of this process. If you have any comments regarding how we could improve the quality of this book, or otherwise alter it to better suit your needs, you can contact us through e-mail at feedback@ciscopress.com. Please make sure to include the book title and ISBN in your message.

We greatly appreciate your assistance.

CISCO SYSTEMS

Corporate Headquarters
Cisco Systems, Inc.
170 West Tasman Drive
San Jose, CA 95134-1706
USA
www.cisco.com
Tel: 408 526-4000
     800 553-NETS (6387)
Fax: 408 526-4100

European Headquarters
Cisco Systems International BV
Haarlerbergpark
Haarlerbergweg 13-19
1101 CH Amsterdam
The Netherlands
www-europe.cisco.com
Tel: 31 0 20 357 1000
Fax: 31 0 20 357 1100

Americas Headquarters
Cisco Systems, Inc.
170 West Tasman Drive
San Jose, CA 95134-1706
USA
www.cisco.com
Tel: 408 526-7660
Fax: 408 527-0883

Asia Pacific Headquarters
Cisco Systems, Inc.
Capital Tower
168 Robinson Road
#22-01 to #29-01
Singapore 068912
www.cisco.com
Tel: +65 6317 7777
Fax: +65 6317 7799

Cisco Systems has more than 200 offices in the following countries and regions. Addresses, phone numbers, and fax numbers are listed on the
Cisco.com Web site at www.cisco.com/go/offices.

Argentina • Australia • Austria • Belgium • Brazil • Bulgaria • Canada • Chile • China PRC • Colombia • Costa Rica • Croatia • Czech Republic
Denmark • Dubai, UAE • Finland • France • Germany • Greece • Hong Kong SAR • Hungary • India • Indonesia • Ireland • Israel • Italy
Japan • Korea • Luxembourg • Malaysia • Mexico • The Netherlands • New Zealand • Norway • Peru • Philippines • Poland • Portugal
Puerto Rico • Romania • Russia • Saudi Arabia • Scotland • Singapore • Slovakia • Slovenia • South Africa • Spain • Sweden
Switzerland • Taiwan • Thailand • Turkey • Ukraine • United Kingdom • United States • Venezuela • Vietnam • Zimbabwe

Copyright © 2003 Cisco Systems, Inc. All rights reserved. CCIP, CCSP, the Cisco Arrow logo, the Cisco *Powered* Network mark, the Cisco Systems Verified logo, Cisco Unity, Follow Me Browsing, FormShare, iQ Net Readiness Scorecard, Networking Academy, and ScriptShare are trademarks of Cisco Systems, Inc.; Changing the Way We Work, Live, Play, and Learn, The Fastest Way to Increase Your Internet Quotient, and iQuick Study are service marks of Cisco Systems, Inc.; and Aironet, ASIST, BPX, Catalyst, CCDA, CCDP, CCIE, CCNA, CCNP, Cisco, the Cisco Certified Internetwork Expert logo, Cisco IOS, the Cisco IOS logo, Cisco Press, Cisco Systems, Cisco Systems Capital, the Cisco Systems logo, Empowering the Internet Generation, Enterprise/Solver, EtherChannel, EtherSwitch, Fast Step, GigaStack, Internet Quotient, IOS, IP/TV, iQ Expertise, the iQ logo, LightStream, MGX, MICA, the Networkers logo, Network Registrar, *Packet*, PIX, Post-Routing, Pre-Routing, RateMUX, Registrar, SlideCast, SMARTnet, StrataView Plus, Stratm, SwitchProbe, TeleRouter, TransPath, and VCO are registered trademarks of Cisco Systems, Inc. and/or its affiliates in the U.S. and certain other countries.

All other trademarks mentioned in this document or Web site are the property of their respective owners. The use of the word partner does not imply a partnership relationship between Cisco and any other company. (0303R)

Printed in the USA

About the Author

Bill Parkhurst, Ph.D., CCIE No. 2969, is an advisory engineer at Cisco Systems and a technical advisor for Cisco certifications. Bill has taught networking to students on five continents at all levels, from beginner to advanced. Before joining Cisco, Bill taught networking at Wichita State University and now has the pleasure of working with many of his former students.

About the Technical Reviewers

Mark Gallo is a technical manager with America Online where he leads a group of engineers responsible for the design and deployment of the domestic corporate intranet. His network certifications include CCNP and CCDP. He has led several engineering groups responsible for designing and implementing enterprise LANs and international IP networks. He has a bachelor of science degree in electrical engineering from the University of Pittsburgh. Mark resides in northern Virginia with his wife, Betsy, and son, Paul.

Kevin Turek, CCIE No. 7284, joined Cisco in 2000 and is currently working as a network consulting engineer in the Cisco Federal Support Program in Research Triangle Park. He has been involved with several Cisco Press projects, including co-authoring the Cisco Press title *Cisco Catalyst QoS: Quality of Service in Campus Networks*. Kevin earned his bachelor of science degree in business administration at the State University of New York, Stony Brook.

Dedications

This book is dedicated to my daughter, Laura. I want to congratulate her on graduating from Kansas State University and taking her own first step. Now, if I can only get her to read this book.

Acknowledgments

I would like to acknowledge the effort and support of all those involved with the development of this book. From Cisco Press, I want to thank John Kane for having the confidence in me to suggest that I write this book; and Dayna Isley for her unmatched efforts in the development process, and for never letting me take the easy road. The technical reviewers, Mark Gallo and Kevin Turek, for diplomatically finding and pointing out errors, and for their insight regarding the content and flow. I want to especially thank my friend Tyler Hodges for reviewing this book from the perspective of a young and open mind. Tyler's comments were extremely helpful in ensuring this book was appropriate for the intended audience, and that everything was explained clearly. Finally, I want to thank my wife, Debbie, for her support during the writing of this book, and for the initial proofreading she did to make sure I appeared literate to my editors and reviewers.

Contents at a Glance

Contents

Introduction

Over the last decade, the Internet has grown from an interesting research project to a ubiquitous form of communication that has forever changed our world. E-mail, instant messaging, IP telephony, music and video on-demand, online banking, gaming, and travel planning are but a few of the many applications that have made many of our lives more convenient. In time, the Internet will eventually be available to everyone—and we can only guess what applications are to come. But whatever form the Internet takes, and whatever applications become available, there is an ever-increasing need for people to design, deploy, support, manage, teach, and sell these technologies.

The Cisco Press First-Step series is the starting point for understanding the basics of computer networking, and this book covers the concepts and protocols that enable the transfer of information from anywhere to anywhere using computer networks. No prior knowledge is assumed and each new concept is explained in understandable terms, allowing you to grasp the concepts without getting lost in the lingo. Of course, you will learn some of the lingo of the trade, but I assure you that it will be painless (mostly). The following description of the chapters in this book will give you an idea of what is in store for you:

- Chapter 1, "Routing and Switching in Everyday Life"—Examines familiar systems, such as postal, highway, and phone, that route information similar to the Internet. These systems are used to present an understanding of the concepts and terminology of routing and switching.

- Chapter 2, "$A_{16} B_{16} C_{16}$, As Easy As 01_2, 10_2, 11_2"—Covers number systems used by networking professionals. If you like numbers, this chapter should be fun. If you don't like numbers, hopefully this chapter will change your mind.

- Chapter 3, "Internet Addressing and Routing"—Uses the concepts learned in the first two chapters to discuss the addressing scheme used in computer networks in detail.

- Chapter 4, "Routing IP"—Introduces network routing, basic configuration of Cisco routers, and RIP, one of the first network routing protocols.

- Chapter 5, "Cisco Interior Gateway Protocols"—Describes the basic concepts and configuration of the Cisco routing protocols: IGRP and EIGRP.

- Chapter 6, "Open Shortest Path First—Better, Stronger, Faster"—Introduces OSPF, a popular standards-based routing protocol used in many networks. After reading this chapter, you will understand the concepts, operation, and configuration of OSPF.

- Chapter 7, "Intermediate System-to-Intermediate System—Better, Stronger, Faster, and Scarier"—Describes IS-IS, which is similar to OSPF but has a few differences that tend to scare people away from using it. This chapter will remove the mystery and darkness that surrounds IS-IS.

- Chapter 8, "Border Gateway Protocol—The Glue That Holds the Internet Together"—The routing protocols covered in Chapters 4 through 7 are used in the networks of companies, universities, government agencies, and so on. The Internet is what ties all these networks together, and BGP is the protocol that holds it all together.

- Chapter 9, "Multicast—What the Post Office Can't Do"—Presents the concepts and routing protocols used to simultaneously send information to more than one recipient, something the post office can't do.

- Appendix A, "Answers to Chapter Review Questions"—Each chapter ends with a "Chapter Review Questions" section that helps reinforce your understanding of the topics discussed. This appendix repeats the questions and provides the answers.

- Glossary—Throughout this book many new terms will be introduced and defined. These new terms are all listed in the glossary for easy reference.

Who Should Read This Book

This book, and this series, is for anyone interested in starting down the road of learning about the many facets of computer networking. The First-Step series can give you a solid foundation to forge ahead into any area of networking you find interesting. If you are in high school and are exploring possible career goals, if you are a college student and want to see if this field is something you might be interested in pursuing, if you are already working in another hi-tech field and are considering a career change, or if your company depends on computer networks but you only need to understand the basics for making the right business decisions, this book is for you.

If you are interested in checking out other books in the First-Step series, visit http://www.ciscopress.com/firststep for more information.

What You Will Find in This Book

This book includes several features to help ease the process of learning about routing:

- **Chapter objectives**–Every chapter begins with a list of objectives that are addressed in the chapter. The objectives are revisited in the chapter summary.

- **Highlighted key terms and Glossary**–Throughout this book, you will see terms formatted with bold and italic. These terms are particularly significant in routing. If you find that you aren't familiar with the term or that you need a refresher, look up the term in the Glossary toward the end of the book to find a full definition.

- **Chapter summaries**–Every chapter concludes with a comprehensive summary that reviews chapter objectives, ensuring complete coverage.

- **Chapter review questions**–Every chapter concludes with review questions. These questions test the basic ideas and concepts covered in each chapter. You can find the answers to the questions in Appendix A.

- **Examples**—In networking, you will encounter router configurations and output. To help prepare you, this book provides basic configuration and output examples that are thoroughly explained in the text and, when necessary, annotated.

The illustrations in this book use the following icons for networking devices:

PC   Router   Switch   Network Cloud

What You Will Learn

After reading this chapter, you should be able to

- ✔ Understand the concepts of routing and switching using familiar systems (postal, road, and telephone)

- ✔ Understand the properties of a routable address and how various parts of the address are used to route something from point A to point B

- ✔ Understand the concept of route summarization, or aggregation, at the core and distribution level for reducing the amount of information required in the routing tables at these levels

CHAPTER 1

Routing and Switching in Everyday Life

The Internet is nothing new. Think about that statement. Certainly the technologies are new and applications such as e-mail, instant messaging, web sites, and video on demand are new, but the concepts are not. How the Internet operates is conceptually no different than how the postal, highway, and telephone systems operate. They all perform the same function—getting things from one place to another. The postal system does this with mail, the highway system does this with families on vacation and produce from California, and the phone system does this with phone calls. This book is about getting things from here to there. If you understand the concepts behind the postal, highway, and phone systems, you can understand the concepts of computer networks. After the concepts are mastered, learning the details of how it all works is easy. So before we jump off into the amazing world of the Internet, let's take the time to look at systems you are already familiar with.

Postal System

First, let's take an imaginary trip back in time and pretend it's your job to develop a system for delivering letters and packages, and whatever else people can think of sending, to anyone anywhere in the country. So, where do you start? I think the best place to start is to establish rules. If your system has any chance of working, you need everyone to follow a clear set of rules. You also want to give your set of rules a fancy name so when you present your plan you sound somewhat authoritative.

Consulting your pocket dictionary, you find that a set of rules is also a set of conventions that is referred to as a *protocol*. That sounds fancy enough, so let's call your set of rules a protocol.

How many protocols do you need? That depends on how you structure the mail delivery system, so you need to think about how the system operates. Ultimately, you need to deliver something from point A to point B. These points can be located anywhere in the country.

After some serious thought, you decide you need to develop the following protocols:

- **Package Protocol (PP)**—The type and parameters (size, weight, contents, and so on) of the mail that can be delivered.

- **Addressing Protocol (AP)**—Where is the item coming from and where is it going to.

- **Delivery Protocol (DP)**—What is the most efficient way to deliver an item from point A to point B.

- **Transportation Protocol (TP)**—How to physically deliver the mail to the proper recipient.

These are not protocols used by the post office, of course, but are used for the purpose of the discussion regarding the routing of mail.

In addition, the protocols should be as independent as possible and scalable. Independence means that the operation of one protocol should not depend on other protocols. For example, the type of mail sent should not affect the addressing protocol. You don't want to use one addressing protocol for letters and another for packages. If you send a letter to your mother and a birthday present to your sister, you would have to use the same format for the address on both. For example, you might change the protocol specifying the location of the address on a letter, or package, or include additional information in the address (a ZIP code, for example). You should be able to do this without affecting which route the mail takes to its final destination.

The delivery protocol will make a delivery, or routing, decision based on the address. In that sense, the delivery protocol is dependent on the addressing protocol. You, however, want the freedom to change the addressing protocol without having to change the delivery protocol. Finally, the means that you use for the physical delivery of the mail (horse and wagon, truck, and so on) should not be dependent on what is actually being sent. With these constraints in mind, you can create a layered model called the Mail System Layered Protocol Model shown in Figure 1-1.

Figure 1-1   Mail System Layered Protocol Model

Package	What is being sent?
Address	Where is it going? Where is it from?
Delivery	What is the best route to use for delivery?
Transportation	How will the mail physically be delivered?

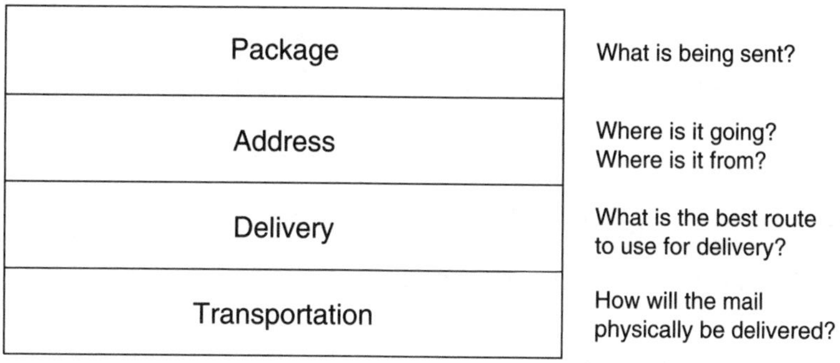

A *scalable protocol* means that the protocols still work well as the size of the system grows. For example, assume that mail will be delivered only between Chicago and Kansas City, and you will allow only one piece of mail every week. Because this is a small volume of mail, you hire someone with a horse to make the delivery. Assume this system works well, and you increase the volume to two pieces of mail per week. You could hire another person with a horse, but now you have two people to pay and two horses to feed. If you follow this method, you cannot scale your system to deliver thousands of pieces of mail because this would require thousands of people and thousands of horses! This system does not scale. You should require each rider to carry as much mail as possible so the system can scale to accommodate higher volumes of mail.

Now that you have decided which protocols are required, you need to determine the details of each protocol.

Package Protocol

The Package Protocol, or PP, is a relatively straightforward protocol. You have to decide what can be sent and the physical limitations of a piece of mail, such as size and weight.

Addressing Protocol

To deliver mail, you need to know where a particular piece of mail is going. In addition, it would be nice to know where a piece of mail came from in case it has to be returned. Therefore, you need a set of addressing rules that are part of our Addressing Protocol (AP). The two rules you need for the AP are the following:

- To Address rule that identifies where the mail is going

- From Address rule that identifies where the mail came from

But again, To Address and From Address are not sophisticated terms. Remember you do want your plan to sound sophisticated. Instead of To Address and From Address, use *destination address* and *source address* in your AP.

The addresses in the protocol need a defined structure. In other words, what information must be contained in a destination or source address? If an address contains multiple pieces of information, in what order should this information be presented? For the destination address, you need to know

- Who the mail is going to

- Where they live (state, city, street, and street number)

For the source address, you need to know

- Who the mail is from

- Where they live (state, city, street, and street number)

The addressing protocol needs to describe the exact location on the package for the source and destination addresses so they can easily be found. You also need to decide the placement order of the information contained in an address. After experimenting with a number of address placement schemes, as shown in Figure 1-2, you decide to use the format shown in Figure 1-2 d. The beauty of this scheme is that it applies regardless of the type of letter or package sent through our mail system. Could the other schemes have been used? Yes. You only need to choose one and be consistent.

Figure 1-2   Rules for Source and Destination Address Placement

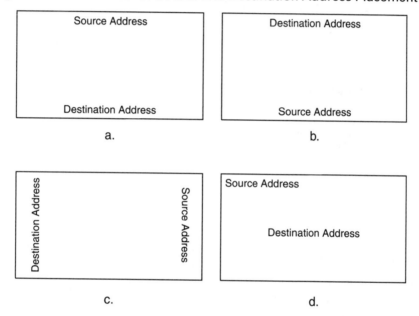

Various address information-ordering schemes were examined. (See Figure 1-3.) You have decided on the scheme in Figure 1-3 c. The other schemes would work just as well, of course, but you need to choose one and be consistent.

Figure 1-3 Address Ordering Schemes

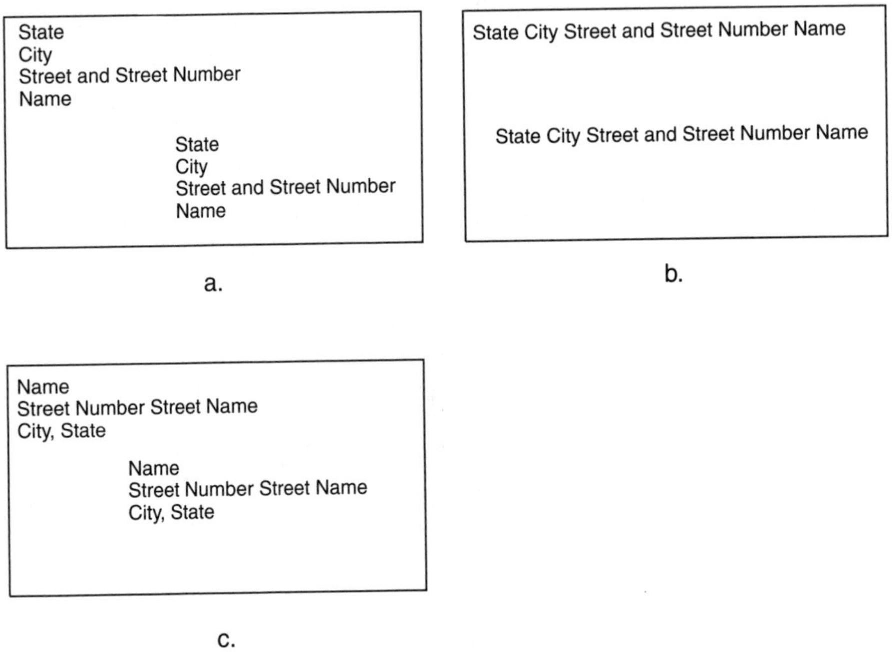

```
State
City
Street and Street Number
Name

            State
            City
            Street and Street Number
            Name
```
a.

```
State City Street and Street Number Name


State City Street and Street Number Name
```
b.

```
Name
Street Number Street Name
City, State

          Name
          Street Number Street Name
          City, State
```
c.

The previous comment might seem obvious, but it is extremely important. Imagine a mail delivery system where the addressing information and placement are different for each type of letter, or package, that is delivered. By having an address-ordering scheme, it doesn't matter what you send—the addressing scheme is the same, independent of the type of letter or package.

Now that you have a workable addressing protocol, the next step is to develop a protocol for mail delivery.

Mail Delivery Protocol

The Mail Delivery Protocol, or MDP, is concerned with examining the information required by the AP and making a delivery decision. Mail will be delivered based on the destination address portion of the AP. The source address is needed if the mail needs to be returned. In that situation, the source address would become the destination address. Let's look at the information contained in the destination address, and see what you can use to make a delivery decision. The destination address contains

- Who the mail is going to

- Where they live (state, city, street, street number)

Further assume that all delivery facilities (post offices) will use all the information in the destination address to determine how to deliver the package. This being the case, every post office needs to maintain a list of every possible destination address—which would be every person in the country. This approach has many problems. The first problem is that each post office will need to maintain a big book that contains everyone's address. The second problem is that whenever any-one moves, or when someone immigrates to the United States, or emigrates from the United States, every address book at every post office would need to be updated. This scheme will simply not work. It is, in fact, unscalable. What you need is a MDP that will scale.

Go back and look at the information contained in the destination address and see if you can devise a delivery system that scales. You have already seen that main-taining a list of every person at every post office will not work. Can you devise a system that uses only parts of the destination address? The geographical relation between the source and the destination might provide us with ideas for setting up a scalable system for the delivery of mail at the local, city, state, and country levels.

Local Delivery

Local delivery is for mail with the same street name, city name, and state name in both the destination and source addresses. The additional information that is needed to deliver the mail is the house number. You do not need the information regarding to whom the package is being delivered. The MDP's job is over when the package arrives at the proper address. Consider two schemes for local mail delivery. The first scheme is called the Broadcast Local Delivery Protocol (BLDP) as shown in Figure 1-4.

Figure 1-4   Broadcast Local Delivery Protocol (BLDP)

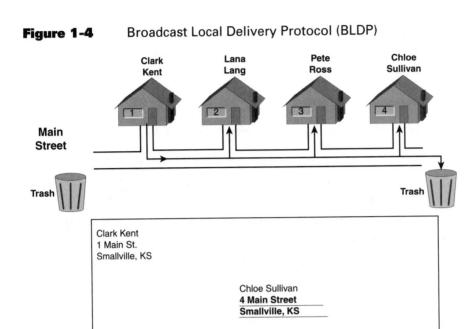

In Figure 1-4, Clark sends a letter to Chloe. The mail carrier looks at all the information in the destination address except for the "who" component. If the street name is Main, the city name is Smallville, and the state name is Kansas, the letter carrier will take the letter to every house on Main Street and ask the resident if the letter is for them. If it is, the letter has been delivered. If not, the carrier moves on to the next house. If the letter has not been delivered after visiting the last house, the carrier will throw the letter away or return it to Clark.

What if the street name is not Main? Or the destination address has a different city or state name? At this point, you haven't come up with a way to handle this situation, but you will in the following sections.

You're probably wondering why you would even consider such a goofy way to deliver the mail. In the early days of computer networking, this is essentially how computers exchanged mail. As shown in Figure 1-5, a coaxial cable, like the type used for cable television, connected local computers.

Figure 1-5   Shared LAN

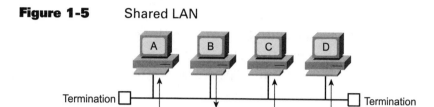

If computer B wanted to send a message to computer A, computer B would set the destination and source addresses to A and B, respectively. (Yes, computers have addresses. In fact, they typically have more than one address. We will get to that in Chapter 3, "Internet Addressing and Routing.") The message was transmitted on the cable, and every computer connected to the cable received the message. Every computer had to take the time to examine the destination address and decide if the message was for them. If it wasn't, the message was discarded. The terminations shown in Figure 1-5 serve the same purpose as the trashcans in Figure 1-4. They absorb the signal on the cable having the effect of throwing the signal away.

This was an inexpensive way to create a network of local computers, or a local-area network (LAN). All you had to do was buy a network card for each computer, run a cable from computer to computer, and connect the computers to the cable. It was inexpensive, but it had a number of annoying problems. If there was a break anywhere in the cable, the communication was lost between all computers. And if your cable was running between computers on multiple floors, it could take some time to find the break. The longer it took to find the break, the more upset the computer users became.

In addition, because the cable was a shared media, only one computer at a time could use the cable for communication. How did the computers know whose turn it was to use the cable? They didn't. So they had to be able to detect a collision, which happens when two or more computers try to send something at the same time. As more people were connected to the network, the number of collisions increased, and the network became slower. Result? More upset computer users.

Ethernet was the name given to the predominant technology used for computer communication on a LAN. Before Einstein, scientists thought that the universe had to contain a substance through which light could travel. Otherwise, how could the light from distant stars reach Earth? This substance was given the name ether. The existence of ether was later disproved, but I guess someone involved with the early development of networks liked the term. Because computer communication had to travel through something, why not call it the ether? And because we are talking about networks, just use the term *Ethernet*.

Every Ethernet network card has an address called an Ethernet address. An example of an Ethernet address is 00-03-47-92-9C-6F. We make sense of that in Chapter 3.

Obviously, you do not want to use the previous method for local mail delivery. You would need a mail carrier for every street, and that does not scale. A better method is to use a local post office that has the responsibility for receiving and delivering mail to the local area. In Figure 1-6, Clark sends a letter to Pete. The letter is first sent to the local post office where the destination address is examined. Because the street, city, and state in the destination address is a street that this local post office serves, the letter is switched back to Pete's house on Main Street. The street names are the same, so the switch has to use only the house number to deliver the mail.

As technology improved, a better method for connecting computers on a LAN was developed, and it is similar to the local "switching" of mail. The switch in Figure 1-7 serves the same purpose as the local post office.

Figure 1-6   Switched Local Mail Delivery

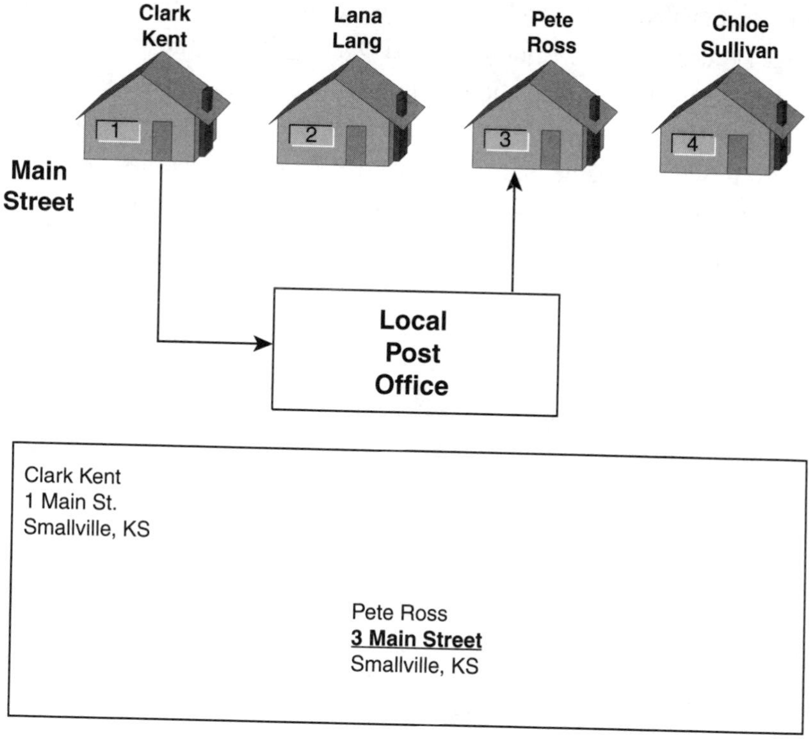

Clark
Kent

Lana
Lang

Pete
Ross

Chloe
Sullivan

1   2   3   4

Main
Street

Local
Post
Office

Clark Kent
1 Main St.
Smallville, KS

Pete Ross
3 Main Street
Smallville, KS

Figure 1-7   Switched LAN

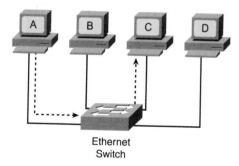

A   B   C   D

Ethernet
Switch

When computer A wants to send a message to computer C, the message is sent to the Ethernet switch. The switch looks at the destination address and sends the message to computer C. Computers B and D never receive the message. How does the switch know which connection, or port, goes to computer C? Initially, it doesn't. The switch has to learn the location of every computer on the network, and build a switching table that contains a listing of each computer's address, and the port to which it is connected. When the switch in Figure 1-8 is first installed, the switching table is empty.

Figure 1-8   LAN Switching Table

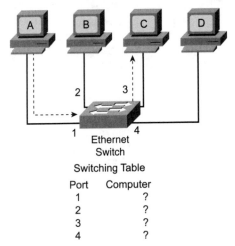

When the switch receives a message from computer A, the switch learns that computer A is on port 1. How? The message was received on port 1, and the source address is A, so the switch knows which computer sent the message. The destination address is computer C, but the switch does not know to which port computer C is connected. In this case, the switch sends the message out all ports except for the one on which it was received. Therefore, computers B and D receive the message even though it was not addressed to them. Eventually, the switch learns on which port each computer is connected. Of course, that assumes that each computer eventually sends a message. After the switching table is complete, the switch is able to forward the message to the computer for which it was meant. Table 1-1 contains the final switching table.

Table 1-1   Final Switching Table

Port	Computer
1	A
2	B
3	C
4	D

Because the switching method of delivering mail seems to make the most sense, you adopt that as your local mail delivery method. Time to move on to local off-street delivery.

Local Off-Street Delivery

Local off-street delivery is for mail on different streets in the same city and state that can be accessed by the same post office. The information required to deliver the package is the street, city, state, and house number. You still do not need the who from the destination address. Previously, you ignored the issue of what to do if the source address was on a different street. Figure 1-9 shows how you can handle local off-street mail. Because it doesn't make sense to have a separate post office act as a switch for every street (it does not scale), you assign a number of streets in an area to a single post office. Each post office has access to more than one street, and acts as the switch when sending mail between houses on the same street.

Figure 1-9 Mail Switched Between Houses on the Same Street and Routed Between Houses on Different Streets

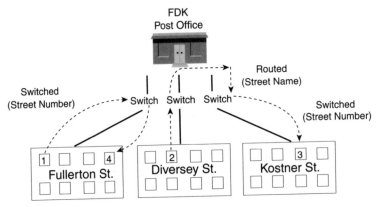

When a letter is sent from 1 Fullerton St. to 4 Fullerton St., the post office examines the destination street, city, and state names. The destination street, city, and state names are the same as the source street, city, and state names; so the letter is switched back to the proper house on Fullerton Street. If a letter is sent from 2 Diversey St. to 3 Kostner St., the local switch determines that it is not connected to Kostner Street. In this case, the switch forwards the letter to the FDK post office. Although the switch is located at the FDK post office, you can think of the post office having a separate switch and router department.

Upon receipt of the letter by the FDK post office, the source address is examined to make a decision on where to route the letter. Therefore, the FDK post office is acting as a router. Because the FDK post office has direct access to the street switches, the FDK post office is an *access router*. The layer in the mail delivery process containing the access router is called the *access layer*.

Just as the switches used a switching table, a router needs a routing table to determine how to route a particular piece of mail. The FDK post office is connected to three streets, and we will call the connection to these streets an interface. (See Table 1-2.)

Table 1-2   FDK Post Office Routing Table

Street	City	State	Interface
Fullerton	Chicago	Illinois	1
Diversey	Chicago	Illinois	2
Kostner	Chicago	Illinois	3

When a letter arrives at the FDK post office, the letter is routed on the street name and sent to the appropriate switch through the proper interface. The switch then switches the letter to the proper house using the house number. Off-street mail delivery is analogous to how multiple LANs can be connected using routers. If you replace the FDK post office with a router, you will have the configuration necessary for delivering messages between computers on different LANs in the same location. In Figure 1-10, an access router has replaced the FDK post office, and the computer network counterparts have replaced their respective switches.

Figure 1-10   Router Enables Communication Between LANs

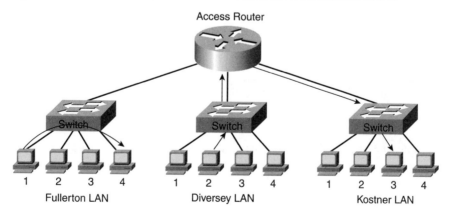

As with mail delivery, when computer 1 on the Fullerton LAN sends a message to computer 4 on the Fullerton LAN, the message is sent to the local switch. Because both computers are on the same LAN, the switch sends the message out the proper port to computer 4. When computer 2 on the Diversey LAN sends a message to computer 3 on the Kostner LAN, the switch forwards the message to the router because the destination is on a different LAN. The access router is directly connected to the switch that services the Kostner LAN, so the router forwards the message out the selected interface to the appropriate switch that switches the message out the proper port to computer 3.

Now you are able to use your off-street mail delivery scheme to develop a citywide mail delivery system.

Citywide Delivery

A citywide mail delivery system can be realized by connecting the access post offices together using a *distribution post office*. (See Figure 1-11.)

Figure 1-11   System for Citywide Mail Delivery

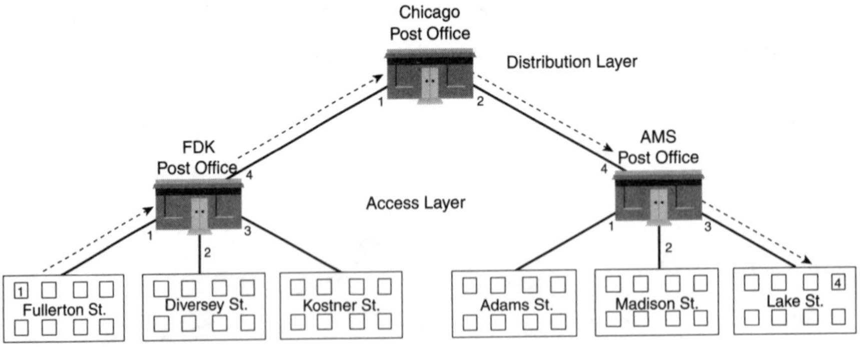

To see how the distribution layer operates, you will trace the delivery of the letter shown in Figure 1-12.

Figure 1-12   Street, City, and State Are Used to Make a Delivery Decision

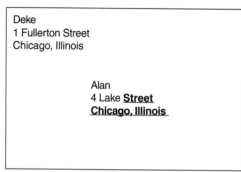

The letter is sent to FDK, the local access post office. Because the destination street is not connected to one of the FDK interfaces, the FDK post office must send the letter to the Chicago distribution post office. How does FDK know to send the letter to the Chicago distribution post office? There must be a rule telling FDK that if it receives a letter for a street that it is not connected to, by default, the letter is sent to the distribution post office. But what if the letter has a destination address that is not in the same city or state? The same rule applies. Any destination address that an access post office is not aware of is sent to the distribution post office. By default, any destination address that is not on Fullerton, Diversey, or Kostner streets is sent to the distribution post office.

For delivery to be successful between access post offices, the *default route* must be added to the routing tables for FDK and AMS. (See Tables 1-3 and 1-4.)

Table 1-3   FDK Post Office Routing Table

Street	City	State	Interface
Fullerton	Chicago	Illinois	1
Diversey	Chicago	Illinois	2
Kostner	Chicago	Illinois	3
Default	Default	Default	4

Table 1-4   AMS Post Office Routing Table

Street	City	State	Interface
Adams	Chicago	Illinois	1
Madison	Chicago	Illinois	2
Lake	Chicago	Illinois	3
Default	Default	Default	4

When the Chicago post office receives the letter, a routing decision must be made based on the destination address. It is not sufficient to examine only the street name as the same street name can exist in different cities. Also, it is not sufficient to examine only the street and city names because there can be more than one city with the name Chicago. The distribution router must use the state, city, and street names to make a delivery decision—but not the street number or name of the recipient.

The Chicago post office knows about FDK and AMS because they are directly connected. To know about the street names that are serviced by FDK and AMS, Chicago needs a delivery or routing table similar to the routing table for the FDK and AMS post offices. (Refer to Tables 1-3 and 1-4.) The routing table for Chicago needs to contain a list of street names, and the interface to be used to reach these street names. (See Table 1-5.)

Table 1-5   Chicago Distribution Post Office Routing Table

Street	City	State	Interface
Fullerton	Chicago	Illinois	1
Diversey	Chicago	Illinois	1
Kostner	Chicago	Illinois	1
Adams	Chicago	Illinois	2
Madison	Chicago	Illinois	2
Lake	Chicago	Illinois	2

How do these values get into the routing table? The first way is to use static routes. A static route is manually entered into the routing table and does not change unless someone manually makes the change. The major problem with a static route is that there is no way to determine if the route actually exists. If the AMS post office burns down, Chicago thinks it still has a route to AMS because there is a static route in the routing table pointing to AMS. Mail could be delivered to a post office that is no longer there. Another method of placing routes in the routing table is to do so dynamically using a routing protocol. A routing protocol can be used to dynamically change the contents of the routing table when changes occur. We are not ready to discuss routing protocols just yet, so for now you will use only static routes.

Now consider the delivery of the letter with the Chicago routing table in place. FDK examines the street, city, and state names in the destination address. The street name is not known, so FDK consults its routing table and determines that the default says to use interface 4 and send the letter to the Chicago post office. The Chicago post office consults its routing table, looking for an entry that matches the street, city, and state names in the destination address. A match is made, and the letter is sent to the AMS post office using interface 2. AMS receives the letter, and routes it out interface 3 to the Lake Street switch. The Lake Street switch then switches the letter to the destination based on the street number.

You created a citywide mail delivery system by adding another layer of delivery, or routing, called the distribution layer. Using the same process, you can now build a statewide mail delivery service by adding another routing layer to our system.

Statewide Delivery

Statewide delivery is for mail having the same state in both the destination and source addresses. The information required to deliver the mail is the city name, street name, and street number. Who receives the mail is still not used. To enable statewide delivery, another routing layer is added above the distribution layer. (See Figure 1-13.) This additional layer is called the core layer and is used for interstate and statewide delivery. For clarity, the AMS post office is not shown in Figure 1-13, although the routes for AMS are included in the routing table. (See Table 1-6.)

Figure 1-13 Core Delivery Layer Is Used for Statewide Delivery

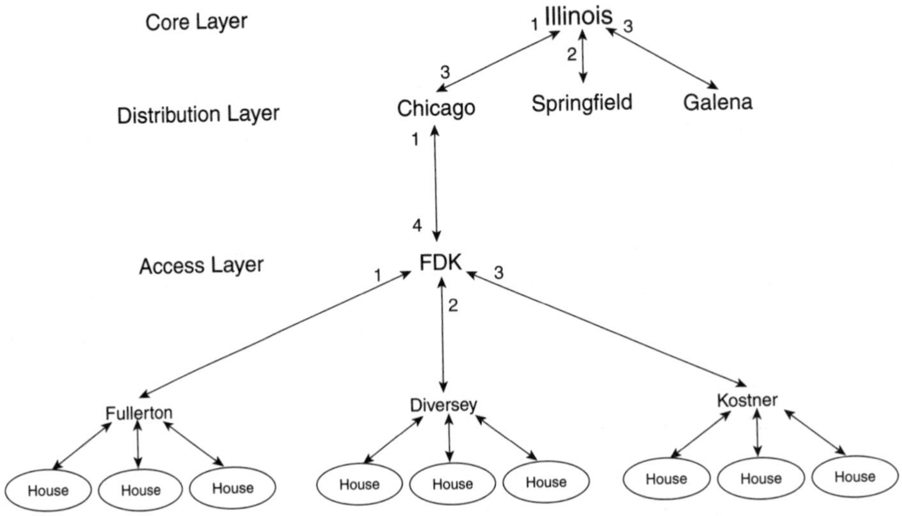

When the *core post office* is added for the state of Illinois, a default route needs to be added to the routing table for the Chicago post office (See Table 1-6.)

Table 1-6 New Chicago Distribution Post Office Routing Table

Street	City	State	Interface
Fullerton	Chicago	Illinois	1
Diversey	Chicago	Illinois	1
Kostner	Chicago	Illinois	1
Adams	Chicago	Illinois	2
Madison	Chicago	Illinois	2
Lake	Chicago	Illinois	2
Default	Chicago	Illinois	3

When a letter is sent between cities in the same state, both the access and distribution routers will use their default routes and the letter will be delivered to the core router for the state. At this point, the function of the core router is to route mail between cities in the same state, so the only information that is required in the routing table is the city name (assuming the cities are in the state of Illinois).

Table 1-7 State of Illinois Post Office Routing Table

City	State	Interface
Chicago	Illinois	1
Springfield	Illinois	2
Galena	Illinois	3

The core router for the state of Illinois will only examine the city and state information in the destination address to make a delivery or routing decision. Now that you have a scalable model for statewide delivery of the mail, you can easily expand your system to handle mail delivery for the country by connecting the core routers for each state.

Countrywide Delivery

Figure 1-14 shows a partial view of our countrywide mail delivery system. The core routers for Illinois, Missouri, and Kansas have been interconnected to enable the delivery of mail between these states.

Figure 1-14 Core Layer Is Used for Interstate Mail Delivery

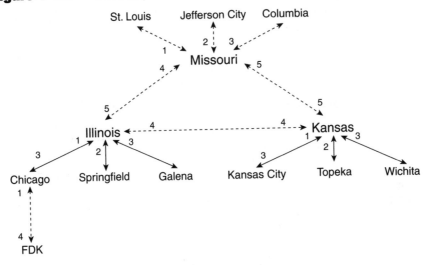

Previously, when you added a new layer of routing, you had to add a default route to the routing table of the post office at the next lowest layer. For the core routers to deliver mail between states, you need to add specific routes for specific states (as shown in Table 1-8) for the state of Illinois post office. Now that there are two routes from Illinois to Kansas, and two routes from Illinois to Missouri (a direct connection to the state and an indirect connection through the other state), you need to determine how to handle multiple routes. The best connection to Kansas is directly to Kansas. But if that route is unavailable because of a bridge or road being out, you need to be able to use the other route as a backup. You can accomplish this by adding a cost to the route, and using the route with the lowest cost. If the route with the lowest cost is unavailable, use the other route. The cost of a route could represent distance, time, or any other factor that can be used to determine if one route is better than another route.

Table 1-8   State of Illinois Post Office Routing Table

State	City	Interface	Cost
Illinois	Chicago	1	1
Illinois	Springfield	2	1
Illinois	Galena	3	1
Kansas	Not Needed	4	1 (Best)
Kansas	Not Needed	5	2
Missouri	Not Needed	5	1 (Best)
Missouri	Not Needed	4	2

Notice in the routing table for the state of Illinois, as shown in Table 1-8, that less specific information is needed for delivery between states than is needed for delivery within the state. Mail destined for a different state than the core post office does not need to know the city name.

Finally, our plan for delivering mail throughout the United States is almost complete. Let's revisit how much information is required at each level of the system: core, distribution, and access.

At the beginning of the chapter, you decided that every post office did not need to know about every destination because this approach will not scale. Why is that?

If the core router for the state of Illinois needed to know about every destination, the routing table would be enormous. Every city in every state in the United States would have an entry in the routing table associating each city/state combination with an interface that is used to forward the mail along the proper route. If a new city is built or an old one ceases to exist, every routing table in every core post office would need to change, and this is not feasible. What you have achieved with your scheme is called *aggregation*, which is also known as *information hiding* or *summarization*.

Aggregation means that at the core post office level, the routing table entry for an interstate destination contains only the state information and an output interface. The core router does not need to maintain a route for every destination in the state. The core post office does need to maintain a route for cities in the state it services, and not the final destination in each of those cities. This makes the core routing table scalable; and it hides information regarding changes to destinations in other states, or connected cities. Therefore, if new houses are built or people move, the core post office does not care. What it needs to know is how to get mail to that state or city–and not who lives there or where they live.

Distribution post offices need only to know about the access-level post offices they are connected to and what streets they serve. As you have seen, a default route can be used to reach other destinations.

At the lowest level, the access routers maintain routes for streets that they service and have a default route for all other destinations.

Our system relies on static routing table entries to move the mail along in the proper direction. As the system grows, this will become an administrative nightmare. Eventually, you need to replace static routing with dynamic routing, but you have to wait a few chapters before we get there.

Before moving on to the next familiar system, you will trace a letter from Illinois to Kansas to see how the various layers of our postal delivery system operate. You will use a trace letter as shown in Figure 1-15, and see how it moves through our system illustrated in Figure 1-16.

Figure 1-15   Letter from Chicago to Kansas City

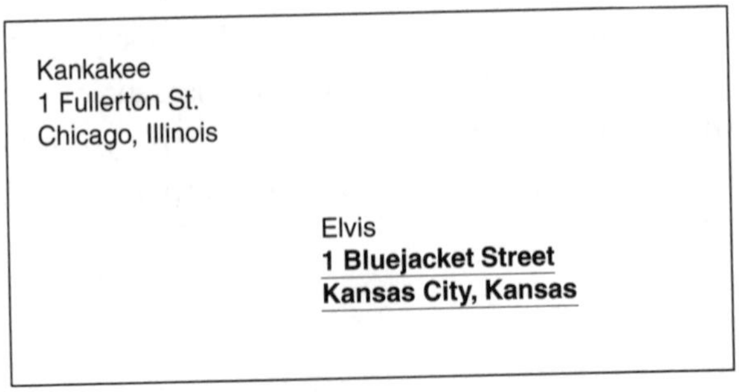

Kankakee
1 Fullerton St.
Chicago, Illinois

Elvis
1 Bluejacket Street
Kansas City, Kansas

Figure 1-16   Tracing a Letter from Chicago to Kansas City

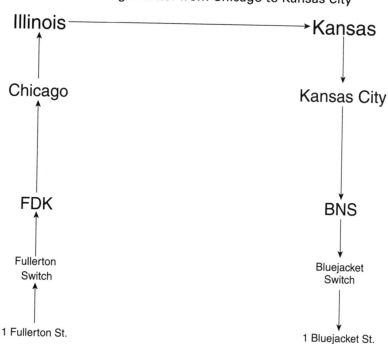

The following describes the process for delivering the letter from Illinois to Kansas:

1. Deliver the letter from Fullerton Street to the Fullerton switch.

2. The Fullerton switch must make a delivery decision on the street, city, and state names:

   Elvis

   1 Bluejacket Street

   Kansas City, Kansas

3. The Fullerton switch does not know the street name, so it forwards to the FDK post office.

4. The FDK post office must make a delivery decision on the street, city, and state names:

Elvis

1 Bluejacket Street

Kansas City, Kansas

5. The FDK post office does not know the street name, so it forwards to the Chicago post office.

6. The Chicago post office must make a delivery decision on the city name:

Elvis

1 Bluejacket Street

Kansas City, Kansas

7. The Chicago post office doesn't know the city name, so it forwards to the state of Illinois post office.

8. The state of Illinois post office must make a delivery decision on the state name:

Elvis

1 Bluejacket Street

Kansas City, Kansas

9. The Illinois post office forwards the letter to the Kansas post office.

10. The Kansas post office must make a delivery decision on the state and city names:

Elvis

1 Bluejacket Street

Kansas City, Kansas

11. The state of Kansas post office forwards to the Kansas City post office.

12. The Kansas City post office must make a delivery decision on the street, city, and state names:

    Elvis

    1 Bluejacket Street

    Kansas City, Kansas

13. The Kansas City post office forwards to the BNS post office.

14. The BNS post office must make a delivery decision on the street, city, and state names:

    Elvis

    1 Bluejacket Street

    Kansas City, Kansas

15. The BNS post office forwards to the Bluejacket switch.

16. The Bluejacket switch sends the letter to the destination using the street number.

The concept to take away from this exercise is that as the mail moves toward a core post office, less information is used in the destination address to make a forwarding decision. As the letter moves from the core post office to the local switch post office, more specific information is needed to make a delivery or routing decision. This concept of core, distribution, and access can be applied to other systems as well. Are you ready for a trip?

Highway System

Now plan a road trip from Chicago to San Jose. Assume you have just moved to Chicago, you are not yet familiar with the area, and you need help getting out of the city. Before you plan your route, you first need to know where you are going and where you are coming from. Does that sound familiar? This is not unlike using the source and destination addresses in your postal system. Certainly to begin planning the route, you must know where you are starting; but after you begin to drive, your route is determined by where you are going.

To help plan your trip, you need a road map. How many road maps do you need? Assume that you can find one map that can be used to plan your route. A map of the United States—with every road in every city—would be perfect. One map for all our planning needs. Yet, there would be several problems in having just one map. First, the amount of information that one map would need to contain would be astronomical. Second, it would be hard to fold.

So, the one-map solution is not scalable. A map containing every destination in a city is possible, but this will not scale to the state or national level. Just as requiring every post office to know everyone's address was not scalable. You need to have a scalable map solution, so let's turn to the structure of our postal delivery system and see if you can get some ideas.

The postal system was divided into three general components:

- An access layer for routing mail to or from local postal customers, and for routing mail to the distribution layer for deliveries outside the local area.

- A distribution layer for routing mail between access layers, or between the access and core layers.

- A core layer for routing mail between distribution layers or other core post offices.

If you follow the postal scheme for your map scheme, you need three types of maps—access, distribution, and core.

The access map would be used for our local area, or city. So call this a city map. The distribution map would take us from the city to the state highway system, so you need a state map. Finally, you need a core map that you can use to route yourself from the state highway system to the interstate highway system—or a U.S. map. Using the U.S. map in Figure 1-17, you determine that Interstate 80 is the core highway to use to get from your starting point in Chicago to your destination point in San Jose.

Figure 1-17   Interstate 80 Is the Core Routing Component Between Chicago and San Jose

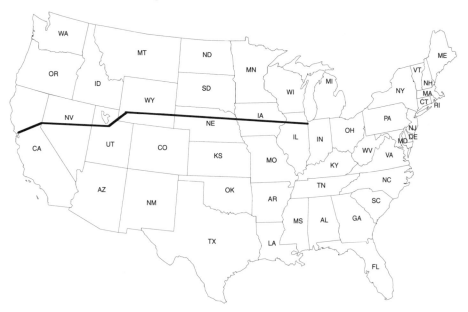

At the distribution layer, you will use the state maps of California and Illinois to determine your route from the respective state highway systems to the interstate. From Figure 1-18, you determine that Highway 66 in Illinois will get you from Chicago to Interstate 80; and Highway 101 in California will get you from Interstate 80 to San Jose.

Figure 1-18 Distribution Highways Used for Chicago and San Jose

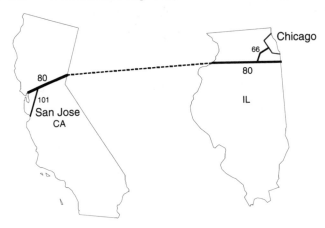

To start and end your journey, you use the city maps of Chicago and San Jose. (See Figure 1-19.)

Figure 1-19 City Maps Show the Access Layer in the Highway System

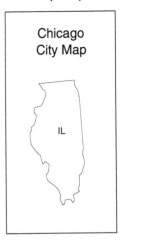

From a conceptual point of view, there is no difference in the structure and operation of the postal system and the highway system. In fact, the source and destination

addresses for both systems are identical. If you write a letter to your friend in San Jose and then drive to San Jose to see that friend, both you and your letter arrive at the same place.

Both systems operate at three distinct layers: access, distribution, and core. The information required at each layer becomes less specific—as far as a final destination is concerned—as you move toward the core from the access layer. Information is hidden, summarized, or aggregated at the core layer. For both systems, the core layer is responsible for routing between states and distribution layers. Specific destination information is not needed for the core to make a routing decision.

When you arrive in San Jose safely, what is the first thing you should do? Phone home.

Telephone System

How is the telephone system similar to the postal and highway systems? The answer to this question can be found by reviewing the properties of the first two systems we examined to see if similarities with the phone system exist. The first property the postal and highway systems have in common is a routable address. The second common property of these systems is a multiple part routable address that can be used to scale the system as the system grows. A routable address has a hierarchical structure that is used to route things from A to B. The hierarchical structure for the mail and highway systems consisted of access, distribution, and core layers. Each system used a source and destination address; and the destination address was used to make a routing decision to move a thing from point A to point B.

The source and destination addresses in the telephone system are telephone numbers. The destination address is the called number, and the source address is the calling number. Are telephone numbers routable? Yes. Years ago, telephone numbers began with two letters. These two letters were the first two letters of a telephone exchange name. A telephone exchange was the access layer that your phone was connected to. For example, a phone number starting with the exchange name **CL**earbrook represents the numbers 2 and 5; because on a telephone keypad, C is associated with the 2 key, and L is associated with the 5 key. The exchange name in the phone system served the same function as the street name in the postal system. The remaining digits in the phone number serve a similar purpose to the street number in a postal address. Although exchange names are no longer used, they do illustrate how the first few digits are used to route a phone call.

For the phone number **CL**earbrook **5**–5555, the CL portion and the first digit identifies the local exchange switch or access layer. The remainder of the phone number, 5555, identifies a phone in that exchange area. This is similar to a street name and street number. Figure 1-20 is a simplified diagram of the access, distribution, and core layers in the telephone system.

Figure 1-20 Access, Distribution, and Core Layers in the Telephone System

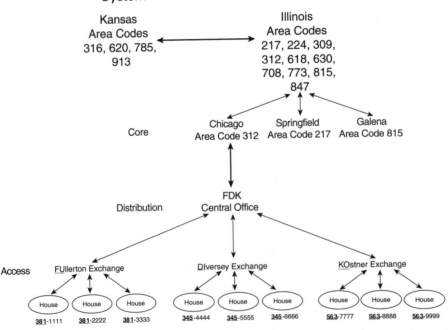

When a call is made from **381**-1111 to **381**-2222, the Fullerton exchange will switch the call based on the exchange number to a locally connected telephone. A call placed from **381**-1111 to **345**-4444 will be initially received by the Fullerton exchange. The exchange numbers in the called and calling numbers do not match, so the Fullerton exchange routes the call to the FDK central office. The FDK central office is directly connected to the Diversey exchange, so the call is routed to the Diversey exchange. The Diversey exchange switches the call to the proper phone.

For a call to reach the core level of the phone system, an area code is required. Using an area code for local calls is optional. If it is used, the access exchanges make a routing decision based on the area code and exchange number. A call from **312 381**-1111 to **312 381**-2222 or **312 345**-4444 will be routed the same as if an area code was not used. A call from any phone in area code 312 to any other area code will be routed to the core level based on the area code only. This is similar to sending a letter to a different city, or different state and city, in the postal system. A routing decision can be made on a portion of the address.

Exchange names are no longer used in the phone system, only numbers. A comparison of postal addresses to phone numbers illustrates the similarity between the structure and components of these addresses. (See Figure 1-21.)

Figure 1-21   Comparing the Structure of Postal Addresses and Phone Numbers

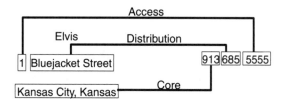

An area code serves the same function as the city and state names. Both are used to route between the core and distribution layers. The exchange name, or number, and the street name are used to route to the proper point in the access layer. Finally, the street number and remaining digits in the phone number are used to switch to the final destination.

Summary

The main goal of this chapter was to understand the concepts of routing and switching in everyday life. The routing of mail, the routing of telephone calls, and the routing of yourself when taking a trip share common concepts. Each system has a hierarchical address used to produce a scalable system. Each system is scalable because a hierarchy consisting of an access, distribution, and core layer is used so complete address information does not need to be maintained at each level.

The access layer only needs complete addressing information for the endpoints to which it is directly connected (as in houses or telephones). All other destinations are reached using a default route to the distribution layer. The distribution layer maintains information to reach specific routers in the access layer based on city names or telephone exchange numbers. Everything else can be routed to the core level using a default route. Finally, the core layer maintains the minimum information to reach either other core routers or the correct distribution router.

Chapter Review Questions

You can find the answers to these questions in Appendix A.

1. Describe why postal addresses and telephone numbers are routable.

2. What is the purpose of a default route?

3. Describe the difference between routing and switching.

4. What does the term information hiding mean in relation to route summarization?

5. How does the use of a hierarchical routing structure (access, distribution, and core) enable a scalable delivery system?

6. Why are multiple protocols used, such as a package, addressing, delivery, and transportation, instead of using one protocol defining everything?

7. Can you think of another familiar system that routes using a hierarchical delivery system?

8. Explain how a letter from New York City to San Diego is routed using the address information.

9. What are the access, distribution, and core components of a postal address?

10. What are the access, distribution, and core components of a North American phone number?

What You Will Learn

After reading this chapter, you should be able to

✔ Understand the number systems that are commonly used with computer networks—binary, octal, and hexadecimal

✔ Convert between the binary, octal, decimal, and hexadecimal number systems

✔ Understand the title of this chapter

CHAPTER 2

A_{16} B_{16} C_{16}, As Easy As 01_2, 10_2, 11_2

In everyday life, you work with the decimal number system using the symbols 0 through 9. The decimal number system has 10 symbols and is, therefore, referred to as the *base 10 number system*. There is nothing preventing you from using other number systems with a different number of symbols. A base 2 number system uses 2 symbols, a base 8 number system uses 8 symbols, and a base 16 number system uses 16 symbols. You can use any number systems—such as base 3 or base 7 or base 11—but these systems are not useful in the world of digital computers.

In reading this chapter, you discover that it is easier for a computer, or router, to work with a number system other than the decimal number system. The number system used in computers is base 2 using only two symbols. Two symbols are used because a computer is made up of millions of tiny devices that need only two values—off and on. Computers, therefore, need only two symbols to represent the values off or on. Because humans must deal with computers, other number systems are needed to represent the numbers computers use in a more readable form. The number systems you will use contain ten or sixteen symbols.

Decimal Numbering System

Every number in the decimal number system can be represented using ten symbols: 0, 1, 2, 3, 4, 5, 6, 7, 8, and 9. You are familiar with these symbols and how to use them to represent a number. For example, when you see the number 123, you know that it represents one hundred and twenty-three. But what are the rules that tell you that the symbols 123 represent one hundred twenty-three? The rule you use is the rule of positional value. Start counting and see what happens:

0

1

2

3

4

5

6

7

8

9

How do you represent a number larger than 9? You have only 10 symbols and you don't have a single symbol for the number 10. The rules tell us that the rightmost digit (assuming no decimal point) represents the one's position. More precisely, the rightmost digit has a value of the digit times 10^0 because $10^0 = 1$. The second digit has a value of the digit times 10^1 or digit times 10 and so on. So the number 123 is equal to

$$(1 * 10^2) + (2 * 10^1) + (3 * 10^0) = 100 + 20 + 3 = 123$$

Using the concept of positional notation, you can work with numbers using a base other than 10.

Binary Numbering System

As mentioned earlier, computers cannot use the familiar base 10 numbering system. Computers are essentially constructed using millions of devices that can have only two positions—on or off. It is logical to represent the value of a switch by the symbols 0 and 1 representing off and on. This is called the *base 2* or *binary* numbering system. Base 2 means there are only two symbols as opposed to the base 10 numbering system that has ten symbols. In the base 10 system, you work with ten symbols called decimal digits; and in the base 2 system, you work with two symbols called *bi*nary dig*its*, or *bits*, for short. Start counting in the binary number system:

0

1

Now what? You have run out of symbols. In the decimal system when you counted to 9, the first digit went back to 0; and the second digit was increased to 1. You might not have seen it, but the second digit is 0.

08

09

10

Each time the first digit goes from 9 to 0, you add one to the second digit. When the second digit goes from 9 to 0, you add one to the third digit, and on and on.

098

099

100

Following the same process for the binary number system allows us to count higher than 1:

000

001

010

011

100

Using positional value, the value represented by the first bit is the bit (0 or 1) * 2^0 (remember, this is base 2), or bit (0 or 1) * 1. Because the bit can have only a value of 1 or 0, the value represented by the first bit is either 0 or 1.

The value represented by the second bit is the bit value (0 or 1) * 2^1 , or bit (0 or 1) * 2. Again, because the bit can have only a value of 0 or 1, the second bit represents either 0 or 2. The third bit represents a value of the bit (0 or 1) * 2^2 or bit (0 or 1) * 4, which has a value of either 0 or 4. Notice that each higher position has a value that is twice the previous position. In the decimal number system, the positional values are powers of 10: 1, 10, 100, and so on. In the binary numbering system, the positional values are powers of 2: 1, 2, 4, 8, 16, and so on. See Table 2-1 to find out how high you can count with four bits.

Table 2-1   Counting with Four Bits

Binary	Decimal	Binary	Decimal
0000	0	1000	8
0001	1	1001	9
0010	2	1010	10
0011	3	1011	11
0100	4	1100	12
0101	5	1101	13
0110	6	1110	14
0111	7	1111	15

As you can see, unless you have experience working with binary numbers, it is not easy to look at a string of 1s and 0s and know what the equivalent decimal value is for the binary number. It even becomes more difficult when the number of bits is increased. For example, what is the value of 1101100101110011? If you said 55,667 without using a calculator, you can move on to Chapter 3, "Internet Addressing and Routing." To figure out the decimal value, just use positional notation. Starting from the right you have:

1 * 1 +

1 * 2 +

0 * 4 +

0 * 8 +

1 * 16 +

1 * 32 +

1 * 64 +

0 * 128 +

1 * 256 +

0 * 512 +

0 * 1024 +

1 * 2048 +

1 * 4096 +

0 * 8192 +

1 * 16384 +

1 * 32768 = 55,667

Now, wasn't that easy? Not really. We need an easier way to deal with binary numbers. Otherwise we might go insane.

Octal Numbering System

If you take the previous binary number and write it down in groups of three— add two 0s on the left—you might notice something:

001 101 100 101 110 011

Each grouping of three bits has a value between 0 and 7. (See Table 2-1.) If you could represent each set of three bits with one symbol, life might be a bit (get it?) easier. How many symbols will you need? The answer is eight. We already have eight symbols we are familiar with (0–7), so let's use them. Counting to 135 using the symbols 0–7 gives you:

000 = 0

001 = 1

010 = 2

011 = 3

100 = 4

101 = 5

110 = 6

111 = 7

When you get to seven, you run out of symbols. This is not a problem. Just follow the rules for the other number systems; first digit becomes 0, second digit becomes 1:

001 000 = 10 = 8 decimal

001 001 = 11 = 9 decimal

001 010 = 12 = 10 decimal

001 011 = 13 = 11 decimal

001 100 = 14 = 12 decimal

001 101 = 15 = 13 decimal

This new representation is the octal numbering system or base 8 numbering system. The positional value of our octal digits is now in powers of 8: 1, 8, 64, 512, 4096, and so on.

The binary number you were working with can be represented in octal as:

001101100101110011

1 5 4 5 6 3 base 8

Converting to decimal should give you the same answer as before:

$$3 * 8^0 = 3$$

$$6 * 8^1 = 48$$

$$5 * 8^2 = 5 * 64 = 320$$

$$4 * 8^3 = 4 * 512 = 2048$$

$$5 * 8^4 = 5 * 4096 = 20480$$

$$1 * 8^5 = 1 * 32768 = 32768$$

$$3 + 48 + 320 + 2048 + 20480 + 32768 = 55667$$

Although you can represent binary numbers using the octal numbering system, this method is not used much. Computers manipulate binary numbers in either groups of four, eight, or sixteen bits; but not three bits as represented by octal numbers.

Hexadecimal Numbering System

If you use groups of four bits, instead of three you get

1101 1001 0111 0011

Each grouping of four bits has a value between 0 and 15. (See Table 2-1.) You represent each set of four bits with one symbol. You need sixteen symbols. You already have ten symbols that you are familiar with (0–9), but that leaves us six short. We do have an alphabet with twenty-six symbols, so let's borrow six symbols from the alphabet. Doing this gives us the symbols we need. (See Table 2-2.)

Table 2-2   Representing Groups of Four Bits

Binary	Decimal	New Symbol	Binary	Decimal	New Symbol
0000	0	0	1000	8	8
0001	1	1	1001	9	9
0010	2	2	1010	10	A
0011	3	3	1011	11	B
0100	4	4	1100	12	C
0101	5	5	1101	13	D
0110	6	6	1110	14	E
0111	7	7	1111	15	F

The symbols aren't new, but the way you are using them is new. And while you are at it, you need a better name than New Symbol. The new scheme has sixteen symbols, so it is natural to call this the hexadecimal numbering system because hexa is the prefix for six. Using the hexadecimal number system, you can now represent base 2 in base 16 form, as follows:

1101100101110011 base 2

D 9 7 3 base 16

To determine the decimal value of the hexadecimal number D973, you use positional value again:

$3 * 16^0 = 3 * 1 = 3$

$7 * 16^1 = 7 * 16 = 112$

$9 * 16^2 = 9 * 256 = 2304$

$D * 16^3 = 13 * 4096 = 53248$

$3 + 112 + 2305 + 53248 = 55667$

You get the same answer, but it was easier to produce. Computers do not use the hexadecimal numbering system. Humans use the hexadecimal system to make binary numbers easier to read and manipulate.

Dotted Decimal Notation

Another method of representing binary numbers is called *dotted decimal notation*. Each group of eight bits, or one ***byte***, is represented by a decimal number with a dot between each decimal number. The range of values for an eight-bit number is 0–255. The lowest value using eight bits is

$$0000\ 0000 = 0$$

The highest value is

$$1111\ 1111 = 128 + 64 + 32 + 16 + 8 + 4 + 2 + 1 = 255$$

Therefore, the binary number 11011001 01110011 can be represented in dotted decimal by 217.115.

Conversions Between Number Systems

Mastering the number bases that we have discussed is a useful skill to have if your goal is to be a networking expert. Certainly, you have tools to do these conversions for you. You can use a calculator to convert from one base to another, but if you don't have experience doing this with paper and pencil you will not have a feel for the result. If you have an idea what the answer should be before using the calculator, and somehow you input the wrong number, you can feel that the answer is not correct. If you do not have that experience, you will believe any answer your calculator gives you. My advice is to practice with pencil and paper now, and use a calculator later.

Binary to Octal

One octal digit represents three binary digits. The first step in converting a binary number to octal is to write down the binary number in groups of three digits starting at the right. If the number of binary bits is not a multiple of three, add zeros on the left-hand side of the number.

Convert 1101011 to octal by following these steps:

Step 1   Write the binary number in groups of three bits:

001 101 011

Step 2   Represent each group of three bits with an octal digit (0–7):

001	101	011	Binary
1	5	3	Octal

Answer: 1101001 binary = 153 octal

Binary to Hexadecimal

One hexadecimal digit represents four binary digits. The first step in converting a binary number to hexadecimal is to write down the binary number in groups of four digits starting at the right. A group of four binary digits, or bits, is called a *nibble*. If the number of binary bits is not a multiple of four, add zeros on the left-hand side of the number.

Convert 1101011 to hexadecimal by following these steps:

Step 1   Write the binary number in groups of four bits:

0110 1011

Step 2   Represent each group of four bits with a hexadecimal digit (0–9 or A–F):

0110	1011	Binary
6	B	Hexadecimal

Answer: 01101011 binary = 6B hexadecimal

Binary to Decimal

For binary to decimal, we do not have a nice three- or four-bit relation between number of bits and a decimal digit. The conversion must be done using the positional value of each bit.

To convert 1101011 to decimal, determine the value of each one bit and add the values. (The 4 and 16 positions have a 0 so their value is 0.)

$$1 + 2 + 8 + 32 + 64 = 107$$

Answer: 1101011 binary = 107 decimal

Binary to Dotted Decimal

One decimal number represents eight binary digits, or one byte. The first step in converting a binary number to dotted decimal is to write down the binary number in groups of eight bits starting at the right. If the number of binary digits is not a multiple of eight, add zeros on the left-hand side of the number.

Convert 10011100000110100010000000000001 to dotted decimal by following these steps:

Step 1   Write the binary number in groups of eight bits:

10011100 00011010 00100000 00000001

Step 2   Convert each byte to decimal using the binary to decimal conversion sequence:

10011100 = 4 + 8 + 16 + 128 = 156

00011010 = 2 + 8 + 16 = 26

00100000 = 32

00000001 = 1

Answer: 10011100000110100010000000000001 binary = 156.26.32.1 dotted decimal

You could also convert each binary byte into two hexadecimal digits and then use the hexadecimal digits to determine the decimal value.

Convert 10011100000110100010000000000001 to dotted decimal by first converting to hexadecimal following these steps:

Step 1   Write the binary number in groups of eight bits:

10011100 00011010 00100000 00000001

Step 2   Represent each byte using two hexadecimal digits:

1001 1100 0001 1010 0010 0000 0000 0001

9 C 1 A 2 0 0 1

Step 3   Convert each pair of hexadecimal digits to decimal.

$9C = 9 * 16 + 12 = 156$

$1A = 16 + 10 = 26$

$20 = 2 * 16 + 0 = 32$

$01 = 1$

Answer: Again the result is 156.26.32.1.

Octal to Binary

One octal digit represents three binary bits. All that is needed for the conversion from octal to binary is to represent each octal digit using three binary digits.

Convert 153 octal to binary by converting each octal digit to a three-bit binary number, as follows:

153

001 101 011 = 001101011

Answer: 153 octal = 1101011 binary

Octal to Hexadecimal

The easiest way to convert an octal number to a hexadecimal number is to first convert each octal digit to a three-bit binary number. Then convert groups of four bits in the resulting binary number to hexadecimal.

Convert 153 octal to hexadecimal by following these steps:

Step 1   Convert each octal digit to a three-bit binary number.

       1   5   3

     001   101   011 = 001101011

Step 2   Convert each group of four bits to a hexadecimal number.

     0000 0110   1011

       0   6   B = 6B

     Answer: 153 octal = 6B hexadecimal

Octal to Decimal

For octal to decimal conversion, you do not have a nice relation between octal and decimal digits. The conversion must be done using the positional value of each octal digit.

To convert 153 octal to decimal, determine the value of each octal digit and add the values:

     153 = (1 * 64) + (5 * 8) + 3 = 107

     Answer: 153 octal = 107 decimal

Octal to Dotted Decimal

For octal to dotted decimal conversion, convert the octal number to its binary equivalent first, then group the bits into groups of eight, and then convert each group of eight bits to its decimal equivalent.

Convert 13767736 octal to dotted decimal following these steps:

Step 1 Convert octal to binary. One octal digit equals three binary digits:

1	3	7	6	7	7	3	6
001	011	111	110	111	111	011	110

Step 2 Group the binary digits into groups of eight bits:

00101111 11101111 11011110

Step 3 Convert each byte to decimal:

$1 + 2 + 4 + 8 + 32 = 47$

$1 + 2 + 4 + 8 + 32 + 64 + 128 = 239$

$2 + 4 + 8 + 16 + 64 + 128 = 222$

Answer: 13767736 octal = 47.239.222 dotted decimal

Hexadecimal to Binary

For hexadecimal to binary conversion, each hexadecimal digit can be represented by four binary digits.

To convert ABACAB32 to binary, convert each hexadecimal digit into four binary digits, as follows:

A = 1010 B = 1011 A = 1010 C = 1100 A = 1010

B = 1011 3 = 0011 2 = 0010

Answer: ABACAB32 hexadecimal = 1010 1011 1010 1100 1010 1011 0011 0010 binary

Hexadecimal to Octal

For hexadecimal to octal, convert each hexadecimal digit into four binary digits. Then convert groups of three binary digits to an octal digit.

Convert ABACAB32 to octal by following these steps:

Step 1   Convert each hexadecimal digit into four binary digits:

A = 1010 B = 1011 A = 1010 C = 1100 A = 1010

B = 1011 3 = 0011 2 = 0010

Step 2   Group the binary digits into groups of three bits:

010 101 011 101 011 001 010 101 100 110 010

Step 3   Convert each group of three binary digits into one octal digit:

010 101 011 101 011 001 010 101 100 110 010

2   5   3   5   3   1   2   5   4   6   2

Answer: ABACAB32 hexadecimal = 25353125462 octal

Hexadecimal to Decimal

For hexadecimal to decimal conversion, convert each hexadecimal digit to its decimal value using positional value, and then sum the values.

To convert ABACAB32 to decimal, use positional value to determine the value of each hexadecimal digit in decimal:

$A * 16^7 = 10 * 268,435,456 = 2,684,354,560$

$B * 16^6 = 11 * 16,777,216 = 184,549,376$

$A * 16^5 = 10 * 1,048,576 = 10,485,760$

$C * 16^4 = 12 * 65,536 = 786,432$

$A * 16^3 = 10 * 4,096 = 40,960$

$B * 16^2 = 11 * 256 = 2,816$

$3 * 16^1 = 3 * 16 = 48$

$2 * 16^0 = 2 * 1 = 2$

Answer: ABACAB32 hexadecimal = 2,880,219,954

Hexadecimal to Dotted Decimal

A dotted decimal number represents eight bits or two hex-digits. Convert pairs of hexadecimal numbers to their decimal equivalent.

Convert ABACAB32 to dotted decimal by following these steps:

Step 1   Group into pairs of hexadecimal digits:

AB AC AB 32

Step 2   Determine the decimal value of each pair:

AB = 10 * 16 + 11 = 171

AC = 10 * 16 + 12 = 172

AB = 10 * 16 + 11 = 171

32 = 3 * 16 + 2 = 50

Answer: ABACAB32 hexadecimal = 171.172.171.50 dotted decimal

Decimal to Binary

A decimal number can be converted to binary by repeatedly dividing the decimal number by 2 and using the remainders as the binary digits starting with the least significant bit.

Convert 19 decimal to binary by following these steps:

Step 1   Divide 19 by 2:

19/2 = 9 remainder 1

Step 2   Divide 9 by 2:

9/2 = 4 remainder 1

Step 3   Divide 4 by 2:

4/2 = 2 remainder 0

Step 4   Divide 2 by 2:

2/2 = 1 remainder 0

Step 5 Divide 1 by 2:

 $1/2 = 0$ remainder 1

Stop when the result of the division is 0 (Step 5). The resulting binary number is constructed from the remainders, with the remainder from Step 1 being the least significant bit.

Answer: 19 decimal = 10011 binary

Now, do one more.

Convert 123 decimal to binary by following these steps:

Step 1 Divide 123 by 2:

 $123/2 = 61$ remainder 1

Step 2 Divide 61 by 2:

 $61/2 = 30$ remainder 1

Step 3 Divide 30 by 2:

 $30/2 = 15$ remainder 0

Step 4 Divide 15 by 2:

 $15/2 = 7$ remainder 1

Step 5 Divide 7 by 2:

 $7/2 = 3$ remainder 1

Step 6 Divide 3 by 2:

 $3/2 = 1$ remainder 1

Step 7 Divide 1 by 2:

 $1/2 = 0$ remainder 1

Answer: 123 decimal = 1111011 binary

Decimal to Octal

You can convert a decimal number to octal by repeatedly dividing the decimal number by 8 and using the remainders as the octal digits starting with the least significant digit.

Convert 19 decimal to octal by following these steps:

Step 1 Divide 19 by 8:

19/8 = 2 remainder 3

Step 2 Divide 2 by 8:

2/8 = 0 remainder 2

Answer: 19 decimal = 23 octal

Follow the next steps to convert 123 decimal to octal:

Step 1 Divide 123 by 8:

123/8 = 15 remainder 3

Step 2 Divide 15 by 8:

15/8 = 1 remainder 7

Step 3 Divide 1 by 8:

1/8 = 0 remainder 1

Answer: 123 decimal = 173 octal

Decimal to Hexadecimal

You can convert a decimal number to hexadecimal by repeatedly dividing the decimal number by 16 and using the remainders as the hexadecimal digits starting with the least significant digit.

Convert 19 decimal to hexadecimal by following these steps:

Step 1 Divide 19 by 16:

19/16 = 1 remainder 3

Step 2   Divide 1 by 16:

1/16 = 0 remainder 1

Answer: 19 decimal = 13 hexadecimal

Follow these steps to convert 123 decimal to hexadecimal:

Step 1   Divide 123 by 16:

123/16 = 7 remainder 11 or B

Step 2   Divide 7 by 16:

7/16 = 0 remainder 7

Answer: 123 decimal = 7B hexadecimal

So, what have you learned about converting from decimal to binary, octal, and hexadecimal? Use a calculator!

Fun Binary Number Facts

This section describes a few interesting facts regarding binary numbers that will be useful during your networking career. Table 2-3 points out these interesting tidbits.

Table 2-3   Patterns in the Bits

Binary	Decimal	Binary	Decimal
00000	0	10000	16
00001	1	10001	17
00010	2	10010	18
00011	3	10011	19
00100	4	10100	20
00101	5	10101	21
00110	6	10110	22

Table 2-3   Patterns in the Bits (continued)

Binary	Decimal	Binary	Decimal
00111	7	10111	23
01000	8	11000	24
01001	9	11001	25
01010	10	11010	26
01011	11	11011	27
01100	12	11100	28
01101	13	11101	29
01110	14	11110	30
01111	15	11111	31

Fun Fact Number One. If a binary number is even, the least significant or right-most digit is 0. If a binary number is odd, the least significant, or rightmost, digit is 1.

Fun Fact Number Two. When counting in binary, each binary digit toggles with the frequency of its positional value. When counting in the decimal number system, the least significant digit changes on every count. The second digit changes on every 10th count, the third digit changes on every 100th count, and so on. In the binary number system, the least significant bit changes on every count, the next bit changes on every 2nd count, the 3rd bit changes on every 4th count, and so on.

- In the 2^0 or 1s position, the bit changes on every count.
- In the 2^1 or 2s position, the bit changes every two counts.
- In the 2^2 or 4s position, the bit changes every four counts.
- In the 2^3 or 8s position, the bit changes every eight counts.
- In the 2^4 or 16s position, the bit changes every sixteen counts.

Fun Fact Number Three. 255.255.255.255 = FF FF FF FF = 11111111 11111111 11111111 11111111. Just something you should remember.

Fun Fact Number Four. The value of a binary number having a continuous sequence of 1s starting with the least significant bit is equal to the positional value of the first 0 bit minus 1.

- 00000001 = 2 − 1 = 1

- 00000011 = 4 − 1 = 3

- 00000111 = 8 − 1 = 7

- 00001111 = 16 − 1 = 15

- 00011111 = 32 − 1 = 31

- 00111111 = 64 − 1 = 63

- 01111111 = 128 − 1 = 127

- 11111111 = 256 − 1 = 255

Fun Fact Number Five. Well, this might not be fun, but memorize the following binary and decimal number pairs. They will be useful later in the book and in your career:

- 1 0 0 0 0 0 0 0 = 128

- 1 1 0 0 0 0 0 0 = 192

- 1 1 1 0 0 0 0 0 = 224

- 1 1 1 1 0 0 0 0 = 240

- 1 1 1 1 1 0 0 0 = 248

- 1 1 1 1 1 1 0 0 = 252

- 1 1 1 1 1 1 1 0 = 254

- 1 1 1 1 1 1 1 1 = 255

Fun Fact Number Six. (Thanks to reviewer Mark Gallo for this one.)

$31_8 = 25_{10}$ or Oct 31 = Dec 25

Summary

You shall see in the following chapters that being able to convert between number systems is an important skill to have if you want to design and implement computer networks. You have learned to convert between the binary, octal, decimal, and hexadecimal number systems to represent the numbers used in a computer in a human readable form.

Before proceeding, you should now know the meaning of the title of this chapter. If not, then phone a friend. Remember, it's as easy as 01_2 10_2 11_2.

Chapter Review Questions

You can find the answers to these questions in Appendix A.

1. This is a speed drill. Using only your head, convert the following binary numbers to decimal.

   11100000

   11111100

   10000000

   11110000

   00111111

2. Convert $FACE1234_{16}$ to dotted decimal.

3. Convert $10100010111101011001110110001011_2$ to hexadecimal.

4. Convert $10100010111101011001110110001011_2$ to dotted decimal.

5. Convert $10100010111101011001110110001011_2$ to octal.

6. True or False. Converting between number bases is fun.

7. Convert 12345670_8 to hexadecimal.

8. Convert 734215_8 to binary.

9. Convert 734215_{16} to binary.

10. Convert 262988031_{10} to hexadecimal.

What You Will Learn

After reading this chapter, you should be able to

✓ Understand the IP version 4 (IPv4) addressing protocol, and the similarities to the addresses used in the postal delivery system

✓ Explain why hosts need two addresses, Ethernet and Internet, and how the Address Resolution Protocol (ARP) is used to determine the Ethernet address of a host given the host's IP address

✓ Understand the TCP and UDP protocols, and how they are used to deliver data to a destination host

✓ Explain the TCP/IP layered model by comparing it to the layer model that was developed for the postal delivery system

✓ Differentiate between classful and classless IP addresses

✓ Learn how to subnet and summarize IP networks

✓ Learn how routers forward packets using the longest match operation

✓ Describe the IP version 6 (IPv6) addressing protocol

CHAPTER 3

Internet Addressing and Routing

In Chapter 1, you examined systems for delivering the mail, planning a road trip, and making telephone calls. Chapter 2 introduced the binary, octal, and hexadecimal numbering systems. You need to understand how computers represent information, and how you can move between number systems to represent binary numbers in a more readable form. In this chapter, the concepts from the first two chapters will be combined to understand the schemes that are necessary to create a scalable computer communication system — the Internet.

Internet Addressing

To begin our discussion on computer communication over a network, this section looks at the similarities between mail delivery between houses, and data delivery between computers. The endpoints in mail delivery are houses, and the endpoints between electronic data delivery are computers. Certainly there can be other endpoints in both systems. Letters can be delivered from a house to a business, from a business to a house, between two businesses, and so on. Electronic data delivery can be from a news service to your cell phone or personal data assistant (PDA), from your computer to your friend's pager, from environmental sensors in a building to the heating and cooling control systems for that building, and so on. But to keep the discussion simple, it will suffice to concentrate on mail delivery between houses, and electronic data delivery between computers. The first analogy is that an endpoint in a mail delivery system, a house, is equivalent to the endpoint in a computer communication system, a PC. (See Figure 3-1.)

Figure 3-1 Equivalent Endpoints in the Mail and Data Communication Systems

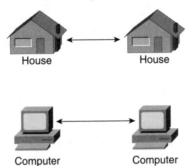

In the mail delivery system, the function of the post office is to deliver mail to a particular house. In the computer communication system, the function of the Internet is to deliver data to a particular PC. Yet, in both systems, the endpoint is not the ultimate destination. For mail, the ultimate recipient is a person. For data, the ultimate recipient is an application such as an e-mail program, a web browser, an audio or video program, an instant messaging program, or any number of wonderful applications that exist today. (See Figure 3-2.)

Figure 3-2 Final Destinations in the Postal and Electronic Data Delivery Systems

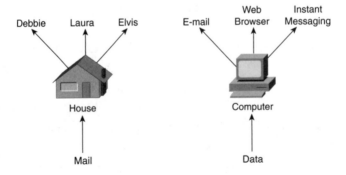

Although the ultimate recipient is a person or a software application, the responsibility of the systems stops when the mail, or data, is delivered to the proper house, or computer. However, as part of the address, you still need the ultimate recipient; either a person or an application, even though this information is not used for delivery to an endpoint. The endpoint uses the name or application to enable delivery to the recipient.

Because the two systems are analogous, it is instructive to revisit the format of an address in the mail delivery system and see if you can use a similar format for electronic data delivery:

> Name
>
> Street Number, Street Name
>
> City, State

Although there are five distinct pieces of information in the mail address (name, street number, street name, city, and state), you can consider an address to contain only four pieces of information. For endpoint delivery, you can ignore the name field. You are left with

> Street Number
>
> Street Name
>
> City
>
> State

The postal system routers (core, distribution, and access) use the state, city, and street names to deliver the mail from the source access post office to the destination access post office. The street number is not needed until the mail arrives at the access post office that is directly connected to the destination street. So, the address can be broken down into

> State, City, Street Name
>
> and
>
> Street Number

The state, city, and street name information enables the mail to get close to the destination (a particular street). The street number is used to deliver the mail to the proper house. What is the analogy in the computer world to houses on a street? Recall from Chapter 1 that a group of computers can directly communicate with each other through a switch residing on a local-area network (LAN). So a LAN is the computer equivalent to a street. (See Figure 3-3.)

Figure 3-3   LAN of Computers Is Similar to a Street of Houses

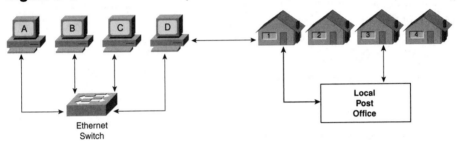

Chapter 1 also mentioned that computers have an address, and the most common technology used for computer communication is Ethernet. The sample Ethernet address that was presented in Chapter 1 was 00-03-47-92-9C-6F.

Before you learn more about Ethernet addresses, take the following quiz to make sure you understand the concepts described so far:

1. What number base is used to represent the Ethernet address?

   Answer: Hexadecimal, because the symbols C and F are not used in the other number bases that we discussed. Computers compute using binary. The hexadecimal representation is for our benefit because it is easier to read and write.

2. How many bytes are in an Ethernet address?

   Answer: Six. One hexadecimal digit contains 4 bits, or 1/2 bytes. Two hexadecimal digits contain 8 bits, or 1 byte. An Ethernet address contains 12 hexadecimal digits or 6 bytes.

3. How many bits are in an Ethernet Address?

   Answer: 48 (8 bits per byte).

4. How many Ethernet addresses are possible?

   Answer: 2^{48} or 281 trillion, 474 billion, 976 million, 710 thousand, 6 hundred fifty-six (281,474,976,710,656).

An Ethernet address is not a property of your PC. An Ethernet address is a property of the Ethernet card, or built in Ethernet port in your PC. If you put a new Ethernet card in your PC, the Ethernet address of your PC changes.

By itself, an Ethernet address cannot deliver data between two endpoints on the Internet. The reason is that there is no structure to an Ethernet address. There are many manufacturers of Ethernet cards for computers, and each manufacturer is assigned a block of Ethernet address to use for their particular brand of card.

An analogy would be to have 281,474,976,710,656 postal addresses that are sold in a local postal address store. Each local postal address store is given a block of numbers from the total range of numbers that are possible. A postal address is just a number between 0 and 281,474,976,710,655. When you build a house, you would go to the local postal address store and your house would be assigned one of the numbers that hasn't yet been assigned. Everyone in your city would need to get a number assigned from the local postal address store. Because people will not be going to the store in any order, numbers will be assigned randomly throughout the city. The only way that these numbers can be used to deliver mail is if every post office at every level (core, distribution, and access) maintained a list of every number, and the route to reach that number. Therefore, every post office would need to maintain a list of 281,474,976,710,656 addresses and the route to get there. Obviously, this is not scalable. So in addition to an Ethernet address, you need another address that has a structure analogous to the structure of the postal address. What you need is an Internet addressing protocol.

Internet Addressing Protocol

The Internet addressing protocol, or Internet Protocol (IP), is an additional addressing scheme. By following this protocol you can have an address with a structure that will allow you to build a scalable data communication system analogous to the postal system. Because this discussion is about computers, you need to decide how many bits you need for an Internet address, and how many Internet addresses you need. Computers can easily work with byte size pieces of data, so the number of bits in the IP should be a multiple of 8 bits or 1 byte. How many IP addresses will you need? That is, and was, a difficult question. When the IP was developed more than 20 years ago, the PC was not common, and it was difficult to imagine the explosion that would take place in the number of computers used throughout the world.

If you placed yourself back in 1980, and had to determine the size, in bits, of an IP address, what would you have picked? You might have started by determining how many addresses are possible based on the number of bytes that are used. And you might have created a table similar to Table 3-1.

Table 3-1   Number of IP Addresses Versus Number of Bytes

Number of Bytes	Number of Bits	Number of Addresses
1	8	$2^8 = 256$
2	16	$2^{16} = 65,536$
3	24	$2^{24} = 16,777,216$
4	32	$2^{32} = 4,294,967,296$
5	40	$2^{40} = 1,099,511,627,776$
6	48	$2^{48} = 281,474,976,710,656$

In 1980, there were more than 256 computers in use, so 1 byte would not be sufficient. Two bytes would give us 65,280 more addresses, but the number is still not sufficient. Although 3 bytes allow more than 16 million addresses, you know that computers are happier with even numbers of things than odd numbers of things. An ideal size is 4 bytes. Four is an even number and you can have in excess of 4 billion IP addresses, which should be sufficient. Now that you have settled on using a 32-bit address for the Internet address, you next need to determine a structure for those 32 bits.

The postal addressing and delivery schemes worked quite well for mail delivery, so let's try and impose the same type of structure on the Internet addresses. You know that a postal address has two components. The first component consisted of the state, city, and street names. The second component was the street or house number. Although the entire address was needed to identify a particular endpoint, or house, you did not need the street number for delivery until the mail reached the street containing the house. Using the same philosophy for the Internet address, use part of the 32 bits to designate the LAN or local network where the computer resides (the ***network address***); and the remaining bits in the address to identify a particular computer, or host (the ***host address***), on that LAN.

The next step is to determine how many bits to use for the network address and how many bits to use to identify a computer, or host, on that network. The easiest approach is to work with bytes, and then use the dotted decimal notation to represent network and host addresses using decimal numbers. You can't use all the bytes for the network address, and you can't use all the bytes for the computer address so the possibilities that remain are listed in Table 3-2.

Table 3-2   Internet Address Structures

Network Address Size	Number of Possible Networks	Host Address Size	Number of Possible Hosts
1 Byte	$2^8 = 256$	3 Bytes	$2^{24} = 16,777,216$
2 Bytes	$2^{16} = 65,536$	2 Bytes	$2^{16} = 65,536$
3 Bytes	$2^{24} = 16,777,216$	1 Byte	$2^8 = 256$

After some thought, you decide that you want to make some modifications to the range of host addresses. It would be nice if you had a broadcast capability where a message could be sent to every host on a network. Therefore, you need a **broadcast address** for the network, and you want the broadcast address to be easy to remember. This can be achieved by using a host address of all 1s for the broadcast address. In addition, you want an address that points to the network itself, or "this" network. This can be achieved by using a host address of all 0s. To accommodate the new broadcast and "this" network addresses, the number of hosts listed in Table 3-2 must now be reduced by two. (See Table 3-3.)

Table 3-3 Number of Hosts Possible

Network Address Size	Number of Possible Networks	Host Address Size	Number of Possible Hosts
1 Byte	$2^8 = 256$	3 Bytes	$2^{24} - 2 = 16{,}777{,}214$
2 Bytes	$2^{16} = 65{,}536$	2 Bytes	$2^{16} - 2 = 65{,}534$
3 Bytes	$2^{24} = 16{,}777{,}216$	1 Byte	$2^8 - 2 = 254$

Try working through the next exercises to reinforce your understanding.

For the first type or class of networks that use 1 byte for the network address and 3 bytes for the host address, the range of addresses in dotted decimal notation are:

> 0.0.0.1–0.255.255.254 for network 0
>
> 1.0.0.1–1.255.255.254 for network 1
>
> 2.0.0.1–2.255.255.254 for network 2
>
> ...
>
> 255.0.0.1–255.255.255.254 for network 255

1. What is the address for host 8 on network 129?

Answer: 129.0.0.8

2. What is the broadcast address for network 129?

> **Answer:**   129.255.255.255

For the second class of networks that use 2 bytes for both the network and host addresses, the range of addresses in dotted decimal notation are

> 0.0.0.1–0.0.255.254 for network 0
>
> 0.1.0.1–0.1.255.254 for network 1
>
>
> ...
>
> 255.254.0.1–255.254.255.254 for network 65,534
>
> 255.255.0.1–255.255.255.254 for network 65,535

3. What is the address for host 8 on the 258th network?

> **Answer:**   Answer.1.1.0.8. The 258th network is network number 257 because network numbering started at 0; 257 in binary = 0000 0001 0000 0001 = 256 + 1 = 257 = 1.1 in dotted decimal notation.

4. What is the broadcast address for the 258th network?

> **Answer:**   1.1.255.255

> For the third class of networks that use 1 byte for the host address and 3 bytes for the network address, the range of addresses in dotted decimal notation are

> 0.0.0.1–0.0.0.254 for network 0
>
> 0.0.1.1–0.0.1.254 for network 1
>
> ...
>
> 0.1.0.1–0.1.0.254 for network 256
>
> ...
>
> 1.0.0.1–1.0.0.254 for network 65536
>
> ...
>
> 255.255.255.1–255.255.255.254 for network 16,777,215

5. What is the address for host 8 on network 25?

   Answer: 0.0.25.8

6. What is the address for host 12 on network 103,481?

   Answer: 103,481 in hexadecimal $= 019439.01_{16} = 1_{10}.94_{16} = 148_{10}.39_{16}$ $= 57_{10}$. 103,481 in dotted decimal $= 1.148.57$ so the address for host 12 on network 103,481 is 1.148.57.12

7. What is the broadcast address for network 103,481?

   Answer: 1.148.57.255

Classful IP Addresses

You must decide which scheme you are going to use for the Internet addresses. You could pick just one, but why not use all three? That way, you would have the flexibility of having networks with a few hosts (254), networks with a moderate number of hosts (65534), and networks with many hosts (16,777,214). This does sound like a good idea, but you need to be able to mix the three address types. A simple way is to use part of the first byte to signal the type of address used. The first byte, like all bytes, contains 8 bits. Using the first few bits to identify the type of network gives you the following rules:

- If the first, or most significant, bit of the first byte is 0, then 1 byte is used for the network address and 3 bytes are used for the host, broadcast, and "this" network address.

- If the most significant bit of the first byte is 1 and the next bit is 0, 2 bytes are used for the network address and 2 bytes are used for the host, broadcast, and "this" network address.

- If the first 2 bits of the first byte are 1, then 3 bytes are used for the network address and 1 byte is used for the host, broadcast, and "this" network address.

Three types of addresses are called Class A, B, and C. In a Class A address, the most significant bit of the first byte is 0. Additionally, you want to reserve two addresses from the Class A address space. Address 0.0.0.X (where X can be any value from 0–255) is reserved. Address 127.X.X.X is reserved for what is called a *loopback address*. The loopback address is used by a host to send a message to itself without even being connected to a network. This can be used for testing applications without interfering with the network. So the range of values for the first byte in a Class A address is 0000–0001–0111 1110 or 1–126 (0 and 127 are reserved).

The entire range of Class A addresses is – 126.255.255.255.

In a Class B address, the most significant bit of the first byte is 1 and the next bit is 0. So the range of values for the first byte in a Class B address is 1000 0000–1011 1111 or 128–191.

The entire range of Class B addresses is: 128.0.0.0–191.255.255.255.

In a Class C address, the first two most significant bits of the first byte are 1 and the next bit is 0. So the range of values for the first byte in a Class C address is 1100 0000–1101 1111 or 192–223.

The entire range of Class C addresses is: 192.0.0.0–223.255.255.255.

This Internet Protocol addressing scheme is called *classful* because every address falls into one of three classes of addresses as summarized in Table 3-4.

Table 3-4   Classful Internet Protocol Address Ranges

Address Class	First Host Address	Last Host Address
A	1.0.0.1	126.255.255.254
B	128.0.0.1	191.255.255.254
C	192.0.0.1	223.255.255.254

A Class A address is identified by the first bit being a 0, as follows:

0XXX XXXX

A Class B address is identified by the first 2 bits being 1 0, as follows:

10XX XXXX

And a Class C address has the first 3 bits set to 1 1 0, as follows:

110X XXXX

One question might have popped into your mind at this point: What about addresses that are not Class A, B, or C? In other words, what about addresses where the first four bits are 1 1 1 0 or 1 1 1 1? Addresses beginning with 1110 are a different class of addresses, Class D, which you will learn about in Chapter 9, "Multicast—What the Post Office Can't Do." The Class D, or multicast, address space is in the range **1110** 0000–1110 1111 or 224–239.

Addresses beginning with 1111 are reserved for future use and cover the remaining address space starting at 240.0.0.0.

Figure 3-4 summarizes the structure of the classful IP addresses scheme.

Figure 3-4   Classful IP Addressing Structures

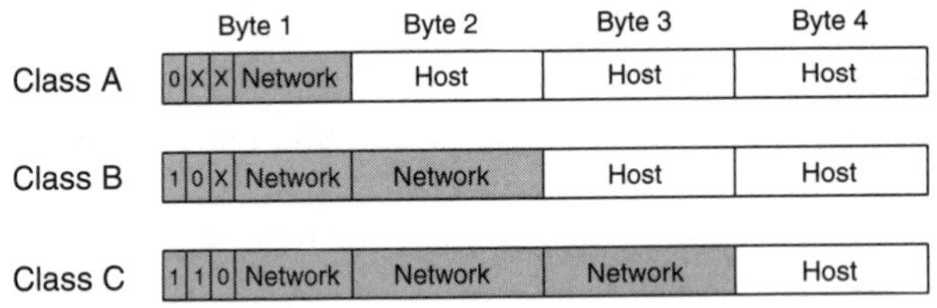

	Byte 1	Byte 2	Byte 3	Byte 4
Class A	0 x x Network	Host	Host	Host
Class B	1 0 x Network	Network	Host	Host
Class C	1 1 0 Network	Network	Network	Host

Private IP Addresses

The final addition to the Internet addressing protocol is that of private IP addresses. A public IP address is one that is reachable on the Internet, and therefore must be globally unique (two computers cannot use the same public IP address). You can have LANs that are not connected to the Internet, but the computers on these LANs are using IP for communication. It doesn't make sense to waste public IP addresses on these computers, so a range of addresses has been set aside for these private networks to use. (See Table 3-5.) Because they are private, the same addresses can be used on more than one LAN with the realization that communication between LANs using the same private IP addresses is not possible.

Table 3-5   Private IP Address Ranges

Class	Range
A	10.0.0.0– 10.255.255.255
B	172.16.0.0– 172.31.255.255
B (Used by Microsoft)	169.254.0.0– 169.254.255.255
C	192.168.0.0– 192.168.255.255

Address Resolution

An IP address is routable. Routers can use the network portion of an IP address to make a delivery, or routing decision, to the destination network. Ethernet addresses are not routable (unless every router knows how to reach every Ethernet address). Ultimately, electronic data must be delivered to a host using the host's Ethernet address. To do this, you need a protocol to determine, or resolve, the Ethernet address associated with a host's IP address. There is an analogy for address resolution that you are familiar with. Assume that you want to call your friend Steve and you do not know his telephone number, but you know where he lives. What do you use to resolve Steve's telephone number from his address? A telephone book. With a computer network, you need to do essentially the same thing when resolving between Ethernet and IP addresses. In Figure 3-5, there are three LANs with four hosts each.

Figure 3-5 Address Resolution Matches a Host's Ethernet Address with a Host's IP Address

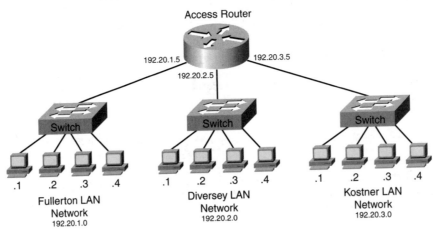

The Fullerton, Diversey, and Kostner LANs have been assigned networks 192.20.1.0, 192.20.2.0, and 192.20.3.0 (remember the 0 designates "this" network). The host addresses on these LANs are .1, .2, .3, and .4. This is a shorthand notation for IP addresses 192.20.1.1, 192.20.1.2, 192.20.1.3, and 192.20.1.4 on the Fullerton LAN—and the same shorthand notation is used on the other two LANs. Also notice that the three Ethernet interfaces on the access router have also been assigned an IP address taken from the range of addresses associated with each LAN.

This section uses the networks in Figures 3-5 and 3-6 to trace through the steps a host uses to send data to a host on the same LAN and to a host on a different LAN. Tables 3-6, 3-7, and 3-8 contain the IP and Ethernet addresses for the hosts and router on the three LANs.

Table 3-6 Fullerton LAN Address Associations

IP Address	Ethernet Address
192.20.1.1 (Host 1)	00-03-47-92-9C-6F
192.20.1.2 (Host 2)	00-03-47-92-9C-70

Table 3-6   Fullerton LAN Address Associations (continued)

IP Address	Ethernet Address
192.20.1.3 (Host 3)	00-03-47-92-9C-71
192.20.1.4 (Host 4)	00-03-47-92-9C-72
192.20.1.5 (Router)	00-03-47-92-9C-73

Table 3-7   Diversey LAN Address Associations

IP Address	Ethernet Address
192.20.2.1 (Host 1)	00-03-48-AB-61-01
192.20.2.2 (Host 2)	00-03-48-AB-61-02
192.20.2.3 (Host 3)	00-03-48-AB-61-03
192.20.2.4 (Host 4)	00-03-48-AB-61-04
192.20.2.5 (Router)	00-03-48-AB-61-05

Table 3-8   Kostner LAN Address Associations

IP Address	Ethernet Address
192.20.3.1 (Host 1)	00-03-49-C5-12-31
192.20.3.2 (Host 2)	00-03-49-C5-12-32
192.20.3.3 (Host 3)	00-03-49-C5-12-33
192.20.3.4 (Host 4)	00-03-49-C5-12-34
192.20.3.5 (Router)	00-03-49-C5-12-35

Intra-LAN Communication

In Figure 3-6, the host with IP address 192.20.1.1 on the Fullerton LAN wants to send data to the host with IP address 192.20.1.2 on the same LAN. The source and destination IP addresses are

- Source: **192.20.1**.1

- Destination: **192.20.1**.2

The source host knows that the destination IP address is on the same network because

- Both source and destination network numbers are Class C.

- Both Class C network numbers are the same; therefore, they both point to the same network.

Figure 3-6   Intra-LAN Address Resolution

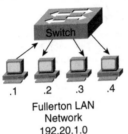

1. Send an Ethernet broadcast asking for the Ethernet address associated with IP address 192.20.1.2. This is an ARP request message.

Fullerton LAN
Network
192.20.1.0

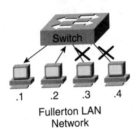

2. Hosts .3 and .4 ignore the message. Host .2 sends an ARP reply containing its Ethernet address to the Ethernet address of host .1

Fullerton LAN
Network
192.20.1.0

The source host knows the destination IP address, but not the destination Ethernet address. The source host needs to resolve the destination Ethernet address from the destination IP address. This is accomplished by using the *Address Resolution Protocol (ARP)*. The source host sends an Ethernet broadcast to the switch. Like the IP broadcast, an Ethernet broadcast is signified by setting the destination Ethernet address to all 1s or FF:FF:FF:FF:FF:FF. The source Ethernet address is set to the Ethernet address of the host sending the broadcast. The ARP message contains the destination IP address or 192.20.1.2. When the Ethernet switch receives the broadcast message, it is sent to all hosts on the network except for the host that sent the message. All hosts on the Fullerton LAN will receive the broadcast and inspect the IP address in the message. If the IP address is not the IP address of the host that received the message, the message will be ignored. When the host with IP address 192.20.1.2 receives the ARP message, it will respond back to the sender with its Ethernet address. Now the host at 192.20.1.1 has resolved the Ethernet address for the host with IP address 192.20.1.2.

Host .1 on the Fullerton LAN receives the ARP request and stores that association between the Ethernet and IP addresses for host .2 in an ARP table. Storing this information allows host .1 to send additional messages to host .2 without having to send an ARP request each time. An example of a typical ARP table is shown in the following output:

```
Interface: 192.20.1.1
Internet Address        Physical Address         Type
192.20.1.2              00-03-47-92-9C-70        dynamic
```

The physical address is the Ethernet address associated with IP address 192.20.1.2. *Dynamic* means that this association was learned using ARP.

At this point, you might be wondering why we have two addresses. Why not use either the IP address or the Ethernet address. Why use both? The clue is in the ARP table shown earlier. An Ethernet address is a physical address. It is "burned in" to the Ethernet card and is sometimes referred to as a burned-in address (BIA). An IP address is a logical address that was assigned to the host. In this case, the host happens to use Ethernet for sending messages on the LAN. Other technologies exist that can be used by the computers to send messages, such as Token ring or Asynchronous Transfer Mode (ATM). If you use ATM on the Fullerton LAN instead of Ethernet, you should expect that you are still able to send messages between computers. An ATM address is 20 bytes while an Ethernet address is 6 bytes. In other words, the logical addressing (IP) should be independent of the physical addressing (Ethernet, Token Ring, ATM). Does this sound familiar? In Chapter 1, "Routing and Switching in Everyday Life," you learned a layered model for the postal delivery system. (See Figure 3-7.)

Figure 3-7   Layered Postal Delivery Model

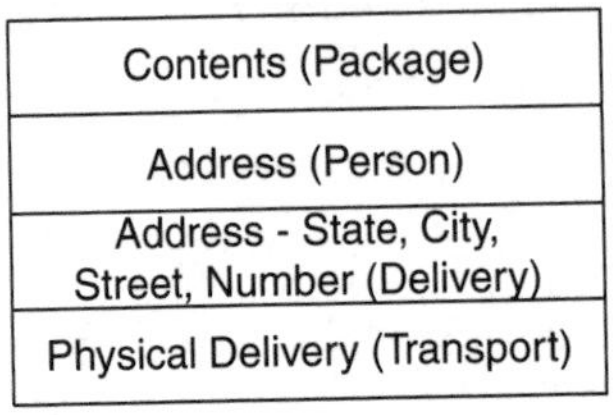

Contents (Package)
Address (Person)
Address - State, City, Street, Number (Delivery)
Physical Delivery (Transport)

For this model, you learned that the address should not be dependent on the contents, and that the physical delivery should not be dependent on the address. The layers in this model are independent. In the same way, you need a layered model for the Internet. With what you've learned, you can start constructing the layer model for the Internet. In Figure 3-8, the lowest layer is the network interface layer.

Figure 3-8   Partial Layered Internet Model

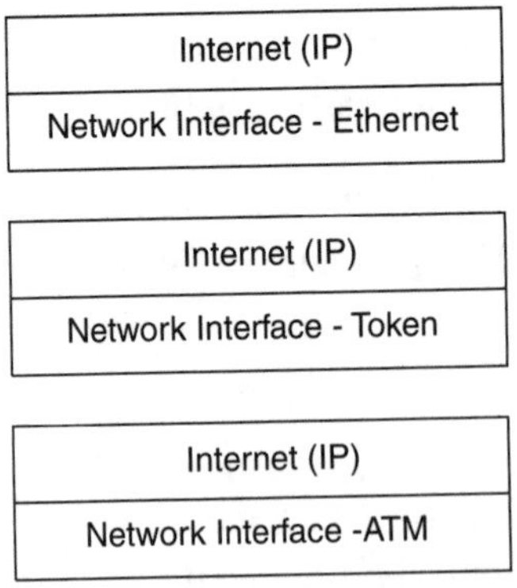

Internet (IP)
Network Interface - Ethernet

Internet (IP)
Network Interface - Token

Internet (IP)
Network Interface -ATM

The network interface layer is concerned with the physical, electrical, and addressing requirements for the particular technology used to deliver the messages. The IP layer is a logical layer concerned with being able to route a message between endpoints. The IP layer in the Internet model should be independent from the network interface layer. This independence allows you to change the technology used at the network interface layer without having to modify the IP layer.

Inter-LAN Communication

The host with IP address 192.20.1.1 on the Fullerton LAN wants to send data to the host with IP address 192.20.3.3 on the Kostner LAN. The source and destination IP addresses are

- Source: **192.20.1**.1

- Destination: **192.20.3**.3

The source host knows that the destination IP address is on a different network because

- Both source and destination network numbers are Class C.

- The source and destination Class C network numbers are not the same; therefore, the source and destination computers are on different networks.

The host on the Fullerton LAN doesn't have to know how to get a message to the host on the Kostner LAN. That is the function of the router. Because the source host knows that the destination is on a different LAN or network, the host knows that it must send the message to the router. Each host has been configured with the IP address of the router interface that connects to their LAN. The router is the gateway to the rest of the world, so the IP address of the router is called the *default gateway*. In other words, if a host is sending a message to a different LAN, the message must first be sent to the default gateway, or router, or last resort. The process for inter-LAN communication is

1. Send an ARP broadcast asking for the Ethernet address associated with the default gateway (192.20.1.5).

2. The router responds with the Ethernet address of the interface that is connected to the source LAN (00-03-47-92-9C-73).

3. Host 192.20.1.1 stores the router's IP address, and associated Ethernet address in its local ARP table. The ARP table now contains

```
Interface: 192.20.1.1
Internet Address        Physical Address       Type
192.20.1.2              00-03-47-92-9C-70      dynamic
192.20.1.5              00-03-47-92-9C-73      dynamic
```

4. The source host sends the message to the router.

5. The router removes the source and destination Ethernet addresses from the message and inspects the destination IP address (192.20.3.3).

6. The router determines that the destination LAN is network 192.20.3.0 and the destination host IP address is 192.20.3.3.

7. The router sends an ARP request on the Kostner LAN asking for the Ethernet address associated with IP address 192.20.3.3.

8. Host 192.20.3.3 on the Kostner LAN sends an ARP reply containing its Ethernet address to the router (00-03-49-C5-12-33).

9. The router sends the message to the Ethernet address of host 192.20.3.3.

This process is similar to how mail is delivered. Figure 3-9 shows the flow of a letter down the protocol stack that was developed for the postal system.

Figure 3-9   Flow of a Letter Down the Mail Protocol Stack

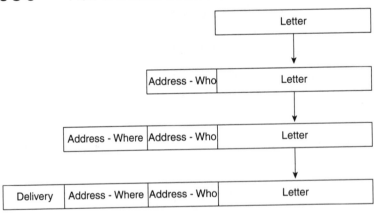

The letter is sent down to the Addressing Person, or Who layer where it is placed, or encapsulated, in an envelope. The envelope is sent to the Addressing Where layer and the state, city, street name, and street number information are added. Remember that you have logically separated the Who from the Where information, because the Who information is not used to deliver the letter. Finally, the envelope is passed to the Delivery layer where it is encapsulated or placed into whatever delivery means is being used (wagon, horse, truck, and so on).

As the letter makes its way through the postal delivery system, it passes through one or more post offices. At each post office the letter is removed from the delivery layer, and the destination address is inspected. Based on the destination address, the post office makes a routing decision and the letter is again sent back to the delivery layer and encapsulated (placed) in a new means of delivery. Between the source of the letter and the letter's destination, the means of delivery at each post office changes, but the source and destination addresses remain the same. This process can be used to better understand the delivery of an electronic message through a network. (See Figure 3-10.)

Figure 3-10   Flow of Data Down the IP Stack

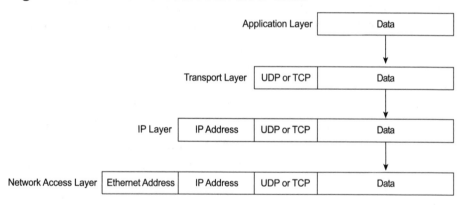

Your application generates the data to be sent to another host. This data could be an e-mail, an instant message, a request for a web page, and so on. The data is sent to the first addressing layer where an application identifier is placed on the data. Think of this as the Who part of the address. As with the postal system, this information is not used to deliver the data, but to identify which application should receive the data after it arrives at the destination. After the application identifier is placed on the data, the next layer in the protocol stack adds the source and destination IP addresses. Finally, the network interface layer adds the source and destination Ethernet addresses on the package (assuming the host is using Ethernet), and the package is transmitted toward the destination. In the Internet, the package of data is called a *packet*.

For intra-LAN communication, the receiving host inspects the destination Ethernet address, and accepts the package if the host sees its own Ethernet address. If it does, the Ethernet addresses (source and destination) will be stripped off, and the remaining package will be sent to the IP layer. The IP layer inspects the destination IP address to verify that the package is meant for this host. If it is, the IP address is stripped off and sent to the application identification layer. After the application has been identified, this information is stripped off and the data is sent to the proper application.

For inter-LAN communication, the package is sent to the router. The router inspects the destination Ethernet address and accepts the package if the router sees its own Ethernet address. If it does, the Ethernet addresses (source and destination) are stripped off and the remaining package is sent to the router's IP layer. The destination IP address is inspected, and the router consults the routing table to determine the interface it needs to use to send the package to the destination. The router looks for the destination IP and Ethernet address association in the ARP table. If the association is not in the ARP table, the router uses ARP to learn the destination Ethernet address associated with the destination IP address. The package is sent back to the network interface layer, and the package is encapsulated using new source and destination Ethernet addresses. Finally, the package is sent to the host, and the host will perform the same functions as mentioned for intra-LAN delivery.

The package might have to travel through more than one router. At each router, the same process takes place. The old Ethernet source and destination addresses are removed, the IP routing table is consulted, and new source and destination Ethernet addresses are applied. But no matter how many routers the package goes through, the source and destination IP addresses do not change. Only the network interface layer addresses change. The analogy between the layers of the mail and data delivery systems is shown in Figure 3-11.

Figure 3-11 Mail and Electronic Data Delivery Protocol Stacks

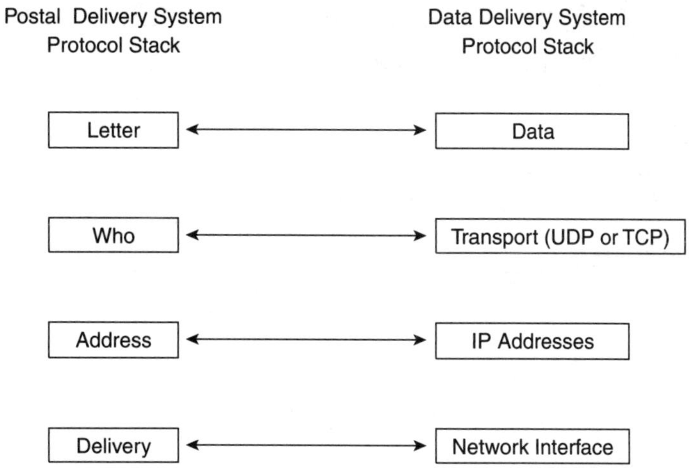

Postal Delivery System
Protocol Stack

Data Delivery System
Protocol Stack

| Letter | ←──────────→ | Data |

| Who | ←──────────→ | Transport (UDP or TCP) |

| Address | ←──────────→ | IP Addresses |

| Delivery | ←──────────→ | Network Interface |

IP Header Format

Unlike the post office, a router or computer cannot determine the size of a package without additional information. A person can look at a letter or box and determine how big it is, but a router cannot. Therefore, additional information is required at the IP layer, in addition to the source and destination IP addresses. Figure 3-12 is a logical representation of the information that is used at the IP layer to enable the delivery of electronic data. This information is called a *header*, and is analogous to the addressing information on an envelope. A header contains the information required to route data on the Internet, and has the same format regardless of the type of data being sent. This is the same for an envelope where the address format is the same regardless of the type of letter being sent.

Figure 3-12   IP Header Format

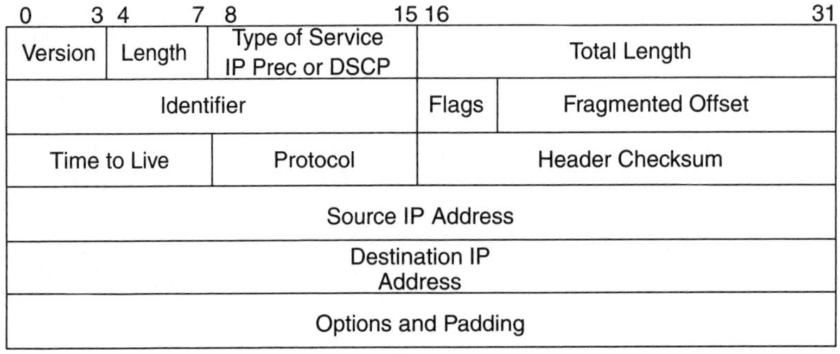

Version	Length	Type of Service IP Prec or DSCP	Total Length	

The fields in the IP header and their descriptions are

- **Version**—A 4-bit field that identifies the IP version being used. The current version is 4, and this version is referred to as IPv4.

- **Length**—A 4-bit field containing the length of the IP header in 32-bit increments. The minimum length of an IP header is 20 bytes, or five 32-bit increments. The maximum length of an IP header is 24 bytes, or six 32-bit increments. Therefore, the header length field should contain either 5 or 6.

- **Type of Service(ToS)**—The 8-bit ToS uses 3 bits for IP Precedence, 4 bits for ToS with the last bit not being used. The 4-bit ToS field, although defined, has never been used.

- **IP Precedence**— A 3-bit field used to identify the level of service a packet receives in the network.

- **Differentiated Services Code Point (DSCP)**-A 6-bit field used to identify the level of service a packet receives in the network. DSCP is a 3-bit expansion of IP precedence with the elimination of the ToS bits.

- **Total Length**—Specifies the length of the IP packet that includes the IP header and the user data. The length field is 2 bytes, so the maximum size of an IP packet is $2^{16} - 1$ or 65,535 bytes.

- **Identifier, Flags, and Fragment Offset**-As an IP packet moves through the Internet, it might need to cross a route that cannot handle the size of the packet. The packet will be divided, or fragmented, into smaller packets and reassembled later. These fields are used to fragment and reassemble packets.

- **Time to Live (TTL)**—It is possible for an IP packet to roam aimlessly around the Internet. If there is a routing problem or a routing loop, then you don't want packets to be forwarded forever. A routing loop is when a packet is continually routed through the same routers over and over. The TTL field is initially set to a number and decremented by every router that is passed through. When TTL reaches 0 the packet is discarded.

- **Protocol**—In the layered protocol model, the layer that determines which application the data is from or which application the data is for is indicated using the Protocol field. This field does not identify the application, but identifies a protocol that sits above the IP layer that is used for application identification.

- **Header Checksum**—A value calculated based on the contents of the IP header. Used to determine if any errors have been introduced during transmission.

- **Source IP Address**—32-bit IP address of the sender.

- **Destination IP Address**—32-bit IP address of the intended recipient.

- **Options and Padding**—A field that varies in length from 0 to a multiple of 32-bits. If the option values are not a multiple of 32-bits, 0s are added or padded to ensure this field contains a multiple of 32 bits.

The IP Precedence field can be used to prioritize IP traffic. (See Table 3-9.) This is the same as the postal system having different classes of mail such as priority, overnight, and 2-day delivery. Routers can choose to use this field to give preferential treatment to certain types of IP traffic.

Table 3-9   IP Precedence Values

Precedence Value	Meaning
000 (0)	Routine or Best Effort
001 (1)	Priority
010 (2)	Immediate
011 (3)	Flash

continues

Table 3-9   IP Precedence Values (continued)

Precedence Value	Meaning
100 (4)	Flash Override
101 (5)	Critical
110 (6)	Internetwork Control
111 (7)	Network Control

The ToS bits were originally designed to influence the delivery of data based on delay, throughput, reliability and cost. (See Table 3-10.) They are usually not used and are therefore set to zero.

Table 3-10   Type of Service Values

ToS Value	Meaning
0000 (0)	Normal Delivery
0001 (1)	Minimize Cost
0010 (2)	Maximize Reliability
0100 (4)	Maximize Throughput
1000 (8)	Minimize Delay

The IP Precedence field can have 8 or 2^3 possible values. Routers use two of these values, 6 and 7, for routing protocol traffic. That leaves six values that can be used to prioritize user traffic. Because the ToS bits are typically not used, the IP Precedence field can be extended from 3 to 6 bits by using 3 bits from the ToS field. (See Figure 3-13.)

Figure 3-13   IP Header Type of Service (ToS) Field

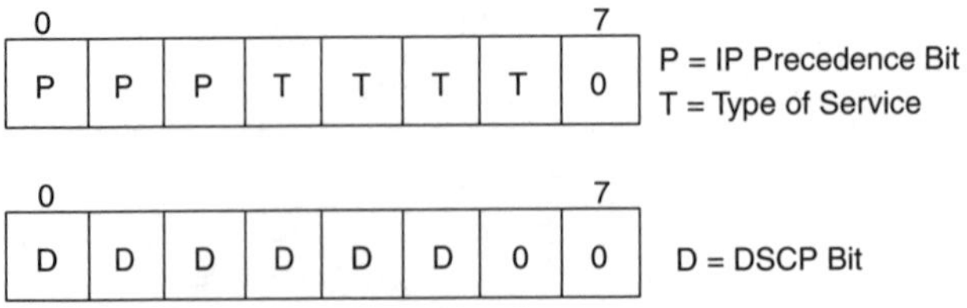

0						7		
P	P	P	T	T	T	T	0	P = IP Precedence Bit T = Type of Service

0						7		
D	D	D	D	D	D	0	0	D = DSCP Bit

This new field is called the Differentiated Services Code Point (DSCP). That gives you 64 or 2^6 possible values that can be used to prioritize traffic. Although there are 64 possible DSCP values, only 14 are used typically. (See Table 3-11 and the explanation that follows.)

Table 3-11 Differentiated Services Code Point Values

DSCP Value	Meaning	Drop Probability	Equivalent IP Precedence Value
101 110 (46)	High Priority Expedited Forwarding (EF)	N/A	101 – Critical
000 000 (0)	Best Effort	N/A	000 – Routine
001 010 (10)	AF11	Low	001 – Priority
001 100 (12)	AF12	Medium	001 – Priority
001 110 (14)	AF13	High	001 – Priority
010 010 (18)	AF21	Low	001 – Immediate
010 100 (20)	AF22	Medium	001 – Immediate
010 110 (22)	AF23	High	001 – Immediate
011 010 (26)	AF31	Low	011 – Flash
011 100 (28)	AF32	Medium	011 – Flash
011 110 (30)	AF33	High	011 – Flash
100 010 (34)	AF41	Low	100 – Flash Override
100 100 (36)	AF42	Medium	100 – Flash Override
100 110 (38)	AF43	High	100 – Flash Override

Notice that the first 3 bits of the DSCP value are the 3 bits from the IP precedence. An IP precedence of 000 maps into a DSCP value of 000 000, and both represent best effort delivery. An IP precedence of 101 (Critical) maps into a DSCP value of 101 110 (High Priority or Expedited Forwarding). The remaining 4 IP precedence values are each mapped into 3 DSCP values. The additional 3-bit portion is used to identify a drop probability within one of the four assured forwarding (AF) classes.

This discussion of the contents of the IP header is meant as an overview. If you are interested in learning more details regarding the IP header, refer to the references at the end of this chapter. The important concept to take away from this discussion is that the IP header contains the source and destination IP addresses. Routers use the destination IP address to determine a route; therefore, the IP layer in the layered model is the routing layer.

At this point, we could stop our discussion of the layered protocol model. This book is about routing, and routing is the second or third layer depending on which model is used. A router does not care what application sent the data, or how the application is going to receive the data. The job of the router is to get the packet to the proper destination. It is then the responsibility of the destination host to deliver the data to the application. The incomplete layered model in Figure 3-8 is sufficient for the remainder of this book. But, to be complete, let's go ahead and finish the model.

TCP/IP Layered Protocol Model

There are different types of service that you can use when delivering a letter. You can use a best effort model. This means that you simply place a stamp on the letter and drop it in a mailbox. How do you know if the letter was delivered? You don't. Not unless the recipient somehow tells you they received the letter. If you want to ensure delivery, you could send a registered letter. After the letter has been delivered, you will receive an acknowledgment from the post office. The layered postal delivery model needs to be modified to include this feature. (See Figure 3-14.) Although IP is used to deliver packets, and TCP and UDP are transport level protocols, the layer model for the Internet is usually referred to as the TCP/IP model.

Figure 3-14   Post Office Layered Protocol Model

Contents	
Addressing - Person	
Normal	Registered
Addressing - Location	
Physical Delivery	

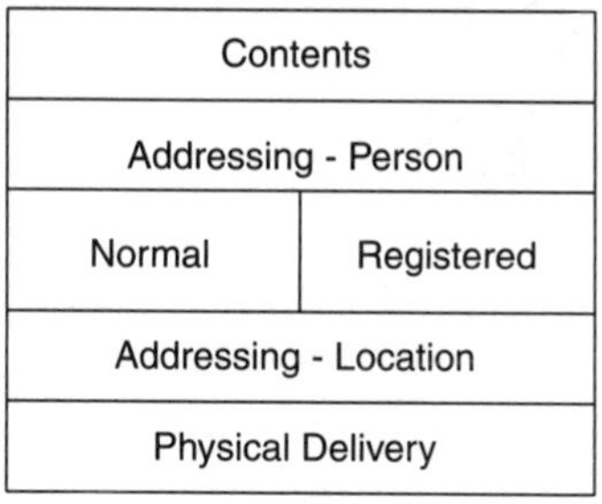

At the Addressing – Person layer, two options have been added:

- **Normal delivery**—The sender will not receive any acknowledgment that the letter has been delivered.

- **Registered mail**– The sender will receive an acknowledgment after the letter has been delivered.

The Internet layered model has two additional protocols that are equivalent to normal and registered mail:

- **Transmission Control Protocol (TCP)**—The equivalent of a registered letter. When data is received at the destination host, an acknowledgment is sent back to the sender.

- **User Datagram Protocol (UDP)**—The equivalent of normal mail. An acknowledgment is not sent back to the sender.

Integrating TCP and UDP into the Internet model gives you the complete TCP/IP layered protocol model. (See Figure 3-15.)

Figure 3-15   TCP/IP Layered Model or Protocol Stack

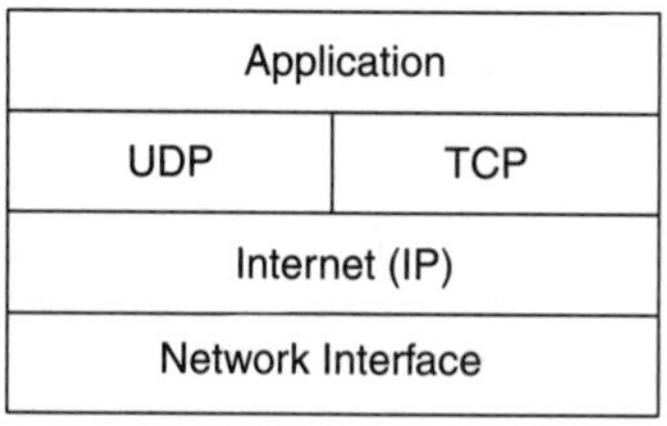

Application	
UDP	TCP
Internet (IP)	
Network Interface	

The port information in the UDP header is used to identify the sending and receiving applications. (See Figure 3-16.)

Figure 3-16   UDP Header Format

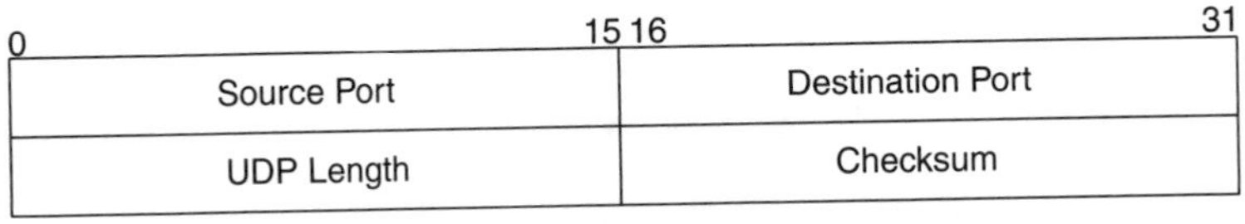

0	15 16	31
Source Port	Destination Port	
UDP Length	Checksum	

The source port is equivalent to the person who is sending the letter. The destination port is equivalent to the person who is to receive the letter. Applications initially will use a well-known port number. For example, if you are using a web browser to contact the Cisco website, your application will send a message to port 80 at IP address 198.133.219.25. The source port is usually assigned dynamically for the application and is included in the UDP header. When the webserver for Cisco.com sends a reply, it will send it back to the dynamic port number that was assigned for the sender's application. The destination IP address is used to reach the host running the web server, and the destination port number is used to reach the proper application. The combination of a port number and an IP address is called a *socket*. A socket is sufficient to identify a particular application on a specific host.

The TCP header is similar to the UDP header with additional fields to enable acknowledgments. (See Figure 3-17.)

Figure 3-17   TCP Header Format

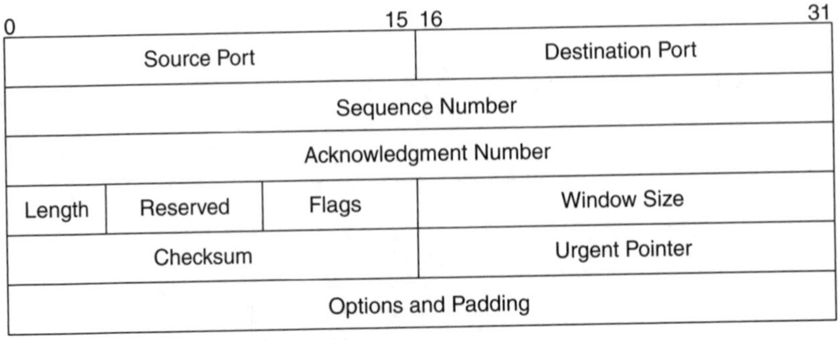

0		15 16	31
Source Port		Destination Port	
Sequence Number			
Acknowledgment Number			
Length	Reserved	Flags	Window Size
Checksum		Urgent Pointer	
Options and Padding			

The source and destination port numbers serve the same function as they did in the UDP header. The remaining fields are used to send the equivalent of registered mail. The operation of the TCP protocol can be complex. If you are interested in learning more, consult the reference list at the end of the chapter.

Before moving on to the next exciting topic, let's trace the flow through the TCP/IP protocol stack. (See Figure 3-18.)

Figure 3-18   Data Flow Through the TCP/IP Protocol Stack

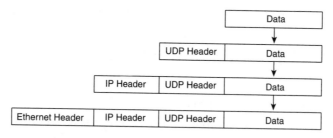

UDP Header - Source and Destination Port Numbers
IP Header - Source and Destination IP Addresses
Ethernet Header - Source and Destination Ethernet Addresses

The application sends the data, such as the text of an e-mail, you are sending to UDP or TCP where the destination and source port numbers are recorded. The IP layer adds the source and destination IP addresses, and sets the protocol field to UDP or TCP depending on what is being used. The IP layer then hands the packet off to the network interface layer. This example uses Ethernet, so the network interface layer adds the source and destination Ethernet addresses. Finally, the entire thing is sent to the network to be sent to the destination.

Upon receipt of an IP packet by a host, the destination Ethernet address is first inspected. If it matches the host's Ethernet address, the Ethernet header is stripped off, and the remaining part of the packet is sent up the protocol stack to the IP layer. The IP layer looks at the destination IP address. If it is the correct IP address, the IP layer strips off the IP header, and sends what is left either to TCP or UDP—depending on the setting of the protocol field. UDP or TCP then uses the destination port number to send the data to the correct application.

Classless Internet Addressing

Using a classful IP addressing format worked well when the Internet was relatively small. But as the number of networks on the Internet grew, the limitations of classful addresses became apparent. The Class A address space contains only 125 usable networks in the range 0–127 because networks 0 and 127 are reserved, and network 10 is used for private addressing. Each of these 125 Class A networks could theoretically contain $2^{24} - 2$ or 16,777,214 hosts, but it's not realistic to have more than 16 million hosts on the same network. Therefore, in the early 1990s, the Internet moved away from a classful address space to a classless address space. In other words, the number of bits used for the network portion of an IP address became variable instead of fixed.

The network portion of classful IP addresses is fixed. For the network portion of an IP address, Class A addresses use 8 bits, Class B addresses use 16 bits, and Class C addresses use 24 bits. A router could determine the address class by inspecting the first byte of the address. A value of 1–126 is Class A, 128–191 is Class B, and 192–223 is Class C.

For classless IP addressing, there is no longer a relationship between the number of bits used in the network portion and the value of the first byte of the address. A different method has to be used to determine the size of the network portion of an IP address. This new method allows you to borrow bits that are normally used for the host portion of an IP address, and use them to extend the network portion of an IP address.

A router is a computer of sorts, and can therefore manipulate binary numbers quite well. It would seem natural to use a 1 to identify a bit in an IP address that is part of the network address, and a 0 to identify a bit that is used as the host address. These bits can be thought of as masking off the network address from the host address. An IP address is 32 bits, so a 32-bit mask is needed to determine the network and host components of an IP address. Figure 3-19 contains the natural mask values for Class A, B, and C addresses.

Figure 3-19   Classful IP Address Masks

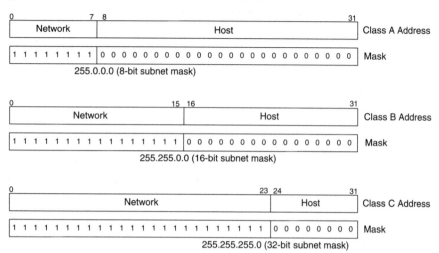

There are two common ways to refer to the mask that is used to determine the number of bits used for the network component of an IP address. The first is to use the number of 1 bits in the mask. A Class A mask is an 8-bit mask, Class B is a 16-bit mask, and Class C is a 24-bit mask. The other way is to represent the mask as / (slash) and then the number of 1 bits in the mask. Class A is /8 (slash 8), Class B is /16 (slash 16), and Class C is /24 (slash 24). An important rule is that the number of 1s and 0s in a mask must be contiguous (all the 1s must be together and all the 0s must be together). For example

11111111 11111111 00000000 00000000 is a valid mask.

11111111 00111111 00000000 00000111 is not a valid mask.

Using a mask to determine the network component of an IP address is called a *bitwise logical AND operation*. Bitwise AND is equivalent to bitwise multiplication:

A * 1 = A

A * 0 = 0 where A = 0 or 1

A router can determine the network component of the classful IP address 156.26.32.1 by using a mask as shown:

156.26.32.1

AND

255.255.0.0

Equals

156.26.0.0

This might seem like a trivial operation. For classful addresses, this is a fair statement because the network component is on an easy-to-use byte boundary. But you want to be able to switch from classful to classless addressing, and you will need a mask to do that.

As an introduction to classless addressing, assume that your company has been assigned the Class B address 156.26.0.0. If you use this as a classful address, you can have one network with $2^{16}-2$ or 65,534 hosts. You would like to have more than one network with fewer hosts on each network. This means you will have to create subnets from the assigned Class B address space. Instead of using a 16-bit mask, or /16, see what happens if you use a 17-bit subnet mask:

IP Address = 156.26.0.0

Subnet Mask = 255.255.128.0

The Class B part, or 156.26, is fixed and cannot be changed. But your company owns the following 16 bits, so they can be any value you want. The seventeenth bit of your network address can either be a 0 or a 1. If it is 0, that identifies network 156.26.0.0. If the seventeenth bit is a 1, that identifies network 156.26.128.0. By borrowing 1 bit from the standard host portion of the IP address and assigning it to the network portion, you have created two subnets of the Class B address space 156.26. The first subnetwork has host addresses in the range 156.26.0.1–156.26.127.254.

The broadcast address is 156.26.127.255.

The second subnetwork has host addresses in the range 156.26.128.1–156.26.255.254.

The broadcast address is 156.26.255.255.

This operation is shown in Figure 3-20.

Figure 3-20   Subnetting a Class B Address with a 17-bit Mask

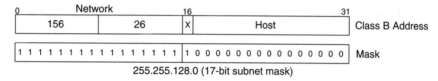

255.255.128.0 (17-bit subnet mask)

If you use 2 additional bits, or a /18 bit mask, you will have four subnets. These four subnets are identified by the four values possible with 2 bits:

    0 0

    0 1

    1 0

    1 1

Remember, the network is identified by setting the host portion of the IP address to 0. So, the first subnet using an 18-bit mask is 156.26.0.0.

The second subnet is determined by calculating the value of the third byte when the most significant bits are 0 1:

0 1 0 0 0 0 0 0 = 64

Subnet 2 has a network address of 156.26.64.0.

The third subnet is determined by calculating the value of the third byte when the most significant bits are 1 0:

1 0 0 0 0 0 0 0 = 128

Subnet 2 has a network address of 156.26.128.0.

And the fourth subnet is determined by calculating the value of the third byte when the most significant bits are 1 1:

1 1 0 0 0 0 0 0 = 192

Subnet 4 has a network address of 156.26.192.0.

If you continue this logic, you obtain the information in Table 3-12.

Table 3-12   Number of Networks and Hosts for a Subnetted Class B Network

Subnet Mask in Bits	Number of Networks	Number of Hosts
16 (Class B)	1	65,534
17	2	32,766
18	4	16,382
19	8	8190
20	16	4096
21	32	2048
22	64	1022
23	128	510
24	256	254
25	512	126
26	1,024	62
27	2,048	30
28	4,096	14
29	8,192	6
30	16,384	2

The first entry is for a Class B network. Increase the subnet mask by 1 bit, and calculate the number of subnetworks and hosts to find the remaining entries. The number of possible subnetworks is 2 raised to the power of the number of extra bits used for the network. The number of hosts is 2 to the power of the bits left over for the host portion of the address – 2 (broadcast and "this" network addresses).

It seems that there are two entries missing in Table 3-12. One for a 31-bit subnet mask and one for a 32-bit subnet mask. You can't have a 32-bit subnet mask because there would be no bits left over for host addresses. A 31-bit mask would leave only 1 bit for the host addresses, either 0 or 1. The broadcast address is obtained by setting all the host bits to 1. The "this" network address is found by setting all the host bits to 0. So, if you used 31-bits, the addresses you would have available are only the broadcast and "this" network addresses.

You do not have to use only one subnet mask to divide the 156.26.0.0 address space in subnetworks. You can use different masks on different networks. For example, assume you have the following requirements for your company's network:

- A maximum of 60 Class C size networks (1–254 hosts)

- A maximum of 14 networks having a maximum of 10 hosts

- Four point-to-point networks

You need to satisfy these requirements, and you want to have addresses in reserve that you can use if your company expands. Where do you start? There is not just one correct way of doing this. You have a Class B address space assigned to you, and you shall see that this will not be that difficult. First, let's subnet the Class B address space into four equal size pieces. For four subnets, you will need to use 2 bits from the host address or a /18 subnet mask. The third byte of the IP address is divided as

N N H H H H H H (2 bits for the network and 6 bits for the host)

To determine the network numbers, first set the host bits to 0:

N N 0 0 0 0 0 0

The possible network values for the third byte are

$00000000 = 0$

$01000000 = 64$

$10000000 = 128$

$11000000 = 192$

The 156.26 address space is now divided into the following networks:

156.26.0.0

156.26.64.0

156.26.128.0

156.26.192.0

To satisfy the first requirement of a maximum of 60 Class C size networks, subnet the 156.26.0.0/18 address into Class C size or /24 subnets. How many Class C size subnets will this provide? We are using an additional 6 bits to subnet the 156.26.0.0/18 network, and $2^6 = 64$ subnets. This will be sufficient to satisfy the first requirement. The Class C networks will have the following addresses:

156.26.0.0/24

156.26.1.0/24

156.26.2.0/24

...

156.26.62.0/24

156.26.63.0/24

How were these network numbers determined? The 156.26.0.0/18 network was derived from the 156.26.0.0/16 network. The first 16 bits are fixed and equal to

156.26. The next 2 bits are fixed and equal to 0 because this is the subnet used for the Class C size networks. Therefore, the possible range of values for the third byte are

00 0 0 0 0 0 0 = 0
00 0 0 0 0 0 1 = 1
00 0 0 0 0 1 0 = 2

...

00 1 1 1 1 1 0 = 62
00 1 1 1 1 1 1 = 63

For the first requirement, use networks 156.26.0.0/24 through 156.26.59.0/24.

To satisfy the second requirement, use the last Class C size network, 156.26.63.0, and subnet it to the proper size. For a maximum of 10 hosts, you will need 4 bits for the host address. With 4 bits, a network can support 14 hosts (16 − 2). Because a Class C size network is being subnetted, there are only 8 bits to work with (the last byte). Four bits are needed for the hosts, which leaves 4 bits for the network. The requirement is 14 networks, and 4 network bits can support 16 networks. The last byte is divided, so 4 bits are used for the network and 4 bits for the host:

N N N N H H H H

The networks addresses are

0 0 0 0 0 0 0 0 =   0 156.26.63.0/28
0 0 0 1 0 0 0 0 = 16 156.26.63.16/28
0 0 1 0 0 0 0 0 = 32 156.26.63.32/28

......

1 1 1 0 0 0 0 0 = 224 156.26.63.224/28
1 1 1 1 0 0 0 0 = 240 156.26.63.240/28

The host addresses are

> 156.26.63.1–156.26.63.14
>
> 156.26.63.17–156.26.63.30
>
> 156.26.63.33–156.26.63.46
>
> ...
>
> 156.26.63.225–156.26.63.238
>
> 156.26.63.241–156.26.63.254

For the final requirement of four point-to-point networks, the 156.26.63.240 network will be subnetted using a 30-bit mask. A point-to-point network requires only two host addresses.

There are 4 bits available on the 156.26.63.240/28 subnet. Two are needed for the host bits. The two remaining bits are sufficient for the four point-to-point networks that are required. The last byte of the 156.26.63.240 is used for the final subnetting operation:

> 1 1 1 1 N N H H

The network numbers using a 30-bit mask are

> 1 1 1 1 0 0 0 0 = 240 156.26.63.240
>
> 1 1 1 1 0 1 0 0 = 244 156.26.63.244
>
> 1 1 1 1 1 0 0 0 = 248 156.26.63.248
>
> 1 1 1 1 1 1 0 0 = 252 156.26.63.252

The host addresses are

> 156.26.63.241 and 242
>
> 156.26.63.245 and 246
>
> 156.26.63.249 and 250
>
> 156.26.63.253 and 254

The final plan is shown in Figure 3-21.

Figure 3-21   Subnetting a Class B Address

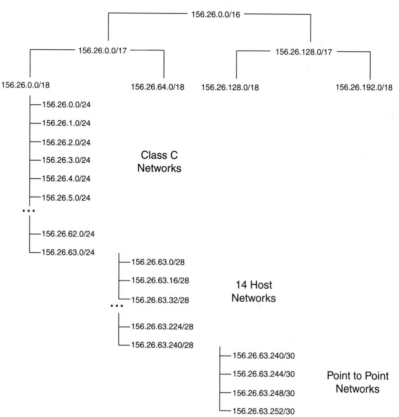

If this is your first experience dealing with subnet masks and you find it a bit confusing, take comfort in the fact that this is normal. Subnets and subnet masks take time to master. Get some paper and a pencil and practice, practice, practice. To aid in your understanding, try the following problems:

1. What is the broadcast address for network 156.26.0.0/16?

    Answer: Set the 16 host bits to 1 to obtain 156.26.255.255.

2. What is the broadcast address for network 156.26.0.0/24?

Answer: Set the 8 host bits to 1 to obtain 156.26.0.255.

3. What is the broadcast address for network 156.26.0.0/28?

Answer: Set the 4 host bits to 1 to obtain 156.26.0.15.

4. The Class C address 195.14.22.0 is subnetted using a 27-bit subnet mask. How many subnets are there and what are the network numbers?

Answer: The natural mask for a Class C address is /24. Therefore, 33 additional bits are used for the subnet, $2^3 = 8$, so there are eight subnets. The 3 additional network bits are taken from the fourth byte so the network numbers are

0 0 0 0 0 0 0 0 = 0 195.14.22.0/27

0 0 1 0 0 0 0 0 = 32 195.14.22.32/27

0 1 0 0 0 0 0 0 = 64 195.14.22.64/27

0 1 1 0 0 0 0 0 = 96 195.14.22.96/27

1 0 0 0 0 0 0 0 = 128 195.14.22.128/27

1 0 1 0 0 0 0 0 = 160 195.14.22.160/27

1 1 0 0 0 0 0 0 = 192 195.14.22.192/27

1 1 1 0 0 0 0 0 = 224 195.14.22.224/27

5. What is the range of host addresses for the network 195.14.22.64/27?

Answer: 195.14.22.65 – 195.14.22.94

6. What is the broadcast address for network 195.14.22.64/27?

Answer: 64 = 0 1 0 0 0 0 0 0, so the broadcast address is:

0 1 0 1 1 1 1 1 = 95 or 195.14.22.95

IP Routing and Route Summarization

The network in Figure 3-22 is a partial implementation of the addressing plan developed for the 156.26.0.0 network.

Figure 3-22   Example Network for Route Summarization

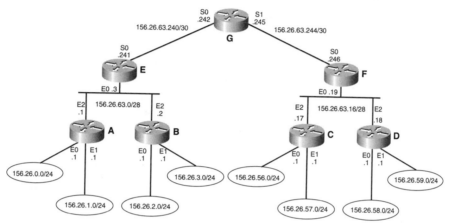

Routers A, B, C, and D are access routers and each one connects to two Class C size networks. Routers E and F are the distribution routers, and Router G is the core router. The terminology used in Figure 3-22 is explained in Figure 3-23.

The network in Figure 3-22 has 12 subnets, so each router will have 12 entries in its IP routing table. The routing table for Router G is listed in Table 3-13. Initially, the only routes in the IP routing table are the directly connected networks. The other subnets need to be learned either statically or dynamically. *Statically* means that every route has to be manually entered on every router. The network has 7 routers so 7 * 12, or 84, routes would need to be entered for IP routing to work. Certainly this can be done, but it would take some time and would be prone to error. Imagine entering all routes statically for a network with hundreds of routers and thousands of routes. This is not a scalable solution. A better solution is to use a dynamic IP routing protocol that will dynamically advertise routes throughout your network. The later chapters will discuss IP routing protocols. For now, assume that all the routes have been entered statically.

Figure 3-23 Network Terminology

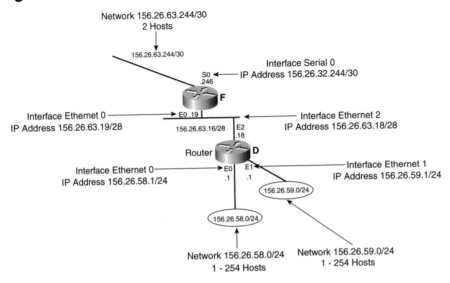

Table 3-13 IP Routing Table for Router G

Route	Output Interface
156.26.63.240/30	Directly connected, Serial 0
156.26.63.244/30	Directly connected, Serial 1
156.26.63.0/28	Serial 0
156.26.63.16/28	Serial 1
156.26.0.0/24	Serial 0
156.26.1.0/24	Serial 0
156.26.2.0/24	Serial 0
156.26.3.0/24	Serial 0
156.26.56.0/24	Serial 1
156.26.57.0/24	Serial 1
156.26.58.0/24	Serial 1
156.26.59.0/24	Serial 1

The network in Figure 3-22 is similar to the network that was developed in Chapter 1 for the statewide delivery of mail. Router G is equivalent to the core post office that routed mail between states, and between cities in a state. Routers E and F are equivalent to the distribution post offices that routed mail between the access post offices and the state post office. Routers A, B, C, and D are equivalent to the access post offices that routed mail between streets (networks) and the distribution post offices. For the statewide postal network, the core post office did not need to know about every street. It was sufficient to route mail based on the city name. For routing between states, the core post office did not need to know the route to every city and every street in another state. It was sufficient to route interstate mail based on the state name alone. This process of information hiding, or route reduction, was called *route summarization* or aggregation. It would be nice if IP routes could be aggregated to reduce the size of the routing tables.

Routes are summarized, or aggregated, by reversing the subnetting process. For example, in Figure 3-21, the 156.26.63.240/28 network was subnetted into 4 /30 networks:

156.26.63.240/30

156.26.63.244/30

156.26.63.248/30

156.26.63.252/30

A router can have these four specific routes in the routing table. Or, a router can have one route, or ***IP prefix***, that summarizes these four specific networks. The summary prefix 156.26.63.240/28 contains every possible subnet of 156.26.63.240/28 in the same way that a state contains every possible city and street name contained within that state. The state name summarizes all the city and street names into one prefix. A summary address allowed the core post office to maintain one route to another state and not a route for every possible destination in the other state.

A summary prefix should only summarize those subnets that are actually being used. The prefix 156.26.0.0/16 summarizes all the subnets of the Class B address space 156.26.0.0. So the prefix 156.26.0.0/16 does summarize the four specific /30 subnets of 156.26.63.240/28, but it also summarizes all other subnets of 156.26.0.0/16. This summary tells a router that all subnets of 156.26.0.0/16 are reachable even though many of the subnets might not be in use.

For the network in Figure 3-22 and subnets in Table 3-13, the subnets can be summarized into one route advertisement.

For Router G, 156.26.0.0/24 through 156.26.3.0/24 can be reached through interface serial 0. If you look at the bit patterns of these four subnets, you can determine the subnet mask to use to summarize these routes. It is sufficient, in this case, to examine only the third byte of the subnets:

$$0 = 0\ 0\ 0\ 0\ 0\ 0\ 0\ 0$$
$$1 = 0\ 0\ 0\ 0\ 0\ 0\ 0\ 1$$
$$2 = 0\ 0\ 0\ 0\ 0\ 0\ 1\ 0$$
$$3 = 0\ 0\ 0\ 0\ 0\ 0\ 1\ 1$$

The subnet mask that needs to be used should include only those bits that do not change. For these four routes, the upper 6 bits do not change. These 6 bits need to be included in the summary subnet mask. The value of the mask for the third byte is 1 1 1 1 1 1 0 0 = 252, so the required subnet mask is 255.255.252.0.

Applying the same process to the subnets 156.26.56.0/24 through 156.26.59.0/24, the values of the third byte are

$$56 = 0\ 0\ 1\ 1\ 1\ 0\ 0\ 0$$
$$57 = 0\ 0\ 1\ 1\ 1\ 0\ 0\ 1$$
$$58 = 0\ 0\ 1\ 1\ 1\ 0\ 1\ 0$$
$$59 = 0\ 0\ 1\ 1\ 1\ 0\ 1\ 1$$

As with the previous example, the upper 6 bits need to be included in the subnet mask and the required mask is again 255.255.252.0. The new routing table for Router G is listed in Table 3-14.

Table 3-14   IP Routing Table for Router G Using Summary Prefixes

Route	Output Interface
156.26.63.240/30	Directly connected, Serial 0
156.26.63.244/30	Directly connected, Serial 1
156.26.63.0/28	Serial 0
156.26.63.16/28	Serial 1
156.26.0.0/22	Serial 0
156.26.56.0/22	Serial 1

The routing table on Router G has been reduced from 12 to 6 routes, a significant reduction. Notice that the two new summary prefixes have a 22-bit subnet mask instead of a 24-bit subnet mask. To see how this works, assume Router G receives a packet for the host at IP address 156.26.2.37. There is no subnet mask information in a destination IP address. The router will find the best match for this route from the routing table. An address with /32 is a host address:

156.26.2.37/32 = 10011100 00011010 00000010 00100101

156.26.0.0/22 = 10011100 00011010 00000000 00000000

There is a 22-bit match between the host address and the prefix 156.25.0.0/22, so this packet will be forward using interface serial 0.

What if subnet 156.26.3.0/24 was moved to Router C? (See Figure 3-24.)

Figure 3-24   Summary and Specific IP Prefixes

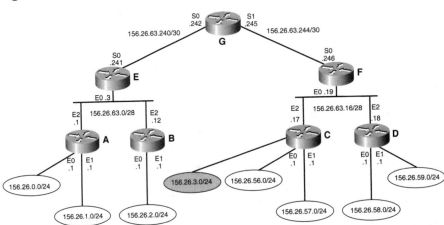

Can we still summarize the networks attached to Routers A and B? Yes. The summary prefix 156.26.0.0/22 contains 156.26.0.0/24 through 156.26.3.0/24, so Router G thinks it can reach the 156.26.3.0/24 network through Router E. You can keep this summary prefix as long as a more specific prefix for network 152.26.3.0/24 is added to the routing table on Router G. (See Table 3-15.)

Table 3-15   IP Routing Table for Router G Using Summary Prefixes and a More Specific Prefix

Route	Output Interface
156.26.63.240/30	Directly connected, Serial 0
156.26.63.244/30	Directly connected, Serial 1
156.26.63.0/28	Serial 0
156.26.63.16/28	Serial 1
156.26.0.0/22	Serial 0
156.26.56.0/22	Serial 1
156.26.3.0/24	Serial 1

Router G now has two routes to subnet 156.26.3.0/24. Which one will it use? Assume Router G receives a packet for host 156.26.3.12/32. Router G will compare this route with the entries in the routing table and there are two that match.

This matches 22 bits in the host address:

156.26.0.0/22 = 10011100 00011010 00000000 00000000

156.26.3.12/32 = 10011100 00011010 00000011 00001100

This matches 24 bits and the longest match wins. Router G will forward the packet to Router F:

156.26.3.0/24 = 10011100 00011010 00000011 00000000

156.26.3.12/32 = 10011100 00011010 00000011 00001100

Try reinforcing the key points with the following questions:

1. How many subnets of the Class C address 197.45.120.0/24 are there that can support at least 12 hosts?

   Answer: Four bits are required for 12 hosts ($2^4 - 2 = 14$). This is a Class C address, so there are 4 bits left for the network. Therefore, there are 16 subnets that can support at least 12 hosts.

2. What are the network numbers for the subnets in the previous question?

   Answer: The first 4 bits of the last byte are included in the network number.

   0 0 0 0 0 0 0 0 = 0 197.45.120.0

   0 0 0 1 0 0 0 0 = 16 197.45.120.16

   0 0 1 0 0 0 0 0 = 32 197.45.120.32

   0 0 1 1 0 0 0 0 = 48 197.45.120.48

   0 1 0 0 0 0 0 0 = 64 197.45.120.64

   0 1 0 1 0 0 0 0 = 80 197.45.120.80

   0 1 1 0 0 0 0 0 = 96 197.45.120.96

0 1 1 1 0 0 0 0 = 112 197.45.120.112

1 0 0 0 0 0 0 0 = 128 197.45.120.128

1 0 0 1 0 0 0 0 = 144 197.45.120.144

1 0 1 0 0 0 0 0 = 160 197.45.120.160

1 0 1 1 0 0 0 0 = 176 197.45.120.176

1 1 0 0 0 0 0 0 = 192 197.45.120.192

1 1 0 1 0 0 0 0 = 208 197.45.120.208

1 1 1 0 0 0 0 0 = 224 197.45.120.224

1 1 1 1 0 0 0 0 = 240 197.45.120.240

3. Summarize the 16 networks from the previous example into two equal size prefixes.

Answer: Examine the bit patterns of the fourth byte of the first 8 subnets.

0 0 0 0 0 0 0 0 = 0 197.45.120.0

0 0 0 1 0 0 0 0 = 16 197.45.120.16

0 0 1 0 0 0 0 0 = 32 197.45.120.32

0 0 1 1 0 0 0 0 = 48 197.45.120.48

0 1 0 0 0 0 0 0 = 64 197.45.120.64

0 1 0 1 0 0 0 0 = 80 197.45.120.80

0 1 1 0 0 0 0 0 = 96 197.45.120.96

0 1 1 1 0 0 0 0 = 112 197.45.120.112

The only bit that is constant is the first bit, so a 25-bit mask is needed. The summary for the first eight subnets is

197.45.120.0/25

The only bit that is constant for the second set of eight subnets is again the first bit and it is always 1. The summary for the second set of eight subnets is

197.45.120.128/25.

Supernets

When more bits are used than the natural mask length for the network portion of a Class A, B, or C address, this process was called *subnetting*. The natural mask for a Class A address is 8 bits. If more than 8 bits are used for the network portion of the IP address, we say that the Class A address has been subnetted.

You can also use fewer bits than the natural mask for the network portion. This process is called *supernetting*. For example, assume your company owns the following four Class C addresses:

> 200.10.4.0/24
>
> 200.10.5.0/24
>
> 200.10.6.0/24
>
> 200.10.7.0/24

You can aggregate the addresses using a 22-bit mask, which is 2 bits less than the natural 24-bit mask. The process is the same as subnetting, but the term that is used depends on whether more or fewer bits than the natural mask are being used. The supernet for these networks is 200.10.4.0/22.

IP Version 4 and IP Version 6

IP version 4 (IPv4) has not changed much since it was defined in 1981. For the last two decades, IPv4 has proven to be a robust and scalable protocol for Internet routing. Unfortunately, the designers of IPv4 did not anticipate the explosive growth of the Internet, or the need for more IP addresses than version 4 could supply.

IPv4 uses 32-bit IP address, and with 32 bits the maximum number of IP addresses is 2^{32} — or 4,294,967,296. This provides a little more than four billion IPv4 addresses (in theory). The number of IPv4 available addresses is actually less than the theoretical maximum number. The reason the actual number of usable IP addresses is less than the maximum is because the broadcast and "this" network addresses cannot be assigned to hosts. A usable IPv4 address is one that can be assigned to a host, implying a unicast IP address. The only unicast IP addresses available are Class A, B, and C addresses. How many unicast IPv4 addresses are there? There are $2^7 - 3$, or 126, possible Class A networks with numbers ranging from 1 to 126. (0 and 127 are not used, and 10 is the Class A private address space.) Each Class A network can have $2^{24} - 2$, or 16,777,216 hosts. (A host address of all 0s signifies the network address, and a host address of all 1s signifies the broadcast address.) The number of Class A hosts is 126 * 16,777,216 or 2,113,929,216. There are $2^{14} - 1$, or 16,383 Class B networks. (172.16.0.0 is the private Class B address space.) Each Class B network can have $2^{16} - 2$, or 65,534 hosts. The number of Class B hosts is 16,383 * 65,534, or 1,073,643,522. There are $2^{21} - 1$, or 2,097,151 possible Class C networks. (192.168.0.0 is the private Class C address space.) Each Class C network can have $2^8 - 2$, or 254, hosts. The number of Class C hosts is 2,097,151 * 254 or 532,676,354. The total number of IPv4 unicast addresses is 3,720,249,092. A Class A, B, or C address identifies one specific host, and these addresses are called unicast addresses. The private addresses can be used in a network, but cannot be advertised on the Internet. This allows many networks to use the same private address as long as the hosts using these addresses do not need to be connected to the Internet.

The actual number of usable IPv4 unicast addresses is less than four billion. But there are usable addresses that will never be used. When IPv4 addresses were first allocated to government agencies, universities, and businesses, the addresses were allocated as classful addresses. If a university received a Class A address, the university had 16,777,216 host addresses that could be used. I cannot imagine any university, business, or government agency using every possible address assigned to them. It is difficult to determine how many IPv4 unicast addresses will never be used, but I'm sure it is more than 1. So the actual number of usable IPv4 addresses is less than 3.7 billion.

At first glance, even 3.7 billion addresses seems like enough. One reason it is not enough is the majority of the IPv4 address space has been allocated to countries that were early implementers of the Internet. The United States and Europe own the majority of the IP address space. Emerging countries like China need more IP addresses than what is available, driving the need for a larger address space.

Also, in the twenty-first century, devices other than computers need an Internet address. Cell phones, PDAs, vehicles, and appliances are all becoming part of the Internet. There simply are not enough IPv4 addresses to go around. So the big question is, how much is enough?

The current world population is more than six billion people, so there are more people than there are IPv4 addresses. If you assume everyone will eventually need at least one IP address, it is easy to see IPv4 does not have enough addresses. For every bit added to an IP address, the size of the address space doubles. A 33-bit IP address has around 8.5 billion addresses. A 34-bit IP address has about 17 billion possible addresses, and so on. IP version 6 (IPv6) uses 128 bits and it is interesting to investigate if 128 bits satisfies the need for more IP addresses.

Using 128 bits gives a theoretical address space of $3.4 * 10^{38}$ addresses. This is 3.4 followed by 38 zeros, or 3,400,000,000,000,000,000,000,000,000,000,000,000,000. Wow! That looks like a BIG number. But how big is it? To put this number in perspective, we need something to compare it to.

There are approximately 100 billion nerve cells in your brain or $1 * 10^{11}$. If you divide the number of possible IPv6 addresses by the number of nerve cells in your brain you get

$3.4 * 10^{38} / 1.0 * 10^{11} = 3.4 * 10^{27}$ IPv6 address for every nerve cell in your brain.

There are approximately $7 * 10^{27}$ atoms in your body. $3.4 * 10^{38} / 7.0 * 10^{27} = 4.86 * 10^{10}$ IPv6 address for every atom in your body. This is more than 48 billion! Of course, you have to share these addresses with 6 billion plus people, so every atom in your body can only have 8 billion IPv6 addresses. By now you should be convinced that the number of possible addresses using 128 bits should last us for quite awhile.

IPv6 Address Format

IPv4 addresses are typically represented using the dotted decimal notation. For example, the 32-bit IPv4 address $10011100000110100010000000000001_2$ can be represented as the dotted decimal number 156.26.21.1.

IPv6 uses eight 16-bit hexadecimal numbers (8 * 16 = 128 bits) separated by a colon to represent a 128-bit IPv6 address using the following rules:

- Leading zeros in each 16-bit field are optional.

  Example: The IPv6 address

  1A23:120B:0000:0000:0000:7634:AD01:004D can be represented by

  1A23:120B:0:0:0:7634:AD01:004D

- Successive fields with the value 0 can be represented by a pair of colons (::).

  Example: The IPv6 address

  1A23:120B:0000:0000:0000:7634:AD01:004D can be represented by

  1A23:120B::7634:AD01:4D

  The double colon :: represents the number of 0s needed to produce eight 16-bit hexadecimal numbers.

- The double colon :: can be used only once to represent an IPv6 address.

  Example: The IPv6 address

  1A23:120B:0000:0000:1234:0000:0000:4D can be represented by

  1A23:120B::1234:0:0:004D or

  1A23:120B:0:0:124::4D, but not by

  1A23:120B::1234::4D because there is no way to determine how many zeros each :: represents.

IPv6 Address Types

IPv4 uses two types of addresses: unicast and multicast. Unicast addresses are the Class A, B, and C addresses and are used to identify a single host on the Internet. Multicast addresses are used to identify multiple hosts for the delivery of multicast traffic (discussed in more detail in Chapter 9, "Multicast—What the Post Office Can't Do"). IPv6 has three major address types: unicast, multicast, and anycast.

IPv6 unicast addresses are divided into five groups:

- Global unicast addresses—Equivalent in function to an IPv4 unicast address using 64 bits for the network ID and 64 bits for the host ID.

- Site-local unicast addresses—Equivalent to the IPv4 private addresses such as 10.0.0.0 and 172.16.0.0.

- Link-local unicast addresses—An IPv6 address that is automatically configured on an interface allowing hosts on the same subnet to communicate with each other without the need for a router.

- IPv4-compatible IPv6 addresses—Used to transport IPv6 messages over an IPv4 network. An IPv4 address is placed in the low-order 32 bits of an IPv6 address. For example, the IPv4-compatible IPv6 address for the IPv4 address 156.26.32.1 is

  0:0:0:0:0:0:156.26.32.1 = ::156.26.32.1 = ::9C1A2001

- IPv4-mapped IPv6 addresses—Similar to an IPv4-compatible address, and used to represent an IPv4 interface as an IPv6 interface using 16 ones before the IPv4 address. For example, the IPv4-mapped IPv6 address for the IPv4 address 156.26.32.1 is

  0:0:0:0:0:FF:156.26.32.1 = ::FFFF:9C1A:2001

IPv6 multicast addresses serve the same function as IPv4 mulitcast addresses (again, more on this in Chapter 9). The anycast address type is a unicast address assigned to a set of interfaces, and a packet is sent to the nearest interface.

IPv6 provides enough addresses to last for a very long time. Eventually, the Internet will move to the use of IPv6; and, for a time, IPv4 and IPv6 will both be used. Routing protocols must be able to handle both address formats. For an in-depth discussion of IPv6, refer to the references at the end of the chapter.

Summary

The delivery of an IP packet is similar in concept to the delivery of a letter in the postal system. The destination address on a letter consists of two parts used to deliver the letter to the final destination. The state, city, and street name are used to route the letter to the proper street. This is analogous to the network portion of an IP address used to route an IP packet to the proper network. The street number is used to determine the proper house while the host portion of an IP address is used to determine the destination host. The name on the letter determines the recipient of the letter, and on the Internet, the UDP or TCP port number serves a similar function. The port number is used to deliver the data to the proper application.

Although the concepts of mail and IP packet delivery are similar, the addressing details of IP are much more complicated and difficult to master. If you are planning on becoming a network professional, it is imperative that you master the details of IP addressing, subnetting, and summarization.

Chapter Review Questions

You can find the answers to these questions in Appendix A.

1. What is the broadcast address for network 142.16.72.0/23?

2. Subnet 198.4.81.0/24 into the maximum number of networks that can support 28 hosts each.

3. What is the broadcast address for network 198.4.81.96/27?

4. What is the prefix and subnet mask that summarizes the following networks:

162.8.0.0/22

162.8.4.0/22

162.8.8.0/22

162.8.12.0/22

5. Using the following routing table, determine the best route to reach the host at address 132.19.237.5.

Network Output Interface

132.0.0.0/8 Serial 0

132.16.0.0/11 Ethernet 1

132.16.233.0/22 Ethernet 2

6. What is the range of host addresses for network 172.16.53.96/27?

7. How many two-host subnets can be made from a /24 network?

8. What is the full IPv6 address represented by FF02::130F:5?

References

Two of these references are RFCs or Requests for Comments. RFC is a misleading name because RFCs are Internet standards that specify every protocol used on the Internet. There are thousands of RFCs, and a searchable index of RFCs can be found at http://www.ietf.org/rfc.html. RFCs are technical documents that are sometimes difficult to follow, so you might want to read the books listed here first.

- Comer, Douglas E. 2000. *Internetworking with TCP/IP, Volume 1: Principles, Protocols, and Architecture*, Fourth Edition. Upper Saddle River, NJ: Prentice Hall.

- Hinden, R. and S. Deering. July 1998. IP Version 6 Addressing Architecture. RFC 2373.

- Postel, J. September 1981, Internet Protocol. RFC 0791.

- Stevens, W. Richard. 1993. *TCP/IP Illustrated*, Volume 1. Upper Saddle River, NJ: Addison-Wesley.

What You Will Learn

After reading this chapter, you should be able to

- ✔ Explain the use of static routes and the concepts of dynamic routing protocols

- ✔ Understand the concepts, operation, and limitations of versions 1 and 2 of the Routing Information Protocol (RIP)

- ✔ Understand the terms convergence, split horizon, poison reverse, and metric as they are used with dynamic routing protocols

- ✔ Differentiate between a classful and a classless routing protocol

CHAPTER 4

Routing IP

Routing IP packets is similar to the routing of mail and phone calls. Each system uses an address with a structure that is routable. The function of routing in the systems is to get something from point A to point B. The postal system address contains state, city, and street information; a phone number contains area code and exchange information; and an IP address contains network and host information. What is common to these three types of addresses is that each can be routed based on a portion of the address. Mail can be routed using the state, state and city, or state, city, and street information. A phone call is routed using the area code, or area code and exchange information. An IP packet is routed using the network portion of the address. The remaining component of the address is not used until the street, exchange, or network has been reached. In addition, each system can be scaled using the concept of core, distribution, and access layers where a portion of the address makes a delivery decision at each layer. (See Table 4-1.)

Table 4-1 Routing Layers and Addresses for Mail, Phone Calls, and IP Packets

Routing Layer	Mail	Phone Calls	IP Packet
Core	State, City	Area Code	Network
Distribution	City	Exchange	Subnetwork
Access	Street	Local Number	Host

Each system is scalable because the address structure allows for a layered, or hierarchical, approach where each layer needs only the information necessary to make a routing decision.

Delivering Snail Mail and E-Mail— Any Difference?

To begin the discussion of routing IP packets, take a look at the network shown in Figure 4-1.

Figure 4-1   Single Router Network and Its Postal Analogy

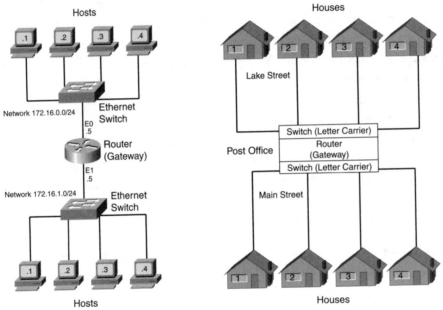

Figure 4-1 shows two systems: a single post office system and a single IP router system. The endpoints for the postal system are houses; the endpoints for the IP network are hosts or computers. Houses have a street address consisting of a street name and house number. Hosts have two addresses: a 32-bit IP address and a 48-bit Ethernet address. The post office is "connected" to two streets, Lake and Main. The router is connected to two IP networks, 172.16.0.0/24 and 172.16.1.0/24. Each IP network can have up to 254 hosts—256 minus the broadcast and "this" network addresses. The letter carrier in the postal system is equivalent to the switch in the IP network. The letter carrier delivers the mail to the proper house, and the switch delivers an IP packet to the proper host. The router routes packets between IP networks; the post office routes mail between streets.

Basic IP Router Configuration

How does the router know how to route between networks 172.16.0.0 and 172.16.1.0? Initially, it doesn't. The router needs to be programmed, or configured, before any routing can occur. Each interface on the router needs to be configured with an IP address and subnet mask. The IP address has to come from the block of addresses for the network that is connected to the router. Network 172.16.0.0 has four hosts with addresses 172.16.0.1, 172.16.0.2, 172.16.0.3, and 172.16.0.4. The addresses that are available for the router interface are 172.16.0.5 through 172.16.0.254. For this scenario, interface Ethernet 0 is configured to use IP address 172.16.0.5. A standard practice for representing router interfaces in a diagram is to use the first letter for the interface type along with a number indicating the actual physical interface. If a router has four Ethernet interfaces, they are represented as E0, E1, E2, and E3. For a Cisco router, the configuration for interface Ethernet 0, or E0, is

```
interface Ethernet0
 ip address 172.16.0.5 255.255.255.0
```

The configuration for interface Ethernet 1 is

```
interface Ethernet1
 ip address 172.16.1.5 255.255.255.0
```

The dotted decimal number 255.255.255.0 represents the 24-bit subnet mask that is used on the two IP networks. The router now knows about the two directly connected networks and can place them in its IP routing table as follows:

```
     172.16.0.0/24 is subnetted, 2 subnets
C       172.16.0.0 is directly connected, Ethernet0
C       172.16.1.0 is directly connected, Ethernet1
```

Each entry in the IP routing table contains a **_prefix_** and a mask. The prefix is determined by the length of the **_subnet mask_**. Networks 172.16.0.0 and 172.16.1.0 have a 24-bit subnet mask indicating that 24 bits are used for the network prefix and 8 bits are used for the host address. Actually, a host address is the full 32-bit

IP address but you can think of the last 8 bits, along with the *IP prefix*, as the host identification portion of the address.

The C in the routing table indicates the network is directly connected to the router. The routing table also contains the interface that is connected to the network. At this point the router does not need a routing protocol because the router knows about all the networks.

Each host has a 48-bit Ethernet address that is burned into the Ethernet card. Each host also has an IP address, subnet mask, and default gateway configured. In this case, the default gateway on network 172.16.0.0 is the IP address of the Ethernet 0 interface on the router—or 172.16.0.5. The default gateway for the hosts on network 172.16.1.0 is the IP address of the Ethernet 1 interface on the router—or 172.16.1.5.

When the host with IP address 172.16.1.1 wants to send a packet to the host with IP address 172.16.1.2, the host knows that the destination IP address is on the same IP subnet because the sending host has an IP address of 172.16.1.1 and a 24-bit subnet mask. Therefore, the sending host's network prefix is

172. 16.   1. 1 32-bit IP address

255.255.255.0 24-bit subnet mask

172. 16.   1.0 IP prefix or network part of the IP address

The range of IP addresses for hosts on this network is 172.16.1.1 through 172.16.1.254. The destination host has an address of 172.16.1.2, which is on the same network as the sending host.

The sending host broadcasts an Address Resolution Protocol (ARP) message on the local network looking for the Ethernet address of the host with IP address 172.16.1.2. The host with IP address 172.16.1.2 responds with its Ethernet address. The sending host can now send a packet to the destination host.

If a host on network 172.16.0.0 wants to send a packet to a host on network 172.16.1.0, the source host knows that the packet must be sent to the default gateway. Why? The range of IP addresses for the sending host is 172.16.0.1 through

172.16.0.254. Any host on the destination network 172.16.1.0 is not in this range, so the packet must be sent to the default gateway.

The source host sends an *ARP request* for the Ethernet address of the default gateway. The router responds with its Ethernet address and the packet is sent to the router.

When the router receives the packet, the Ethernet address information is removed, and the router inspects the destination IP address. The destination IP address is on network 172.16.1.0, so the router sends an ARP request on this network asking for the Ethernet address of the host with the destination IP address. The host replies with its Ethernet address, and the router forwards the packet to the destination host.

Now, add another set of networks, as shown in Figure 4-2.

Figure 4-2   Routing in a Two-Router Network

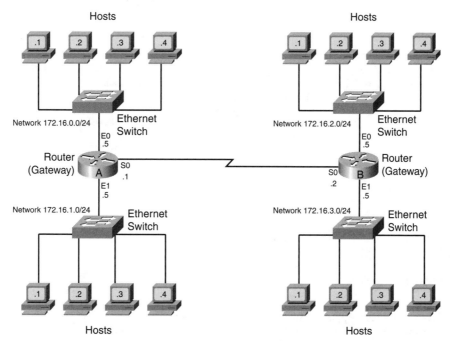

In Figure 4-2, another router with two additional networks has been added. The routers have been connected with a point-to-point serial link. A point-to-point link can have only two hosts, one at each end. In this case, the two hosts are routers. The serial interface on Router A(S0), the two Ethernet interfaces (E0 and E1), and one serial interface on Router B(S0) need to be configured. (See Example 4-1.)

Example 4-1 Interface Configurations for Routers A and B

```
Router A
interface Serial0
 ip address 172.16.4.1 255.255.255.0

Router B
interface Ethernet0
 ip address 172.16.2.5 255.255.255.0
interface Ethernet1
 ip address 172.16.3.5 255.255.255.0
interface Serial0
 ip address 172.16.4.2 255.255.255.0
```

Example 4-2 shows the routing tables on Routers A and B.

Example 4-2 IP Routing Tables for Routers A and B

```
Router A
A#show ip route
Codes: C - connected, S - static, I - IGRP, R - RIP, M - mobile, B - BGP
       D - EIGRP, EX - EIGRP external, O - OSPF, IA - OSPF inter area
       N1 - OSPF NSSA external type 1, N2 - OSPF NSSA external type 2
       E1 - OSPF external type 1, E2 - OSPF external type 2, E - EGP
       i - IS-IS, L1 - IS-IS level-1, L2 - IS-IS level-2, ia - IS-IS inter area
       * - candidate default, U - per-user static route, o - ODR
       P - periodic downloaded static route

Gateway of last resort is not set

     172.16.0.0/24 is subnetted, 3 subnets
C        172.16.4.0 is directly connected, Serial0
C        172.16.0.0 is directly connected, Ethernet0
C        172.16.1.0 is directly connected, Ethernet1

Router B
B#show ip route
Codes: C - connected, S - static, I - IGRP, R - RIP, M - mobile, B - BGP
       D - EIGRP, EX - EIGRP external, O - OSPF, IA - OSPF inter area
       N1 - OSPF NSSA external type 1, N2 - OSPF NSSA external type 2
       E1 - OSPF external type 1, E2 - OSPF external type 2, E - EGP
       i - IS-IS, L1 - IS-IS level-1, L2 - IS-IS level-2, ia - IS-IS inter area
```

Example 4-2   IP Routing Tables for Routers A and B (continued)

```
        * - candidate default, U - per-user static route, o - ODR
        P - periodic downloaded static route

Gateway of last resort is not set

     172.16.0.0/24 is subnetted, 3 subnets
C        172.16.4.0 is directly connected, Serial0
C        172.16.2.0 is directly connected, Ethernet0
C        172.16.3.0 is directly connected, Ethernet1
```

Routers A and B have the three connected prefixes in their routing tables, each
with a 24-bit subnet mask. A default gateway, or gateway of last resort, has not
been configured on the routers. If a router receives an IP packet with a destination
address that is not in the routing table, the packet is dropped.

In Example 4-2, Router A does not know about the two Ethernet networks connected to Router B, and Router B does not know about the two Ethernet networks
connected to Router A. Before communication can occur between all hosts shown
in Figure 4-2, the network prefixes that are not directly connected to a router need
to be in the routing tables. The first method is to use a ***static route***. A static route is
one that is manually configured on the router. You need two static routes on both
Routers A and B. (See Example 4-3.)

Example 4-3   Static Route Configuration on Routers A and B

```
Router A
ip route 172.16.2.0 255.255.255.0 Serial0
ip route 172.16.3.0 255.255.255.0 172.16.4.2

Router B
ip route 172.16.0.0 255.255.255.0 Serial0
ip route 172.16.1.0 255.255.255.0 172.16.4.1
```

The first static route on Router A says that to reach any host on network
172.16.2.0/24 the packet will be sent out interface Serial0. The second static route
on Router A says that to reach any host on network 172.16.3.0/24 the packet will
be sent to the next hop 172.16.4.2—which is also interface Serial0. You might be
wondering what next hop means. ***Next*** hop is just the networking way of saying
where a packet will be sent next on the way to the destination. These are just

different ways of configuring a static route. The routing tables on Routers A and B now contain all the necessary routing information as shown in Example 4-4. In the example, S indicates a static route.

Example 4-4   Routing Tables for Routers A and B

```
Router A
     172.16.0.0/24 is subnetted, 5 subnets
C       172.16.4.0 is directly connected, Serial0
C       172.16.0.0 is directly connected, Ethernet0
C       172.16.1.0 is directly connected, Ethernet1
S       172.16.2.0 is directly connected, Serial0
S       172.16.3.0 [1/0] via 172.16.4.2

Router B
     172.16.0.0/24 is subnetted, 5 subnets
C       172.16.4.0 is directly connected, Serial0
S       172.16.0.0 is directly connected, Serial0
S       172.16.1.0 [1/0] via 172.16.4.1
C       172.16.2.0 is directly connected, Ethernet0
C       172.16.3.0 is directly connected, Ethernet1
```

Well, that was easy enough. All hosts can reach all other hosts. But is this really the best method? For a small network, static routes are fine. For larger networks, static routes are also fine if you assume that nothing will ever change. No networks or routers will break or lose power, network interfaces will never fail, and new networks will never be added. If that is all true, static routes might be the way to go. But if you remember that things fall apart, then maybe using only static routes is not such a good idea. You need a dynamic routing protocol that automatically exchanges routes between routers so you don't have to do it with static routes. If a network is added or if a network fails, you want the dynamic routing protocol to inform the routers of the change so they can update their routing tables. What you need is a protocol that can be used for routing information.

Routing Information Protocol Version 1

There is no better name for a routing information protocol than the *Routing Information Protocol (RIP)*. In this section, you learn the operation and limitations of RIP version 1 (RIPv1). RIPv1 must first be enabled on Routers A and B with the configuration shown in Example 4-5.

Example 4-5 RIPv1 Configuration for Routers A and B

```
Router A
router rip
 version 1
 network 172.16.0.0

Router B
router rip
 version 1
 network 172.16.0.0
```

The command **router rip**enables the RIP routing process. RIP is forced to use version 1 using the command **version 1**. The **network 172.16.0.0**instructs the router to enable RIP on any interface that has an IP address configured from the 172.16.0.0/16 IP address block. All interfaces on both routers have been assigned an IP address from this block; so all interfaces participate in the RIP process. Notice that a subnet mask is not used with the **network**command. RIPv1 is known as a classful routing protocol; therefore, the router assumes a 16-bit subnet mask because 172.16.0.0 is from the Class B address space and the standard mask for Class B addresses is 16 bits. When the RIP process is enabled, the router advertises its entire routing table out every interface that has been enabled for RIPv1. This is seen by turning on debugging on one of the routers. (See Example 4-6.) Debugging is typically used to find problems in the operation or configuration of a router. Debugging can also be used to watch what a router is actually doing, even if no problems exist. Debugging is a useful tool for verifying correct operation, or reinforcing your knowledge of the operation of a protocol.

Example 4-6 Debug RIPv1 Output on Router A

```
Router A
A#debug ip rip
RIP protocol debugging is on
A#
00:58:02: RIP: received v1 update from 172.16.4.2 on Serial0
00:58:02:        172.16.0.0 in 2 hops
00:58:02:        172.16.1.0 in 2 hops
00:58:02:        172.16.2.0 in 1 hops
00:58:02:        172.16.3.0 in 1 hops
```

Example 4-6   Debug RIPv1 Output on Router A (continued)

```
00:58:02:       172.16.4.0 in 1 hops
00:58:13: RIP: sending v1 update to 255.255.255.255 via Ethernet0 (172.16.0.5)

00:58:13: RIP: build update entries
00:58:13:       subnet 172.16.1.0 metric 1
00:58:13:       subnet 172.16.2.0 metric 2
00:58:13:       subnet 172.16.3.0 metric 2
00:58:13:       subnet 172.16.4.0 metric 1
00:58:13: RIP: sending v1 update to 255.255.255.255 via Serial0 (172.16.4.1)
00:58:13: RIP: build update entries
00:58:13:       subnet 172.16.0.0 metric 1
00:58:13:       subnet 172.16.1.0 metric 1
00:58:13:       subnet 172.16.2.0 metric 2
00:58:13:       subnet 172.16.3.0 metric 2
00:58:13:       subnet 172.16.4.0 metric 1
00:58:13: RIP: sending v1 update to 255.255.255.255 via Ethernet1 (172.16.1.5)
00:58:13: RIP: build update entries
00:58:13:       subnet 172.16.0.0 metric 1
00:58:13:       subnet 172.16.2.0 metric 2
00:58:13:       subnet 172.16.3.0 metric 2
00:58:13:       subnet 172.16.4.0 metric 1
```

In Example 4-6, RIP is sending routing updates on the Ethernet interfaces because the router does not know that there are not any other routers on the Ethernet networks. Routing protocols communicate network prefixes between routers, not between routers and hosts. If no routers are on a RIP network, the RIP process can be disabled on these interfaces using the **passive-interface** command under the RIP routing process. (See Example 4-7.) Configuring an interface as passive prevents RIP from advertising routes on the interface, but the network prefix assigned to a passive interface is advertised by RIP on the nonpassive interfaces.

Example 4-7   Using the **passive-interface** Command

```
Router A
router rip
 version 1
 passive-interface Ethernet0
 passive-interface Ethernet1
 network 172.16.0.0

Router B
router rip
 version 1
 passive-interface Ethernet0
 passive-interface Ethernet1
 network 172.16.0.0
```

After implementing the **passive-interface** command, you should see less debugging information. (See Example 4-8.)

Example 4-8   Debugging Output with Passive Interfaces on Router A

```
A#debug ip rip
RIP protocol debugging is on
A#
01:05:02: RIP: received v1 update from 172.16.4.2 on Serial0
01:05:02:        172.16.0.0 in 2 hops
01:05:02:        172.16.1.0 in 2 hops
01:05:02:        172.16.2.0 in 1 hops
01:05:02:        172.16.3.0 in 1 hops
01:05:02:        172.16.4.0 in 1 hops
01:05:18: RIP: sending v1 update to 255.255.255.255 via Serial0 (172.16.4.1)
01:05:18: RIP: build update entries
01:05:18:        subnet 172.16.0.0 metric 1
01:05:18:        subnet 172.16.1.0 metric 1
01:05:18:        subnet 172.16.2.0 metric 2
01:05:18:        subnet 172.16.3.0 metric 2
01:05:18:        subnet 172.16.4.0 metric 1
```

The routers are advertising their IP routing tables only on the serial interface. The routing tables for Routers A and B are now complete, as shown in Example 4-9.

Example 4-9   Verifying the Advertising of RIP Routes

```
Router A
     172.16.0.0/24 is subnetted, 5 subnets
C        172.16.4.0 is directly connected, Serial0
C        172.16.0.0 is directly connected, Ethernet0
C        172.16.1.0 is directly connected, Ethernet1
R        172.16.2.0 [120/1] via 172.16.4.2, 00:00:08, Serial0
R        172.16.3.0 [120/1] via 172.16.4.2, 00:00:08, Serial0

Router B
     172.16.0.0/24 is subnetted, 5 subnets
C        172.16.4.0 is directly connected, Serial0
R        172.16.0.0 [120/1] via 172.16.4.1, 00:00:24, Serial0
R        172.16.1.0 [120/1] via 172.16.4.1, 00:00:24, Serial0
C        172.16.2.0 is directly connected, Ethernet0
C        172.16.3.0 is directly connected, Ethernet1
```

Router A has learned about the two Ethernet networks directly connected to Router B. Router B has learned about the two Ethernet networks directly connected to Router A. The R in the routing table indicates these routes were learned through RIP. The numbers in brackets [120/1] are the *administrative distance* for the prefix (120), and the *metric* for the prefix (1). If one routing protocol is enabled on a router, the administrative distance is not necessary. If more than one routing protocol is enabled on a router, it is possible for the router to learn about the same network prefix from more than one protocol. For example, if a router learns about network 172.16.1.0/24 from RIPv1 and OSPF (an IP routing protocol discussed in Chapter 6, "Open Shortest Path First—Better, Stronger, Faster"), which route to the prefix should be placed in the routing table? RIP has an administrative distance of 120, and OSPF has an administrative distance of 110. A lower administrative distance is considered better, so OSPF routes are better than RIP routes.

Every routing protocol assigns a metric, or cost, to every route. The metric, or cost, is a measure of the goodness of a route. A lower metric is better. If a router receives an advertisement for the same prefix from more than one router using the same routing protocol, the router has to decide which route it places in the routing table. The route with the lowest cost, or metric, is the best and is placed in the routing table.

In summary, the administrative distance determines the best route when a route is learned from more than one routing protocol. Metric determines the best route when multiple routes to the same destination are learned using the same routing protocol.

Table 4-2 lists the administrative distances for the routing protocols discussed in this book.

Table 4-2   IP Routing Protocol Administrative Distance

Route Type	Administrative Distance
Connected	0
Static	1
EBGP (Chapter 8)	20
EIGRP (Chapter 5)	90
IGRP (Chapter 5)	100
OSPF (Chapter 6)	110

Table 4-2   IP Routing Protocol Administrative Distance (continued)

Route Type	Administrative Distance
IS-IS (Chapter 7)	115
RIP (Chapter 4)	120
IBGP (Chapter 8)	200

From the debug output in Example 4-10, you see that Router A is receiving the routing table from Router B.

Example 4-10   RIP Routes Received by Router A from Router B

```
01:05:02: RIP: received v1 update from 172.16.4.2 on Serial0
01:05:02:       172.16.0.0 in 2 hops
01:05:02:       172.16.1.0 in 2 hops
01:05:02:       172.16.2.0 in 1 hops
01:05:02:       172.16.3.0 in 1 hops
01:05:02:       172.16.4.0 in 1 hops
```

In Example 4-10, you see 2 hops and 1 hops. RIP is a ***distance-vector routing protocol,*** and the metric that RIP uses is called a ***hop count.*** A hop count is a measure of how far away a network is. Each router along the path from the source to the destination is called a ***hop***. Router B advertises any directly connected network with a hop count of 0.

The following debug output means that from the perspective of Router A, network 172.16.3.0/24 is one hop away:

```
01:05:02:       172.16.3.0 in 1 hops
```

This means one router is in the path between Router A and network 182.16.3.0:

```
01:05:02:       172.16.1.0 in 2 hops
```

Router A is directly attached to network 172.16.1.0. Why is Router B advertising that it can reach network 172.16.1.0? RIP advertises the entire IP routing table (well, not always, but we will get to that). Router A advertises network 172.16.1.0 with a hop count of 0 because the network is directly connected. Router B adds one to the hop count before placing this prefix in the routing table. When Router B advertises its routing table to Router A, Router A adds one to the hop count of each route. When Router A receives this advertisement, it now has two routes to 172.16.1.0. The first is directly attached, and the second is through Router B with a hop count of 2. The directly attached network has a lower metric or hop count, so Router A rejects the advertisement from Router B for network 172.16.1.0. Simple, isn't it? Well, not always. This can cause an interesting problem called *counting to infinity*.

Counting to Infinity

How long does it take to count to infinity? With RIP, not long, because RIP considers 16 to be infinity. In Figure 4-3, assume that the routers have exchanged their routing tables using RIP.

Figure 4-3   Counting to Infinity

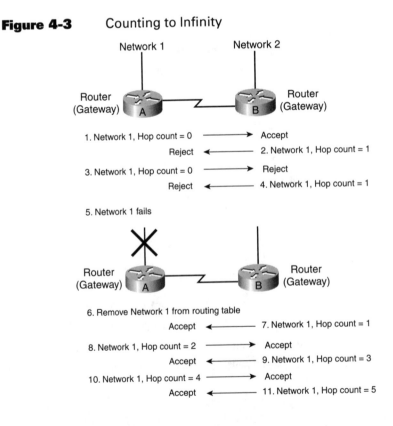

As long as everything is working well, Router A advertises Network 1 with a hop count of 0. Router B accepts the advertisement, and adds one to the hop count. Router B advertises Network 1 back to Router A with a hop count of one. Router A rejects the advertisement because Network 1 is directly attached. If Network 1 fails, Router A removes Network 1 from the routing table. Assume Router B sends its routing table to Router A before Router A can tell Router B that Network 1 is no longer available. Router A accepts the advertisement for Network 1, because Network 1 is no longer in the routing table on Router A. Router A now thinks it can reach Network 1 through Router B. Router A readvertises Network 1 to Router B with a hop count of 2. Router B accepts the route because the route was originally learned from Router A. Router B adds one to the hop count and advertises it back to Router A. This process continues and the hop count is increased by one each time. Fortunately, infinity in RIP equals 16. After the hop count reaches 16, the routers reject the route and remove it from their routing table. Any network that is more than 15 hops away is considered unreachable. This limits the maximum size of a RIP network.

Counting to infinity is an inherent problem with distance-vector routing protocols. Two ways to try to prevent counting to infinity from happening are split horizon and poison reverse, which you learn about in the next sections.

Split Horizon

Split horizon is a rule that states that a router will not advertise a route out an interface if the route was originally learned on that interface. By default, split horizon is disabled on the serial interface between the routers. To prevent the counting to infinity problem, you can enable split horizon on both sides of the serial network, as shown in Example 4-11.

Example 4-11   Enabling Split Horizon on the Router's Serial Interfaces

```
Router A
interface Serial0
 ip address 172.16.4.1 255.255.255.0
 ip split-horizon

Router B
interface Serial0
 ip address 172.16.4.2 255.255.255.0
 ip split-horizon
```

If you examine the debug output in Example 4-12, you see that split horizon has been enabled.

Example 4-12 Verifying the Operation of Split Horizon

```
A#debug ip rip
RIP protocol debugging is on
A#
01:59:32: RIP: received v1 update from 172.16.4.2 on Serial0
01:59:32:        172.16.2.0 in 1 hops
01:59:32:        172.16.3.0 in 1 hops
01:59:48: RIP: sending v1 update to 255.255.255.255 via Serial0 (172.16.4.1)
01:59:48: RIP: build update entries
01:59:48:        subnet 172.16.0.0 metric 1
01:59:48:        subnet 172.16.1.0 metric 1
```

Both Router A and Router B are not readvertising the routes they have learned from their neighbor. Split horizon solves the counting to infinity problem for two routers. If more than two routers are in the network, split horizon will not solve all counting to infinity problems.

Poison Reverse

Poison reverse allows the readvertising of routes out the interface on which they were learned, but the hop count is set to 16, or infinity. This prevents the receiving router from accepting the route. Cisco routers use split horizon with RIP, but not poison reverse.

note

The rest of this chapter discusses networks that contain more than two routers. To keep the diagrams from becoming cluttered, you now see simplified network diagrams as shown in Figure 4-4.

The hosts and switches have been removed, but their presence is implied. Routing is concerned with moving packets between routers, so the switches and hosts are not needed in the diagrams. The IP address block that is being used—172.16.0.0/16—is shown at the top of the figure. The partial IP addresses shown on the interfaces are part of this block. The address shown on the Ethernet 1 interface on Router A is 1.0/24. This is a shorthand way of representing 172.16.1.0/24.

Figure 4-4   Simplified Network Diagram

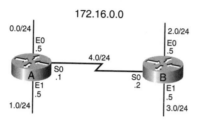

Convergence

An important property of every routing protocol is the time it takes for correct routing information to be propagated to every router in the network. If there is a change, either a new network is added, a network failure, or a router failure, the new information must be advertised to every router. The time it takes for a network to update all the routing tables is called the *convergence time*.

In Figure 4-5, assume that a RIP process is enabled on every router at the same time. Each router initially advertises only a routing table that contains directly connected networks. RIP, by default, transmits the routing table every 30 seconds. It takes 60 seconds for the routing table from Router A to propagate to Router D. So the convergence time for this relatively small network is on the order of minutes. But after the network converges and there are no changes, the network will be stable As the network grows, the convergence time becomes more of a problem. After the network initially converges, the routing table on Router D contains eight RIP routes and three directly connected routes, as shown in Example 4-13.

Figure 4-5   Example RIP Network

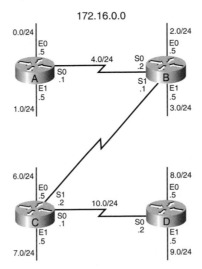

Example 4-13   IP Routing Table—Router D

```
Router D
     172.16.0.0/24 is subnetted, 11 subnets
C        172.16.8.0 is directly connected, Ethernet0
C        172.16.9.0 is directly connected, Ethernet1
C        172.16.10.0 is directly connected, Serial0
R        172.16.4.0 [120/2] via 172.16.10.1, 00:00:01, Serial0
R        172.16.5.0 [120/1] via 172.16.10.1, 00:00:01, Serial0
R        172.16.6.0 [120/1] via 172.16.10.1, 00:00:01, Serial0
R        172.16.7.0 [120/1] via 172.16.10.1, 00:00:01, Serial0
R        172.16.0.0 [120/3] via 172.16.10.1, 00:00:03, Serial0
R        172.16.1.0 [120/3] via 172.16.10.1, 00:00:03, Serial0
R        172.16.2.0 [120/2] via 172.16.10.1, 00:00:03, Serial0
R        172.16.3.0 [120/2] via 172.16.10.1, 00:00:03, Serial0
```

If the interface to network 172.16.0.0 on Router A fails, how long will it take for
the network to converge? That depends. If Router A has sent a routing table
update to Router B just before the interface fails, it will be 30 seconds before the
new routing table on Router A is transmitted to Router B. If Router B sent a routing update just before it received the update from A, another 30 seconds passes
before the change is propagated to Router C. So it could take up to 90 seconds for
Router D to see the change.

A technique used to reduce the convergence time is called ***triggered updates***. Whenever a change to a route occurs on a router, an update is triggered and the router sends a routing table update immediately. If the interface on Router A fails, this change is propagated throughout the network using triggered updates; and the convergence time will be greatly reduced.

Assume Router A loses power and networks 172.16.0.0/24 and 172.16.1.0/24 are no longer available. Router A cannot send a triggered update—it has no power! How do the remaining routers know these networks cannot be reached? For every route received through RIP, an ***update time*** is associated with that route. For example, the update timer value for network 172.16.1.0 on Router B is shown in the routing table as follows:

```
R        172.16.1.0 [120/1] via 172.16.4.1, 00:00:13, Serial0
```

This route was learned 13 seconds ago. The update timer increments every second and is reset to 0 every time an update is received from Router A. If Router A fails, the update timer continues to increase. When the update timer reaches 180 seconds, the route is marked as inaccessible (hop count > 15). The prefix is advertised with a hop count of 4,294,967,295 (the largest 32-bit number), indicating to neighboring routers that the route is invalid. When the update timer expires, two additional timers are started: the holddown and flush timers.

Assume the serial interface on Router A fails in Figure 4-5. Router A can no longer send routing table updates to Router B. The timers on Router B for the prefixes learned from Router A continue to increment, as follows:

```
R        172.16.0.0/24 [120/1] via 172.16.4.1, 00:02:59, Serial0
R        172.16.1.0/24 [120/1] via 172.16.4.1, 00:02:59, Serial0
```

When the update timers reach 180 seconds, or 3 minutes, the routes are marked as inaccessible (hop count > 15), as shown in Example 4-14.

Example 4-14   Verification of the Metric for an Inaccessible RIP Route

```
!Output omitted for brevity
R        172.16.0.0/24 is possibly down,
           routing via 172.16.4.1, Serial0
R        172.16.1.0/24 is possibly down,
           routing via 172.16.4.1, Serial0

B#show ip route 172.16.1.0
Routing entry for 172.16.1.0/26
  Known via "rip", distance 120, metric 4294967295 (inaccessible)
  Redistributing via rip
  Last update from 172.16.4.1 on Serial0/0, 00:03:22 ago
  Hold down timer expires in 162 secs
```

After the prefix has been declared inaccessible, a 180-second holddown timer and 240-second flush timer will start. During the *holddown time*, advertisements for the invalid prefix will not be accepted. There might be routers that have not received a triggered update for the invalid prefix, so they are still advertising the prefix as reachable. The holddown timer allows the new information to be propagated throughout the network. When the holddown timer expires, advertisements for the prefix can be accepted. If the *flush time* expires before an advertisement is received for the prefix, the prefix is removed from the routing table.

Variable-Length Subnet Masks

Variable-length subnet masks (VLSMs) means that different subnet mask lengths are used in the network. In the previous networks in this chapter, all subnets used a 24-bit subnet mask. This means you can have up to 254 hosts on each network. A point-to-point network can have only 2 hosts, the endpoints. If you use a 24-bit mask on a point-to-point network, 2 of the 254 possible addresses are used, and 252 host addresses are unused. In Figure 4-6, the subnet mask on the serial network between Routers A and B has been changed to a 30-bit mask. This allows for two host addresses: the broadcast address and the "this" network address. You can use whatever subnet mask length you want, as long as you can support the number of required hosts, and the same subnet mask length is used on all interfaces connecting to the network.

Figure 4-6   VLSM with RIPv1

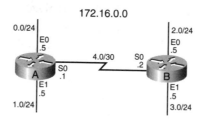

Using a 30-bit mask instead of a 24-bit mask saves 252 host addresses. The new configurations for the serial interface on Routers A and B are shown in Example 4-15.

Example 4-15   RIPv1 VLSM Demonstration—Part 1

```
Router A
interface Serial0
 ip address 172.16.4.1 255.255.255.252

Router B
interface Serial0
 ip add 172.16.4.2 255.255.255.252
```

If you look at the routing table on Router A or B, you will see a problem. (See Example 4-16.)

Example 4-16   RIPv1 VLSM Demonstration—Part 2

```
Router A
     172.16.0.0/16 is variably subnetted, 3 subnets, 2 masks
C       172.16.4.0/30 is directly connected, Serial0
C       172.16.0.0/24 is directly connected, Ethernet0
C       172.16.1.0/24 is directly connected, Ethernet0

Router B
     172.16.0.0/16 is variably subnetted, 3 subnets, 2 masks
C       172.16.4.0/30 is directly connected, Serial0
C       172.16.2.0/24 is directly connected, Ethernet0
C       172.16.3.0/24 is directly connected, Ethernet1
```

The routing table indicates that two masks are being used: /24 and /30. You should also notice there are no RIPv1 routes in either routing table. This illustrates another limitation of RIPv1. The limitation is that subnet mask information is not included in the routing updates. So how does a router know what subnet mask to use? If a network prefix, such as 172.16.1.0, is received on an interface configured with an IP address from the same major network number, assume that the mask of the received prefix is the same as the receiving interface.

For example, the Class B network prefix 172.16.0.0/16 is the major network number for all subnets of 172.16.0.0. The Class A network prefix 12.0.0.0/8 is the major network number for all subnets of 12.0.0.0/8, and 193.1.2.0/24 is the major network number for all subnets of 193.1.2.0/24. The network in Figure 4-6 uses only subnets of the major network prefix 172.16.0.0/16.

RIP assumes that a prefix received on the serial interface that is in major network 172.16.0.0 will have a 30-bit mask. The sending router only advertises routes with a 30-bit mask out the serial interface. The Ethernet networks are using a 24-bit mask so they will never be sent to Router B.

To prove this point, change the subnet mask on the Ethernet interfaces on Router A to 30 bits, as shown in Example 4-17.

Example 4-17 RIPv1 VLSM Demonstration—Part 3

```
Router A
interface Ethernet0
  ip address 172.16.0.5 255.255.255.252
interface Ethernet1
  ip address 172.16.1.5 255.255.255.252
```

These networks are also in the routing table on Router B, as shown in Example 4-18.

Example 4-18 RIPv1 VLSM Demonstration—Part 4

```
     172.16.0.0/16 is variably subnetted, 5 subnets, 2 masks
R       172.16.0.4/30 [120/1] via 172.16.4.1, 00:00:19, Serial0
C       172.16.4.0/30 is directly connected, Serial0
R       172.16.1.4/30 [120/1] via 172.16.4.1, 00:00:06, Serial0
C       172.16.2.0/24 is directly connected, Ethernet0
C       172.16.3.0/24 is directly connected, Ethernet1
```

The Ethernet networks on Router A can have only two hosts, and the router is using one of the host addresses. Now it gets interesting. Change the IP address on the Ethernet 1 interface on Router A using an address from a different major network prefix, as shown in Example 4-19.

Example 4-19   RIPv1 VLSM Demonstration—Part 5

```
Router A
interface Ethernet1
 ip address 156.26.1.5 255.255.255.0
router rip
 network 172.16.0.0
 network 156.26.0.0
```

Now note what is in the routing table on Router B. (See Example 4-20.)

Example 4-20   RIPv1 VLSM Demonstration—Part 6

```
R    156.26.0.0/16 [120/1] via 172.16.4.1, 00:00:04, Serial0
     172.16.0.0/16 is variably subnetted, 4 subnets, 2 masks
R       172.16.0.4/30 [120/1] via 172.16.4.1, 00:00:08, Serial0
C       172.16.4.0/30 is directly connected, Serial0
C       172.16.2.0/24 is directly connected, Ethernet0
C       172.16.3.0/24 is directly connected, Ethernet1
```

Two things to notice are

- The network 156.26.0.0 has been advertised to Router B.

- The subnet mask is /16 not /24 as configured on Router A.

Because the prefix 156.26.1.0 is in a different major network number from the interface connecting the routers, Router A automatically summarizes this advertisement to a classful boundary. The standard mask for a Class B address is 16-bits, and this mask is assumed with the network 156.26.0.0. This brings up another problem. Router B now thinks it can reach the entire Class B address 156.26.0.0/16 through Router A. But Router A is using only one subnet of 156.26.0.0. The rules for how and when RIP advertises a network are listed in Table 4-3.

Table 4-3   RIP Rules for Route Advertisement on an Interface

Major Network Number	Subnet Mask	RIP Action
Same	Same	Advertise
Same	Different	Don't Advertise
Different	Same	Advertise and summarize to a classful boundary
Different	Different	Advertise and summarize to a classful boundary

Hop Count Limitation

The *bandwidth* of an interface is the number of bits per second (bps) that can be transmitted. Table 4-4 lists the bandwidths, in millions of bits per second (Mbps), of various router interfaces. T1 and E1 are serial point-to-point interfaces; with T1 being used mostly in North America, and E1 mostly in Europe and Asia.

Table 4-4   Interface Bandwidths

Interface Type	Bandwidth (Mbps)
Ethernet	10
Fast Ethernet	100
Gigabit Ethernet	1000
T1	1.544
E1	2.048

The network in Figure 4-7 has three routers. Routers A and B and Routers B and C are connected using fast Ethernet. Routers A and C are connected using T1.

Figure 4-7   Limitations of Hop Count

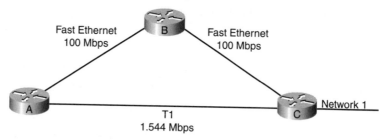

Fast Ethernet
100 Mbps

Fast Ethernet
100 Mbps

B

A

T1
1.544 Mbps

C

Network 1

If RIP is being used in this network, the best path from Router A to Network 1 is through the T1 connection to Router C because the hop count is one. The path from Router B to Network 1 has a hop count of two; but the bandwidth from A to B to C is greater than the bandwidth from A to C. RIP does not take bandwidth into account when determining the best path, only the hop count. This is yet another limitation of RIP.

RIPv1 Algorithm

You have learned about the operation and limitations of RIPv1 a piece at a time. It is time to put all the pieces together and write down the rules for RIP in an orderly manner.

RIPv1 output algorithm:

1. If the prefix to be advertised is in the same major network, and has the same subnet mask as the interface used to advertise the network, advertise the prefix.

2. If the prefix to be advertised is in the same major network, but has a different subnet mask as the interface used to advertise the network, do not advertise the prefix.

3. If the prefix to be advertised is not in the same major network as the interface used to advertise the prefix, advertise the prefix as a classful route.

4. If split horizon is enabled, do not advertise prefixes that were learned on the interface used to advertise the prefix.

RIPv1 input algorithm:

1. Accept a prefix if it is not in the IP routing table. Add one to the hop count before adding the prefix to the IP routing table. If the new metric is 16, reject the prefix.

2. If a prefix is in the IP routing table, accept the prefix and place it in the IP routing table only if the hop count is lower than the prefix currently in the IP routing table.

3. If a prefix is in the IP routing table, accept the prefix and place it in the IP routing table only if the original prefix was received on this interface — regardless of the hop count.

Figures 4-8 and 4-9 illustrate the operation of the RIP algorithm. In Figure 4-8, Router A is advertising Network 1 to Routers B and D with a hop count of 0.

Figure 4-8   The RIP Routing Algorithm, Part 1

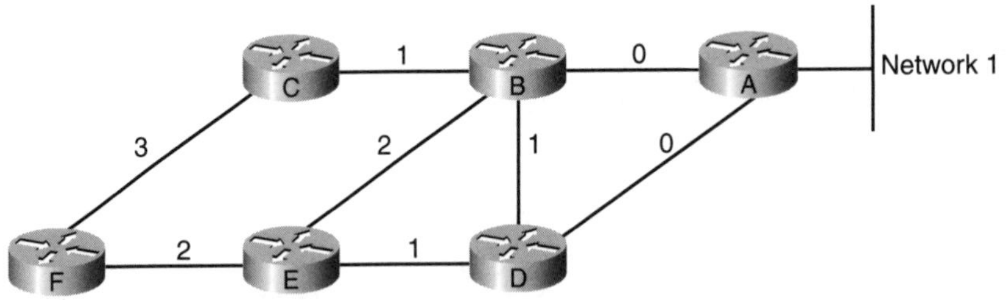

Router D adds one to the hop count and advertises Network 1 to Routers B and E with a hop count of 1. Router E advertises Network 1 to B and F with a hop count of 2; and Router F advertises Network 1 to C with a hop count of 3. Router B is receiving three routes for Network 1. On Router B, the route from A has a hop count of 0, the route from D has a hop count of 1, and the route from E has a hop count of 2. B accepts the route from A because it has the lowest hop count. Router

C receives two advertisements for Network 1: Router B with a hop count of 1, and router F with a hop count of 3. Router C accepts the route from B.

In Figure 4-9, the link between Routers A and B has failed. Router B now advertises Network 1 to Router C with a hop count of 2. Before the failure of the network between A and B, Router B was advertising a hop count of 1. Router C accepts the higher hop count because the route currently in the routing table was learned from Router B.

Figure 4-9   The RIP Routing Algorithm, Part 2

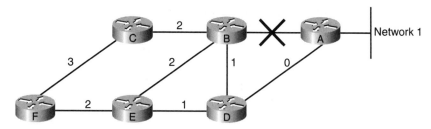

For more details on RIPv1, including packet formats, see the references at the end of the chapter.

The limitations of RIPv1 are listed in Table 4-5.

Table 4-5   RIP Version 1 Limitations

Limitation	Comments
Small network diameter	Hop count must be less than 16
No VLSM support	Subnet masks are assumed, not advertised
Metric	Hop count only, no bandwidth considerations
Convergence	Increases as the network becomes larger
Counting to infinity	A potential problem with more than two routers

RIP Version 2

RIP version 2, or RIPv2, suffers many of the same limitations as RIPv1. The limitations of the RIP metric, convergence time, small network diameter, and the counting to infinity problem still exist with RIPv2. The major limitation of RIPv1, which RIPv2 addresses, is VLSM. RIPv2 routing updates contain subnet mask information. This allows you to use different subnet mask lengths in your network. In Figure 4-10, five different subnet masks are used for the 172.16.0.0 networks.

Figure 4-10   RIP Version 2 Supports VLSM

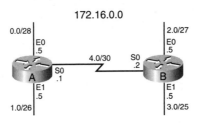

In Example 4-21, the Ethernet interfaces in Figure 4-10 have been configured using the new subnet masks, and the RIP process has been changed to version 2.

Example 4-21   RIPv2 VLSM Demonstration—Part 1

```
Router A
interface Ethernet0
 ip address 172.16.0.5 255.255.255.240
interface Ethernet1
 ip address 172.16.1.5 255.255.255.192

router rip
 version 2
 passive-interface Ethernet0
 passive-interface Ethernet1
 network 172.16.0.0

Router B
interface Ethernet0
 ip address 172.16.2.5 255.255.255.224
interface Ethernet1
 ip address 172.16.3.5 255.255.255.128
```

Example 4-21   RIPv2 VLSM Demonstration—Part 1 (continued)

```
router rip
 version 2
passive-interface Ethernet0
passive-interface Ethernet1
network 172.16.0.0
```

In Example 4-22, the debug output on Router B shows that subnet mask information is being sent and received by the RIPv2 processes (compare this with the debug output in Example 4-12 when we were using RIP version 1).

Example 4-22   RIPv2 VLSM Demonstration—Part 2

```
B#debug ip rip
RIP protocol debugging is on
B#
00:23:26: RIP: received v2 update from 172.16.4.1 on Serial0
00:23:26:        172.16.0.0/28 via 0.0.0.0 in 1 hops
00:23:26:        172.16.1.0/26 via 0.0.0.0 in 1 hops
00:23:26:        172.16.4.0/30 via 0.0.0.0 in 1 hops
00:23:32: RIP: sending v2 update to 224.0.0.9 via Serial0 (172.16.4.2)
00:23:32: RIP: build update entries
00:23:32:        172.16.0.0/28 via 172.16.4.1, metric 2, tag 0
00:23:32:        172.16.1.0/26 via 172.16.4.1, metric 2, tag 0
00:23:32:        172.16.2.0/27 via 0.0.0.0, metric 1, tag 0
00:23:32:        172.16.3.0/25 via 0.0.0.0, metric 1, tag 0
00:23:32:        172.16.4.0/30 via 0.0.0.0, metric 1, tag 0
```

All the RIP routes are now in the routing tables on Routers A and B even though different subnet mask lengths are being used. (See Example 4-23.)

Example 4-23   RIPv2 VLSM Demonstration—Part 3

```
Router A
     172.16.0.0/16 is variably subnetted, 5 subnets, 5 masks
C        172.16.4.0/30 is directly connected, Serial0
C        172.16.0.0/28 is directly connected, Ethernet0
C        172.16.1.0/26 is directly connected, Ethernet1
R        172.16.2.0/27 [120/1] via 172.16.4.2, 00:00:16, Serial0
R        172.16.3.0/25 [120/1] via 172.16.4.2, 00:00:17, Serial0

Router B
     172.16.0.0/16 is variably subnetted, 5 subnets, 5 masks
C        172.16.4.0/30 is directly connected, Serial0
R        172.16.0.0/28 [120/1] via 172.16.4.1, 00:00:17, Serial0
R        172.16.1.0/26 [120/1] via 172.16.4.1, 00:00:17, Serial0
C        172.16.2.0/27 is directly connected, Ethernet0
C        172.16.3.0/25 is directly connected, Ethernet1
```

RIPv2 is called a classless routing protocol, and RIPv 1 is a classful protocol. *Classless* means that the VLSM can be used with the protocol. *Classful* means that assumptions are made about the subnet masks associated with network prefixes because subnet mask information is not advertised.

Another enhancement over RIPv1 is that RIPv2 sends the routing updates to the multicast address 224.0.0.9 instead of the broadcast address 255.255.255.255:

```
01:59:48: RIP: sending v1 update to 255.255.255.255 via Serial0
 (172.16.4.1)
00:23:32: RIP: sending v2 update to 224.0.0.9 via Serial0
 (172.16.4.2)
```

Multicast is discussed later in Chapter 9, "Multicast—What the Post Office Can't Do." The network in Figure 4-11 illustrates the difference between broadcast and multicast routing updates.

Figure 4-11   Broadcast Versus Multicast Routing Updates

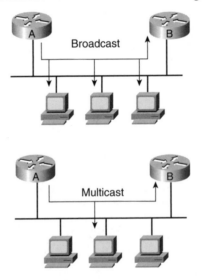

If the routers are attached to a common multi-access network, usually Ethernet, all hosts on the network will have to accept the broadcast update, determine it was

not meant for them, and reject the update. A multicast update is only sent to hosts or routers that are expecting to receive traffic sent to that multicast address. This reduces the traffic sent to the hosts (assuming you are using a switch that only forwards multicast traffic to the proper place).

Security

RIPv2 has the ability to authenticate routing updates. Someone can send fake RIP routing updates by using a program that sends bogus routing updates. RIPv2 has two methods available for authentication of routing updates. The first method, called the simple password method, uses an unencrypted password that is included in the routing updates. An unencrypted password is one that can be read by examining the packet. The second method, called message digest, uses an encrypted password. If someone is able to capture and read the packet, they would not be able to determine the password. For both methods, the same password must be used between routers exchanging routing information. Password authentication is configured on the RIP interfaces as shown in Example 4-24.

Example 4-24   Configuring RIP Simple Password Authentication on Router B

```
Router B
key chain laura
 key 1
  key-string elvis
interface Serial0
 ip address 172.16.4.1 255.255.255.252
 ip rip authentication key-chain laura
```

Authentication, using the key chain laura with password elvis, is enabled on the serial interface on Router B but not on Router A. Router B rejects RIP updates from Router A:

```
00:35:18: RIP: ignored v2 packet from 172.16.4.1
 (invalid authentication)
```

Configure Router A to use the same password as Router B. (See Example 4-25.)

Example 4-25 Configuring RIP Simple Password Authentication on
Router A

```
Router A
key chain Cisco
 key 1
  key-string elvis
interface Serial0
 ip address 172.16.4.1 255.255.255.252
 ip rip authentication key-chain Cisco

Router B
key chain laura
 key 1
  key-string elvis
interface Serial0
 ip address 172.16.4.1 255.255.255.252
 ip rip authentication key-chain laura
```

Router A is configured to use key chain Cisco and Router B uses key chain laura.
A key chain defines the password used by RIP. Multiple key chains can be
defined, and you select the one you want to use when configuring the interface.
The names of the key chains do not need to match on Routers A and B. Only the
password used in the key chains on Routers A and B needs to match. The pass-
words are sent in the clear, so someone can learn the password by intercepting the
update packets. A more secure form of authentication is Message Digest 5 (MD5).
With MD5 authentication, the password is encrypted before it is sent. If someone
intercepts the RIP protocol packets, they will not be able to tell what the password
is. To enable MD5 authentication, configure it on the serial interface on Routers A
and B as shown in Example 4-26.

Example 4-26 Configuring RIP for MD5

```
Router A
interface Serial0/0
 ip address 172.16.4.1 255.255.255.252
 ip rip authentication mode md5
 ip rip authentication key-chain Cisco

Router B
interface Serial0/0
 ip address 172.16.4.2 255.255.255.252
 ip rip authentication mode md5
 ip rip authentication key-chain laura
```

The debug output on Router A shows that MD5 authentication is being used. (See Example 4-27.)

Example 4-27   Verifying RIPv2 Authentication

```
01:15:27: RIP: received packet with MD5 authentication
01:15:27: RIP: received v2 update from 172.16.4.2 on Serial0/0
01:15:27:      156.26.0.0/16 via 0.0.0.0 in 2 hops
01:15:27:      172.16.2.0/27 via 0.0.0.0 in 1 hops
01:15:27:      172.16.3.0/25 via 0.0.0.0 in 1 hops
01:15:27:      172.16.4.0/30 via 0.0.0.0 in 1 hops
```

For more information on additional options that are available with RIPv2 authentication, see the references at the end of the chapter.

Route Summarization

One of the properties that allows for a scalable system is being able to aggregate, or summarize, information. In the postal system, for example, a core post office needs either state or city and state information to make a delivery decision. The core layer in the phone system, for example, needs only area code information for a delivery decision. RIPv2 has the ability to aggregate or summarize IP prefixes. Router A is advertising two prefixes to Router B: 172.16.0.0/24 and 172.16.1.0/24. These two prefixes can be summarized by 172.16.0.0/23. Therefore, Router B will have only one RIP route in the routing table instead of two. Summarization of RIP routes is configured on the router interface. (See Example 4-28.)

Example 4-28   Configuring a RIP Summary Route

```
Router A
interface Serial0/0
 ip address 172.16.4.1 255.255.255.252
 ip summary-address rip 172.16.0.0 255.255.254.0
```

The routing table on Router B now contains only one summarized RIP route with a 23-bit subnet mask. (See Example 4-29.)

Example 4-29   Results of Configuring RIP Summarization

```
Router B
     172.16.0.0/16 is variably subnetted, 4 subnets, 4 masks
C       172.16.4.0/30 is directly connected, Serial0/0
R       172.16.0.0/23 [120/1] via 172.16.4.1, 00:00:21, Serial0/0
C       172.16.2.0/27 is directly connected, FastEthernet0/0
C       172.16.3.0/25 is directly connected, FastEthernet0/1
```

Summarization of RIPv2 routes allows the building of a scalable network using core, distribution, and access layers. In Figure 4-12, 24 networks are at the access layer.

Figure 4-12   Route Summarization Using RIPv2

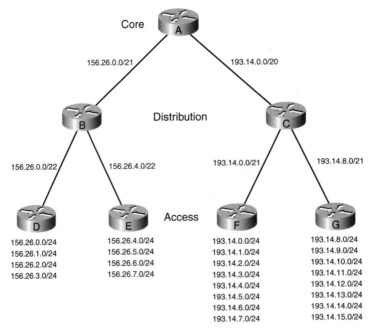

Without summarization, every router at every layer would have 24 RIP routes in the routing table along with the prefixes assigned to the links connecting the routers. For clarity, the addresses of the connecting links are not shown. With summarization, access layer Routers D, E, F, and G advertise one summary prefix to the distribution layer. Distribution Routers B and C advertise one summary prefix to the core layer. Core Router A has only two RIP summary prefixes in its routing table instead of 24.

Route summarization can be thought of as information hiding because the core and distribution routers do not see each individual network. The access routers only see the specific networks that are directly connected. All other prefixes in the routing tables at the access layer are summary prefixes. Another benefit of summarization is that changes in the access layer are hidden from the upper layers. If one of the specific networks at the access layer becomes unreachable, an update will not have to be sent to the distribution layer. As long as one of the specific prefixes in the summary is available, the summary will be advertised. A summary is only removed if all the specific networks that make up that summary become unavailable. This means that changes at the access layer are hidden from the upper layers of the network.

With RIPv1, prefixes not in the same major network number as the interface used to advertise the routing update were automatically summarized to a classful boundary. This is called *autosummarization*. In Figure 4-13, two networks from 156.26.0.0/16 have been added to Router A.

Figure 4-13   RIP Autosummarization

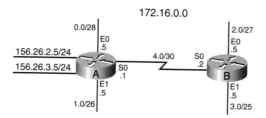

The serial interface is in major network 172.16.0.0, so the 156.26.0.0 prefixes will be summarized to a classful boundary as shown on the routing table on Router B in Example 4-30.

Example 4-30   Autosummarization of a RIPv2 Route

```
Router B
R    156.26.0.0/16 [120/1] via 172.16.4.1, 00:00:17, Serial0
     172.16.0.0/16 is variably subnetted, 4 subnets, 4 masks
C       172.16.4.0/30 is directly connected, Serial0
R       172.16.0.0/23 [120/1] via 172.16.4.1, 00:00:17, Serial0
C       172.16.2.0/27 is directly connected, Ethernet0
C       172.16.3.0/25 is directly connected, Ethernet0
```

With RIPv 2, autosummarization can be disabled. (See Example 4-31.)

Example 4-31   Disabling RIPv2 Autosummarization

```
Router A
router rip
 version 2
 passive-interface Ethernet0
 passive-interface Ethernet0
 network 156.26.0.0
 network 172.16.0.0
 no auto-summary
```

Both 156.26.0.0 routes are advertised with a 24-bit mask instead of a 16-bit mask, as shown in Example 4-32.

Example 4-32   Results of Disabling RIPv2 Autosummarization

```
     156.26.0.0/24 is subnetted, 2 subnets
R       156.26.2.0 [120/1] via 172.16.4.1, 00:00:01, Serial0
R       156.26.3.0 [120/1] via 172.16.4.1, 00:00:01, Serial0
     172.16.0.0/16 is variably subnetted, 4 subnets, 4 masks
C       172.16.4.0/30 is directly connected, Serial0
R       172.16.0.0/23 [120/1] via 172.16.4.1, 00:00:01, Serial0
C       172.16.2.0/27 is directly connected, Ethernet0
C       172.16.3.0/25 is directly connected, Ethernet1
!Output omitted for brevity
```

Router B now knows it can reach only two specific subnets of 156.26.0.0/16, instead of the entire Class B address space. Also, the 156.26.0.0/24 routes can be summarized on Router A, reducing the size of Router B's routing table. (See Example 4-33.)

Example 4-33   Manual Summarization of RIPv2 Routes

```
Router B
     156.26.0.0/23 is subnetted, 1 subnets
R       156.26.2.0 [120/1] via 172.16.4.1, 00:00:01, Serial0
     172.16.0.0/16 is variably subnetted, 4 subnets, 4 masks
C       172.16.4.0/30 is directly connected, Serial0
R       172.16.0.0/23 [120/1] via 172.16.4.1, 00:00:01, Serial0
C       172.16.2.0/27 is directly connected, Ethernet0
C       172.16.3.0/25 is directly connected, Ethernet1
```

Finally, in Figure 4-14, someone has configured network 193.14.7.0/24 on access Router D.

Figure 4-14   Specific and Summary Prefix Advertisement

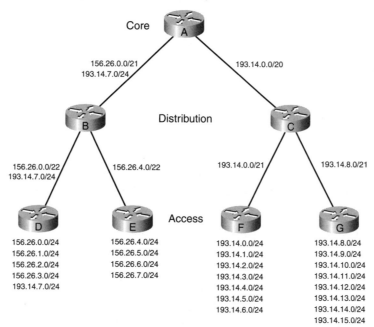

Access Router F is advertising a summary that includes network 193.14.7.0/24. Is this network reachable? The routing table on the core router has the following prefixes:

- 193.14.0.0/20

- 193.14.7.0/24

A packet destined for networks 193.14.0.0 through 193.14.6.0 or networks 193.14.8.0 through 193.14.15.0 will match the summary prefix in the routing table. A packet destined for network 193.14.7.0 will match the second entry in the routing table based on longest match. Therefore, routing works fine as long as Router D advertises the more specific prefix.

Summary

RIP versions 1 and 2 are distance vector interior gateway routing protocols. An organization, such as a company or university, uses one of the interior routing protocols to exchange routes within the organization.

RIP uses a metric called a hop count that cannot account for the bandwidth of the links connecting the routers. The maximum size of a RIP network is limited by the maximum hop count of 16. RIP version 2 is an enhanced version of RIP; it allows the use of VLSM, prefix summarization, and authentication. Because of the limitations of RIP version 1, its use is not recommended. RIP version 2 is recommended for small-to-medium size networks.

The goal of this chapter was not to make you a RIP configuration expert, but to help you understand the concepts, operation, and limitations of RIP. The references at the end of the chapter can be used to learn the configuration options that are available for the protocol.

Chapter Review Questions

You can find the answers to these questions in Appendix A.

1. For the network in Figure 4-15 and the configurations given, determine the contents of the routing table on Router B.

```
Router A
router rip
 version 1
 passive-interface Ethernet0
 passive-interface Ethernet1
 passive-interface Ethernet2
 network 172.16.0.0
 network 64.0.0.0


Router B
router rip
 version 1
 passive-interface Ethernet0
 passive-interface Ethernet1
 network 172.16.0.0
```

Figure 4-15   Review Questions 1 - 3

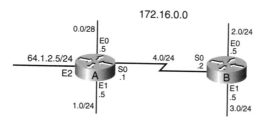

2. For the network in Figure 4-15, and the given configurations, determine the contents of the routing table on Router B.

```
Router A
router rip
 version 2
 passive-interface Ethernet0
 passive-interface Ethernet1
 passive-interface Ethernet2
 network 172.16.0.0
 network 64.0.0.0
Router B
router rip
 version 2
 passive-interface Ethernet0
 passive-interface Ethernet1
 network 172.16.0.0
```

3. For the network in Figure 4-15, and the given configurations, determine the contents of the routing tables on Routers A and B.

```
Router A
router rip
 version 2
 passive-interface Ethernet0
 passive-interface Ethernet1
 passive-interface Ethernet2
 network 172.16.0.0
 network 64.0.0.0
 no auto-summary

Router B
router rip
 version 2
 passive-interface Ethernet0
 passive-interface Ethernet1
 network 172.16.0.0
```

4. For the network in Figure 4-16, determine the interface summary address commands on Routers B, C, D, E, F, and G to summarize the RIP routes. Assume RIP version 2 is being used.

Figure 4-16   Review Question 4

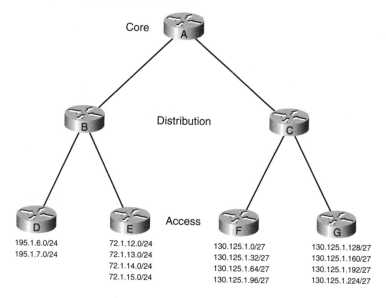

195.1.6.0/24
195.1.7.0/24

72.1.12.0/24
72.1.13.0/24
72.1.14.0/24
72.1.15.0/24

130.125.1.0/27
130.125.1.32/27
130.125.1.64/27
130.125.1.96/27

130.125.1.128/27
130.125.1.160/27
130.125.1.192/27
130.125.1.224/27

References

Use the following references to learn more about the concepts described in this chapter. Note that RFCs are technical documents that are sometimes difficult to follow, so you might want to read the book listed here first:

- Doyle, Jeff. 1998. *Routing TCP/IP*, Volume I. Indianapolis: Cisco Press.

- Hedrick, C. June 1998. RFC 1058, Routing Information Protocol.

- Malkin, G. November 1994. RFC 1723, RIP Version 2.

What You Will Learn

After reading this chapter, you should be able to

✔ Explain the Cisco interior routing protocols: IGRP and EIGRP

✔ Understand the concepts, operation, and limitations of IGRP and EIGRP

✔ Understand the basics of configuring IGRP and EIGRP on Cisco routers

CHAPTER 5

Cisco Interior Gateway Protocols

In general, there are two types of IP routing protocols: *open standard* and *proprietary*. Open-standard documentation, such as Requests for Comments (RFCs), defines the operation and algorithms of the protocol. Any company can implement an open standard on its products as long as it follows the information in the standard. Protocols such as Routing Information Protocol (RIP), Open Shortest Path First (OSPF), Intermediate System-to-Intermediate System (IS-IS), and Border Gateway Protocol (BGP) are all open standards.

A proprietary protocol is developed by one company and is not a published open standard. A proprietary routing protocol is available from only one manufacturer. Cisco has two proprietary *interior routing protocols*. The first was developed as an enhancement to RIP version 1 (RIPv1) and is called the *Interior Gateway Routing Protocol (IGRP)*. The second is an enhanced version of IGRP called the *Enhanced Interior Gateway Routing Protocol (EIGRP)*.

Introducing IGRP

IGRP was developed in the mid-1980s to overcome some of the limitations of RIPv1. The two main limitations of RIPv1 that are addressed by IGRP are the limited hop count; and the inability to chose a path based on the parameters of a link such as bandwidth, reliability, delay, and load. IGRP has increased the maximum hop count to 255, but the hop count in IGRP is not used to select the best path to a network prefix. The hop count is used only to limit the diameter of the network. Any prefix that has a hop count greater than the configured maximum is considered unreachable. The metric or cost of a RIP route is simply the hop count.

The metric of an IGRP route is based on the parameters of the links between routers. These changes aside, IGRP operates the same way as RIPv1. Both are classful, *distance vector* routing protocols. The similarity to RIP is demonstrated with the network in Figure 5-1.

Figure 5-1   Routing in an IGRP Network

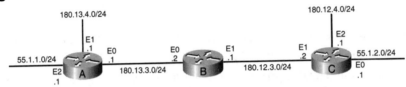

Example 5-1 shows the configurations for Router A, Router B, and Router C.

Example 5-1   Configurations for Router A, Router B, and Router C

```
Router A

router igrp 1
 passive-interface Ethernet 1
 passive-interface Ethernet 2
 network 180.13.0.0
 network 55.0.0.0

Router B

router igrp 1
 network 180.12.0.0
 network 180.13.0.0

Router C

router igrp 1
 passive-interface Ethernet 0
 passive-interface Ethernet 2
 network 180.12.0.0
 network 55.0.0.0
```

The IGRP process must be enabled on every router that is to run IGRP. The first difference with RIP is that a process number is required. Multiple IGRP processes can be configured on the same router, but for routers to be able to exchange routing information the routers must use the same process number. With RIP, only one process can be configured. Interfaces are enabled for IGRP by using classful network statements. For example, when using the configuration command **network 180.13.0.0,** any interface on the router that is configured with an IP address from the Class B address space 180.13.0.0/16 is enabled for IGRP. After an interface is enabled for IGRP, IGRP broadcasts the contents of the routing table on every enabled interface (except for the ones that have been configured as passive). The update time for IGRP is 90 seconds compared to 30 seconds using RIP. This means that IGRP broadcasts its entire routing table on every interface enabled for IGRP every 90 seconds. This is true even if there have been no changes to the routing table. The invalid timer for IGRP is 270 seconds (90 seconds for RIP). When a router receives an update for a prefix, a timer for that prefix is set to 0 and incremented every second. Whenever a new update is received, the counter is reset to 0. If an update is not received for 270 seconds, the prefix is marked as invalid and placed in holddown for 280 seconds. During holddown, advertisements of this prefix are ignored.

IGRP, like RIPv1, does not support variable-length subnet masks (VLSM) because subnet mask information is not advertised with the IP prefix. In this sense, the operation of IGRP is identical to RIPv1. With that in mind, determine the contents of the routing tables for Routers A, B, and C in Figure 5-1. Hint: By default, split horizon is enabled on Ethernet interfaces.

Router A advertises prefix 180.13.4.0 to Router B with an assumed subnet mask of /24. This is because the network between Routers A and B is in the same major network number (180.13.0.0/16) as the prefix assigned to interface E0 on Router A. Router A autosummarizes network 55.1.1.0/24 to an 8-bit classful boundary before advertising to B. So, Router B learns two prefixes from Router A: 180.13.4.0/24 and 55.0.0.0/8 (the subnet masks are assumed by B). Router C advertises the prefixes 180.12.4.0 and 55.0.0.0 to Router B using the same logic as Router A. Router B receives two advertisements for prefix 55.0.0.0/8, one from Router A and one from Router C. Which one will Router B use? Look at the routing table on B in Example 5-2.

Example 5-2 Routing Table on Router B

```
B#show ip route
Codes: C - connected, S - static, I - IGRP, R - RIP, M - mobile, B - BGP
       D - EIGRP, EX - EIGRP external, O - OSPF, IA - OSPF inter area
       N1 - OSPF NSSA external type 1, N2 - OSPF NSSA external type 2
       E1 - OSPF external type 1, E2 - OSPF external type 2, E - EGP
       i - IS-IS, L1 - IS-IS level-1, L2 - IS-IS level-2, ia - IS-IS inter area
       * - candidate default, U - per-user static route, o - ODR
       P - periodic downloaded static route

Gateway of last resort is not set

I    55.0.0.0/8 [100/1200] via 180.12.3.2, 00:00:43, Ethernet1
                [100/1200] via 180.13.3.1, 00:00:49, Ethernet0
     180.12.0.0/24 is subnetted, 2 subnets
C       180.12.3.0 is directly connected, Ethernet1
I       180.12.4.0 [100/1200] via 180.12.3.2, 00:00:43, Ethernet1
     180.13.0.0/24 is subnetted, 2 subnets
C       180.13.3.0 is directly connected, Ethernet0
I       180.13.4.0 [100/1200] via 180.13.3.1, 00:00:49, Ethernet0
```

Both routes to 55.0.0.0/8 are in the routing table. One route has Router A as the next hop. The other route has Router C as the next hop. Is this a good thing? No. Router B thinks it can reach the entire class A network 55.0.0.0/8 through either Router A or C, but it can't. This is one of the inherent problems using a classful routing protocol. Router B does not know that prefix 55.1.1.0/24 can be reached through Router A or that prefix 55.1.2.0/24 can be reached through Router C. Router B believes both these prefixes can be reached through either router!

IGRP Metrics

IGRP uses only hop count to limit the diameter of the network. The default value is 100 hops and can be configured to be between 1 and 255 hops. IGRP uses bandwidth, delay, load, and reliability to determine the metric for a route. The formulas for calculating an IGRP metric are

$A = K1 * Bandwidth_{min}$

$B = (K2 * Bandwidth_{min})/(256 - Load)$

$C = K3 * Delay_{total}$

$$D = K5/(Reliability + K4)$$

$$Metric = (A + B + C) * D$$

The constants K1, K2, K3, K4, and K5 are numbers you can set to a constant value to influence how the IGRP metric is calculated by a router. The following list describes each component of the formula and how the components determine the IGRP metric:

- Bandwidth$_{min}$ is the minimum bandwidth along the route to the destination in kbps divided into 10 million. In Figure 5-1, the bandwidth of the link between Routers A and B and Routers B and C is 10 Mbps, or 10,000 kbps. Therefore, the minimum bandwidth from Router A to C is 10,000,000/ 10,000 = 1,000 kbps.

- Delay is the sum of the end-to-end travel time from source to destination, in ms, divided by 10.

- Reliability is a number between 1 and 255 and measures the reliability of a link. An unreliable link has a value of 1 and a 100-percent reliable link has a value of 255.

- Load measures how busy the interface is. A value of 1 indicates the link is not busy, and a value of 255 indicates the link is extremely busy.

These parameters can be found by looking at the properties of a router interface, as shown in Example 5-3.

Example 5-3   Reviewing the Properties of an Interface

```
A#show interfaces ethernet 0
Ethernet0 is up, line protocol is up
  Hardware is AmdP2, address is 0004.9aac.7d80 (bia 0004.9aac.7d80)
  Internet address is 180.13.3.1/24
  MTU 1500 bytes, BW 10000 Kbit, DLY 1000 usec,
     reliability 255/255, txload 1/255, rxload 1/255
```

For the Ethernet interface on Router A, the parameters are

Bandwidth = 10,000,000/10,000 = 1000 kbps

Delay = 1000/10 = 100 microseconds

Reliability = 255

Load = 1

The values for the link between Routers B and C are identical. You can now calculate the metric for the 180.12.4.0/24 route advertised by Router C from Router A's point of view. Luckily, by default, the constants K1 and K3 are equal to 1; and K2, K4, and K5 are equal to 0. If K5 = 0, the last term in the metric equation is not used. Otherwise, the value of the metric equation would be 0. The IGRP metric formula reduces to:

$$\text{Metric} = A + C = \text{Bandwidth}_{min} + \text{Delay}_{total}$$

For the path from Router A to Router C, the minimum bandwidth is 1000 and the sum of the delays is 100 + 100 = 200. Therefore, the metric from A to C is 1200 as shown in Example 5-4.

Example 5-4　Verifying the IGRP Metric

```
Router A
     55.0.0.0/24 is subnetted, 1 subnets
C       55.1.1.0 is directly connected, Loopback0
I     180.12.0.0/16 [100/1200] via 180.13.3.2, 00:01:12, Ethernet0
     180.13.0.0/24 is subnetted, 2 subnets
C       180.13.3.0 is directly connected, Ethernet0
C       180.13.4.0 is directly connected, Ethernet1
```

The IGRP metric is an improvement over the RIP metric (hop count) because the properties of the connecting links determine the best path. In Figure 5-2, RIP would prefer the path from A to C to reach Network 1 because of the smaller hop count.

Figure 5-2   Best Path in an IGRP Network

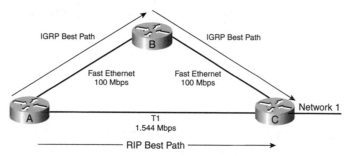

Which path would IGRP prefer? The IGRP bandwidth for the fast Ethernet link is 10,000,000/100,000 = 100. Delay for fast Ethernet is 100 ms; the IGRP delay is 10. The total delay from A to C through B is 20. The IGRP metric for the path from A to C through B is 120.

The IGRP bandwidth for the T1 link is 10,000,000/1544 = 6476. The delay is 20,000 microseconds/10 = 2000. The IGRP metric from A to C using the T1 link is 8476. Therefore, IGRP will prefer the path from A to B to C to reach Network 1.

IGRP Limitations

The network in Figure 5-3 has the ideal structure for IGRP.

Figure 5-3   Ideal IGRP Network

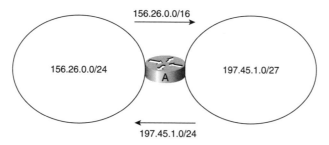

Router A is a border router between two domains. The domain on the left uses the 156.26.0.0/16 Class B address space with all subnets using a 24-bit mask. The domain on the right uses the 197.45.1.0/24 Class C address space with all subnets using a 27-bit mask. Router A automatically summarizes the 156.26.0.0 address space to a classful boundary before advertising into the 197.45.1.0 domain. Router A also summarizes the 197.45.1.0 address space to a classful boundary before advertising into the 156.26.0.0 domain. All networks in Figure 5-3 are reachable, but there are limitations. In the 156.26.0.0 domain, all networks must use a 24-bit mask. If a different subnet mask is used, these networks are not advertised throughout the domain. The same limitation exists on the 197.45.1.0 side. All subnets must use a 27-bit mask. There is no flexibility in scaling subnets based on the number of users. A 24-bit subnet can have up to 254 hosts. A 27-bit subnet can have up to 30 hosts. What if a subnet needs more hosts? What if a subnet needs fewer hosts? There is nothing you can do.

Figure 5-4 shows a routing domain using private IP addresses.

Figure 5-4   Another Ideal IGRP Network

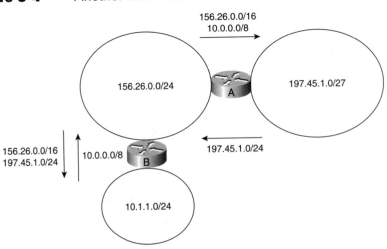

A routing domain using the 10.0.0.0/8 private address space has been added to the network. Router B is the border router between the 10.0.0.0 network and the rest of the IGRP domains. Will this work? Yes. Router B summarizes the private address space to the classful prefix 10.0.0.0/8, and this prefix advertises into the 156.26.0.0 and 197.45.1.0 domains.

Figure 5-5 shows the 10.1.1.0/24 network split into two domains.

Figure 5-5   Broken IGRP Network

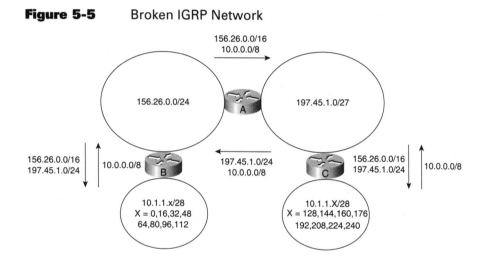

Router A now has two routes to 10.0.0.0: one to Router B and one to Router C. Router A thinks the entire Class A address space can be reached through B and C. Oops! This will not work. This problem would be the same if RIPv1 were used instead of IGRP.

In summary, RIPv1 and IGRP are adequate routing protocols for small, simple networks, but are usually not used for large, complex networks. Although IGRP has a better metric than RIPv1, both suffer serious limitations. The greatest limitation is that both are classful routing protocols—subnet mask information is not advertised. Therefore, the same subnet mask must be used. Second, all route summarization in RIPv1 and IGRP is automatic. There is no way to configure route summarization as you can with RIPv2.

For larger, more complex networks, you need an interior routing protocol that overcomes the limitations of RIPv1 and IGRP. The next protocol presented— EIGRP—is an enhanced version of IGRP designed to overcome those limitations.

Introducing EIGRP

EIGRP is an advanced distance vector routing protocol that guarantees a loop-free routing topology. EIGRP is a classless routing protocol that supports the use of VLSM and *discontiguous subnets*. In Figure 5-5, the 10.0.0.0 network is discontiguous. You see some similarities with IGRP, but the overall operation of EIGRP is quite different.

EIGRP Neighbor Discovery

RIPv1 and IGRP periodically broadcast their routing tables on every interface enabled for the protocol. RIPv2 sends its routing table to a multicast address every update period. Neither RIP nor IGRP are aware that neighboring routers are also enabled for the protocol—except for the fact that they receive protocol updates from them. EIGRP, however, first discovers EIGRP neighbors on an enabled interface before the routing table is sent. (See Figure 5-6.)

When EIGRP is enabled on an interface, EIGRP sends a *hello packet* every 5 seconds on high-speed interfaces and every 60 seconds on low-speed interfaces. The hold time in EIGRP is used to determine if a neighbor has gone away. If a hello packet is not received from a discovered neighbor in three times the hello time (15 seconds), the neighbor is declared dead. For high-speed interfaces, it takes EIGRP 15 seconds to determine if a neighbor has died. With RIP this takes 90 seconds, and with IGRP this takes 270 seconds. Therefore, EIGRP responds much faster than RIP or IGRP when a neighbor disappears.

Figure 5-6   EIGRP Neighbor Discovery and Route Exchange

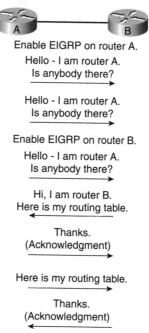

Enable EIGRP on router A.

Hello - I am router A.
Is anybody there?

Hello - I am router A.
Is anybody there?

Enable EIGRP on router B.

Hello - I am router A.
Is anybody there?

Hi, I am router B.
Here is my routing table.

Thanks.
(Acknowledgment)

Here is my routing table.

Thanks.
(Acknowledgment)

RIP transmits its routing table every 30 seconds. IGRP transmits its routing table every 90 seconds. After the initial exchange of routing information with a neighbor, EIGRP sends only *incremental updates*. An incremental update contains only new or changed prefix information and it is sent only to the neighbor that needs it.

Basic EIGRP Configuration

The network in Figure 5-7 is the same network used for IGRP in Figure 5-1. Example 5-5 shows the EIGRP configurations for each router.

Figure 5-7 Basic EIGRP Configuration

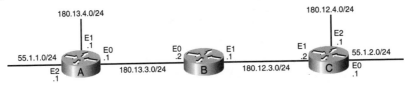

Example 5-5 EIGRP Configurations for Router A, Router B, and Router C

```
Router A
router eigrp 1
 passive-interface Ethernet 1
 passive-interface Ethernet 2
 network 180.13.3.0 255.255.255.0
 network 180.13.4.0 255.255.255.0
 network 55.1.1.0 255.255.255.0

Router B
router eigrp 1
 network 180.12.3.0 255.255.255.0
 network 180.13.3.0 255.255.255.0

Router C
router eigrp 1
 passive-interface Ethernet 0
 passive-interface Ethernet 2
 network 180.12.3.0 255.255.255.0
 network 180.12.4.0 255.255.255.0
 network 55.0.0.0
```

Configuring EIGRP is similar to IGRP. A routing process is configured with an assigned process number. Interfaces with no neighbors are configured as passive. EIRGP advertises the prefix and mask assigned to a passive interface but will not try to discover neighbors using the interface. Network statements inform the router which interfaces to enable for EIGRP, and which connected interfaces will be advertised through EIGRP. The **network**statement now includes a subnet mask. With RIP and IGRP, the network statements are classful. The subnet mask used is the standard mask for that particular class of prefix. For example, **network 55.0.0.0** has an assumed 8-bit Class A mask. Any interface configured in this Class A address space is enabled for RIP or IGRP, and the prefix is advertised. With EIGRP, the **network**statement now includes a subnet mask. This allows for many variations on how to configure an interface for EIGRP.

You can use a 32-bit host address using a 32-bit mask: **network 180.13.4.1 255.255.255.255**.

The network statement informs the router which interfaces to use for EIGRP route exchange. Regardless of the subnet mask used in the network statement, the router advertises the subnet mask assigned to the interface. You could use one 16-bit subnet mask to include both 180.13.0.0 interfaces on Router A just like you did with IGRP. In this case, you do not need to include a subnet mask. EIGRP assumes a classful 16-bit mask: **network 180.13.0.0**

You could use any mask as long as the resulting block of addresses contains the two 180.13.0.0 interfaces on Router A. The following network statements both enable the 180.13.0.0 interfaces for EIGRP:

network 180.0.0.0 255.0.0.0

network 180.0.0.0 255.240.0.0

The second form of the network statement gives you more flexibility when determining which interfaces are enabled for EIGRP.

If you configure the routers as shown in Figure 5-7, the routing table on Router B should contain all the EIGRP routes, as shown in Example 5-6.

Example 5-6   EIGRP Route Verification

```
B#show ip route
Codes: C - connected, S - static, I - IGRP, R - RIP, M - mobile, B - BGP
       D - EIGRP, EX - EIGRP external, O - OSPF, IA - OSPF inter area
       N1 - OSPF NSSA external type 1, N2 - OSPF NSSA external type 2
       E1 - OSPF external type 1, E2 - OSPF external type 2, E - EGP
       i - IS-IS, L1 - IS-IS level-1, L2 - IS-IS level-2, ia - IS-IS inter area
       * - candidate default, U - per-user static route, o - ODR
       P - periodic downloaded static route

Gateway of last resort is not set

D    55.0.0.0/8 [90/307200] via 180.12.3.2, 00:00:03, Ethernet1
                [90/307200] via 180.13.3.1, 00:00:03, Ethernet0
     180.12.0.0/24 is subnetted, 2 subnets
C       180.12.3.0 is directly connected, Ethernet1
D       180.12.4.0 [90/307200] via 180.12.3.2, 00:00:03, Ethernet1
     180.13.0.0/24 is subnetted, 2 subnets
C       180.13.3.0 is directly connected, Ethernet0
D       180.13.4.0 [90/307200] via 180.13.3.1, 00:00:03, Ethernet0
```

Do you see anything wrong? Router B has two routes to the entire 55.0.0.0/8 net-work, just like you saw when using IGRP. The problem is that the 55.0.0.0/8 route is discontiguous. You are using one subnet on Router A and one subnet on Router C. You could not fix this problem with IGRP, but you can fix it with EIGRP. By default, auto-summary is enabled with IGRP and EIGRP. You can't turn it off when using IGRP, but you can disable it with EIGRP. If auto-summary is disabled on Routers A and C, the problem should be fixed, as follows:

```
router eigrp 1
 no auto-summary
```

The routing table on Router B should now contain two routes to the 55.0.0.0 network, as shown in Example 5-7.

Example 5-7   Verifying Auto-Summary Has Been Disabled

```
!Output omitted for brevity
     55.0.0.0/24 is subnetted, 2 subnets
D       55.1.2.0 [90/307200] via 180.12.3.2, 00:00:01, Ethernet1
D       55.1.1.0 [90/307200] via 180.13.3.1, 00:00:01, Ethernet0
     180.12.0.0/24 is subnetted, 2 subnets
C       180.12.3.0 is directly connected, Ethernet1
D       180.12.4.0 [90/307200] via 180.12.3.2, 00:00:01, Ethernet1
     180.13.0.0/24 is subnetted, 2 subnets
C       180.13.3.0 is directly connected, Ethernet0/0
D       180.13.4.0 [90/307200] via 180.13.3.1, 00:00:02, Ethernet0
```

Because EIGRP advertises subnet masks with the IP prefixes and auto-summary is disabled, the network can now use VLSM and discontiguous network prefixes.

EIGRP Metrics

EIGRP uses the same formula as IGRP for a route metric with the addition of a scaling factor of 256. In other words, an EIGRP metric = 256 times the IGRP metric. From the perspective of Router A in Figure 5-7, network 180.12.4.0/24 on Router C has an IGRP metric of 1200:

```
I    180.12.0.0/16 [100/1200] via 180.13.3.2, 00:01:12, Ethernet0
```

Using EIGRP, this network should have a metric of 1200 * 256 = 307,200:

```
D       180.12.4.0 [90/307200] via 180.12.3.2, 00:00:01, Ethernet1
```

IGRP uses 24-bits for the route metric in an update message. EIGRP uses 32-bits or 8 additional bits and $2^8 = 256$.

Because the IGRP metric is lower than the EIGRP metric, does this mean the IGRP route is better than the EIGRP route? No. You cannot compare metrics between routing protocols. What is better? A RIP hop count of 2, an IGRP metric of 1200, or an EIGRP metric of 307,200? Well, that question cannot be answered. If you recall from Chapter 4, "Routing IP," the first number in brackets is the administrative, or admin, distance:

```
I    180.12.0.0/16 [100/1200] via 180.13.3.2, 00:01:12, Ethernet0
D       180.12.4.0 [90/307200] via 180.12.3.2, 00:00:01, Ethernet1
```

IGRP has an admin distance of 100, EIGRP has an admin distance of 90, and RIP has an admin distance of 120. When comparing routes learned from more than one routing protocol, the admin distance determines the best route. The lowest admin distance is considered the best. So EIGRP is better than IGRP, and IGRP is better than RIP.

EIGRP Route Update Algorithm

RIP and IGRP use a simple route update algorithm. When a prefix is received from a neighbor, add the prefix to the routing table if the route is not already in the routing table. If the metric or cost is lower than the metric in the routing table, replace the route. If the metric is higher than a route in the routing table, but the route in the routing table was learned from the advertising neighbor, replace the route. RIP and IGRP cannot detect routing loops. A routing loop is where a packet follows a closed path and loops around in the network. The convergence time if a route or router disappears is long for RIP and IGRP.

EIGRP uses the *diffusing update algorithm (DUAL)* to determine a loop-free path to every destination network. The best way to understand DUAL is by example. In Figure 5-8 the cost, or metric, of the links determines the best path from each router to network 172.16.9.0/24. Router E reports a distance of 2560 to this network. This quantity is called the *reported distance*. Routers B, C, and D receive the reported distance from Router E and add their cost to reach Router E. For example, in Table 5-1, Router B has a metric to reach network 172.16.9.0 of 2560 + 2560 = 5120. This new quantity is called the *feasible distance* (FD). The FD is the reported distance plus the cost to reach the reporting router.

Figure 5-8　　DUAL Determines the Best Path to a Network

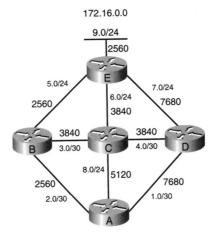

Table 5-1　　Reported and Feasible Distances for Routers B, C, and D

Destination	Router	Reported Distance	Feasible Distance (FD)
172.16.9.0	B	2560	5120
172.16.9.0	C	2560	6400
172.16.9.0	D	2560	7680

Routers B, C, and D use their FD to network 172.16.9.0 as their reported distance when they advertise this route to Router A. Router A has three routes to network 172.16.9.0 as shown in Table 5-2.

Table 5-2   Reported and Feasible Distances for Router A

Destination	Neighbor	Reported Distance	FD
172.16.9.0	B	5120	**7680**
172.16.9.0	C	**6400**	11,520
172.16.9.0	D	10,240	17,920

The next-hop router with the lowest FD to the destination is called the *successor*. In other words, the successor has the best or lowest cost path to the destination. An EIGRP router maintains a list of feasible successors in the *EIGRP topology table*. A *feasible successor* is a router that has a reported distance that is less than the router's FD. In Table 5-2, Router C has an reported distance of 6400, which is less than the FD of 7680. Therefore, Router C is a feasible successor to reach network 172.16.9.0. Router D has a reported distance that is greater than the FD. Router A assumes the path through Router D contains a loop, so Router D is not on the list of feasible successors. If the successor fails, the path through Router B disappears and Router A immediately promotes Router C to successor for that route. In contrast, RIP and IGRP have to wait for the route to time out before installing an alternative route in the routing table.

In Figure 5-9, assume that the link between Routers B and E fails. Router A switches to the feasible successor, Router C, to reach network 172.16.9.0. The reported distance and FD on Router A to 172.16.9.0 are listed in Table 5-3.

Figure 5-9   Operation of DUAL

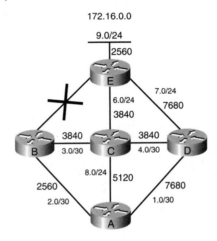

Table 5-3   Reported and Feasible Distances for Router A

Destination	Neighbor	Reported Distance	FD
172.16.9.0	C	6400	**11,520**
172.16.9.0	D	**10,240**	17,920

Router C is now the successor and Router D is the feasible successor to reach network 172.16.9.0.

Any route that has a successor is said to be in the *passive state*. Being in the passive state means the router has a loop-free path and is not actively looking for a route to the destination.

What happens if the successor fails and there is not a feasible successor? In Figure 5-10, the RD and FD on Router C to network 172.16.9.0 are listed in Table 5-4.

Figure 5-10   Using Reported Distance and FD to Determine a Best Path

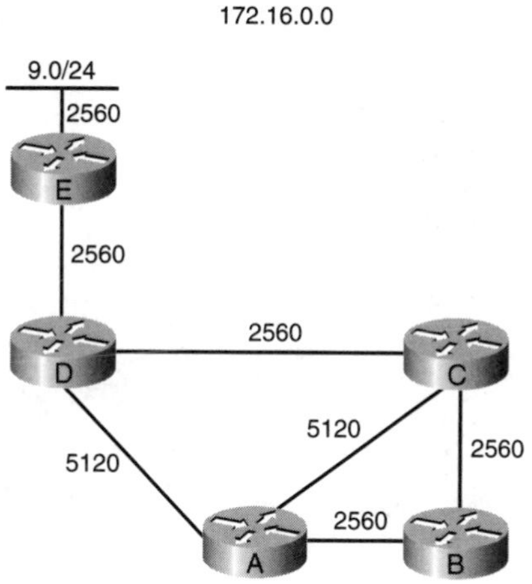

172.16.0.0

Table 5-4   Reported and Feasible Distances for Router C

Destination	Neighbor	Reported Distance	FD
172.16.9.0	D	5120	**7680**
172.16.9.0	A	10,240	15,360
172.16.9.0	B	12,800	15,260

Router D is the successor, no feasible successor exists, and the route to 172.16.9.0 is in the passive state. There is no feasible successor because the reported distances from Routers A and B are higher than the FD of 7680. In Figure 5-11, the successor route to network 172.16.9.0 fails and no feasible successor exists.

Figure 5-11 Router C Does Not Have a Feasible Successor to Network 172.16.9.0

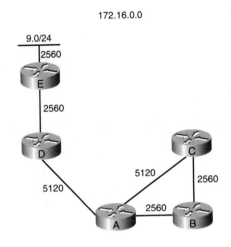

Router C moves network 172.16.9.0 from the passive state to the active state. In the active state, Router C sends queries to its neighbors asking for information regarding network 172.16.9.0. (See Figure 5-12.)

Figure 5-12 Router C has Placed Network 172.16.9.0 in Active Mode

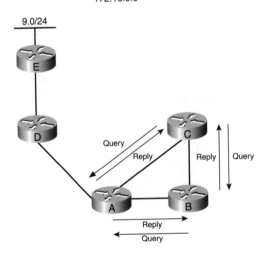

Before the failure of the network between Routers C and D, Routers A and B had the following distances for network 172.16.9.0. (See Table 5-5 and Table 5-6.)

Table 5-5   Reported and Feasible Distances on Router B

Destination	Neighbor	Reported Distance	FD
172.16.9.0	C	7680	10,240
172.16.9.0	A	10,240	12,800

Table 5-6   Reported and Feasible Distances on Router A

Destination	Neighbor	Reported Distance	FD
172.16.9.0	D	5120	10,240
172.16.9.0	C	7680	12,800
172.16.9.0	B	10,240	12,800

Router B has a successor through Router C and no feasible successor. Router A has a successor through D and a feasible successor through C. When the link fails, Router B has no successor and no feasible successor. Router A still has a successor through D. When Router B receives the query from C, Router B queries A because it no longer has a successor and B had no feasible successor. Router A replies to Routers B and C with its route through D. These routes are installed in the routing tables on B and C, and this route to 172.16.9.0 is placed back in the passive state.

The query process stops when all neighbors respond to the query, or it is determined that the network in question is no longer available. After all neighbors have responded to the query then the router determines the best path, or successor, for the route to the network. As long as there are outstanding replies to a query, the route stays in the active state. It is possible for a route to be *stuck in active (SIA)*. When a route becomes active, a timer is started for that route. After 1.5 minutes, if the timer expires and a neighbor has not responded to the query, the neighbor is sent another query. Up to three additional queries can be sent to a neighbor for a total elapsed time of 6 minutes. If a neighbor still has not responded to the query, the neighbor is reset, the EIGRP neighbor relationship is re-established with the neighbor, and all routes that went through that neighbor are placed in the active state.

There are a number of reasons that a neighbor might have not responded to a query, including the following:

- The links between routers could be congested or failed.

- The neighbor might be busy doing other things.

- The neighbor router does not have enough memory to properly handle all its tasks.

- The network diameter might be too big.

Queries are sent to all neighbors if the router that receives a query does not have information regarding the lost route. If the range of the queries is not limited, the originating router could wait a long time before receiving a response from all neighbors. One way to limit the range of queries is to use network summarization.

EIGRP Network Summarization

In Figure 5-13, assume that you are running EIGRP and that automatic network summarization has been disabled.

Without network summarization, all routes are in the routing tables on all routers. The routing table on the core router, Router A, has the 14 specific prefixes from the access layer and the 6 prefixes assigned to the interfaces that interconnect the routers (not shown in Figure 5-13). Twenty routes does not seem like a large number, but without summarization the routing tables grow as the size of the network grows. To summarize, EIGRP routes use the following interface command:

```
ip summary-address eigrp process-number prefix mask
```

Figure 5-13   Route Summarization with EIGRP

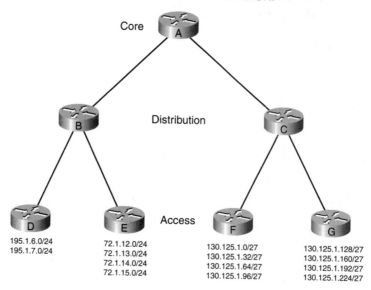

The *process-number* is the number used when the EIGRP process was enabled. The *prefix* and *mask* are the parameters used to summarize the networks. The two 195.1.0.0 networks on Router D can be summarized using the following command:

```
ip summary-address eigrp 1 195.1.6.0 255.255.254.0
```

The first two bytes must match 195.1, so the first two bytes of the mask are 255.255. The last byte is used for the host address—you don't care what its value is. This makes the last byte of the mask a 0. The third byte of the mask is obtained by looking at the third byte of each prefix to be included in the summary address:

$6 = 0\ 0\ 0\ 0\ 0\ 1\ 1\ 0$

$7 = 0\ 0\ 0\ 0\ 0\ 1\ 1\ 1$

The first seven bits of the third byte must equal 0 0 0 0 0 1 1. It doesn't matter what the last bit of the third byte is, so the mask for the third byte is 1 1 1 1 1 1 1 0 (0 = don't care) and the entire mask is 255.255.254.0.

The prefix and mask used to summarize the 72.1.0.0 networks are again found by examining the third byte of each prefix:

12 = 0 0 0 0 1 1 0 0

13 = 0 0 0 0 1 1 0 1

14 = 0 0 0 0 1 1 1 0

15 = 0 0 0 0 1 1 1 1

The first six bits of the third byte must equal 0 0 0 0 1 1 and the last two bits are "don't cares." Therefore, the mask is 1 1 1 1 1 1 0 0 or 252, and the summary address command is as follows:

```
ip summary-address eigrp 1 72.1.12.0 255.255.252.0
```

Finally, to summarize the 130.125.0.0 networks, the first three bytes must match 130.125.1. The first three bytes of the mask are 255.255.255. Three bits of the last byte of the prefix are used for the network portion of the address. For the networks connected to Router F, the last bytes of the addresses are

0 = 0 0 0 0 0 0 0 0

32 = 0 0 1 0 0 0 0 0

64 = 0 1 0 0 0 0 0 0

96 = 0 1 1 0 0 0 0 0

The last 5 bits are the host addresses (they are irrelevant) and the corresponding mask bits are 0. The next two bits are not important and the first bit must be 0. Therefore, the mask for the networks on Router F is 128 = 1 0 0 0 0 0 0 0.

The summary address command for networks 0, 32, 64, and 96 is

```
ip summary-address eigrp 1 130.125.1.0 255.255.255.128
```

For the networks on Router G, the last five bits are host addresses and the corresponding mask bits are 0, as follows:

128= 1 0 0 0 0 0 0 0

160= 1 0 1 0 0 0 0 0

$$192 = 1\ 1\ 0\ 0\ 0\ 0\ 0\ 0$$

$$224 = 1\ 1\ 1\ 0\ 0\ 0\ 0\ 0$$

The next two bits are not important, and the first bit must be one. Therefore, the mask for the networks on Router G is 128 = 1 0 0 0 0 0 0 0.

The summary address command for networks 128, 160, 192, and 224 is

```
ip summary-address eigrp 1 130.125.1.128 255.255.255.128
```

Router C can further summarize the two prefixes that it is receiving from Routers F and G using the following command:

```
ip summary-address eigrp 1 130.125.1.0 255.255.255.0
```

The routing table on Router A contains only the summary routes and not the 14 specific routes as shown in Table 5-7.

Table 5-7 Core Routing Table

Prefix	Next Hop
72.1.12.0/22	B
195.1.6.0/23	B
130.125.1.0/24	C

Comparing IGRP and EIGRP

You have seen that EIGRP is a more robust IP routing protocol than RIP or IGRP. The limitation of IGRP, along with the advantages of EIGRP, should make it obvious that IGRP should only be deployed in small IP networks. The limitations of IGRP include the following:

- Slow convergence time—on the order of minutes

- Cannot guarantee a loop-free topology

- Does not support VLSM or discontiguous networks

- Uses periodic full routing table updates

- Classful routing protocol

- Proprietary routing protocol

The advantages of EIGRP are as follows:

- DUAL algorithm

- Guaranteed loop-free topology

- Fast convergence if a feasible successor is available

- Uses incremental updates instead of full-routing table updates

- Supports VLSM and discontiguous networks

- Supports route summarization for reducing routing table size

- Classless routing protocol

Summary

IGRP and EIGRP are proprietary Cisco interior distance vector IP routing protocols. Distance vector means that each router need not know the topology for the entire network. Each router only advertises destination routes with a corresponding metric, cost, or distance. IGRP is a classful protocol and must use the same subnet mask length throughout the network—limiting the ability to use subnets with varying numbers of hosts.

The IGRP metric is comprised of bandwidth, delay, load utilization, and link reliability. This allows fine-tuning of link characteristics to determine a best path to a destination.

EIGRP is an enhanced version of IGRP and is a classless IP routing protocol. As with IGRP, EIGRP uses same distance vector approach used in IGRP. The convergence properties and the operating efficiency of this protocol have been improved. EIGRP uses the diffusing update algorithm (DUAL) to obtain a loop-free topology.

Chapter Review Questions

You can find the answers to these questions in Appendix A.

1. Determine the successor and any feasible successors for Network 1 in Figure 5-14 for each router in the network.

Figure 5-14   Network for Review Question 1

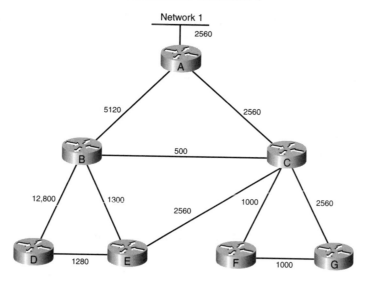

2. Explain the difference between a classful and a classless routing protocol.

3. What are the states that an EIGRP route can be in and what do these states mean?

4. Explain the relationship between reported distance and feasible distance and how they determine successors and feasible successors.

5. For the router in Figure 5-15, configure EIGRP so that it is active on all interfaces. Use a minimum number of network commands.

Figure 5-15   Network for Review Question 5

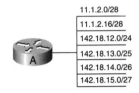

11.1.2.0/28
11.1.2.16/28
142.18.12.0/24
142.18.13.0/25
142.18.14.0/26
142.18.15.0/27

6. Determine the EIGRP command to summarize the following networks:

   10.1.0.0/19

   10.1.32.0/19

   10.1.64.0/19

   10.1.96.0/19

References

Use the following references to learn more about the concepts described in this chapter:

- Aziz, Z., J. Liu, A. Martey, and F. Shamin. 2002. *Troubleshooting IP Routing Protocols*. Indianapolis: Cisco Press.

- Doyle, J. 1998. *Routing TCP/IP*, Volume I. Indianapolis: Cisco Press.

- Cisco Documentation, Cisco.com.

What You Will Learn

After reading this chapter, you should be able to

- ✔ Understand the concepts, terminology, and operation of Open Shortest Path First (OSPF)

- ✔ Understand the basics of configuring OSPF on Cisco routers

CHAPTER 6

Open Shortest Path First— Better, Stronger, Faster

OSPF is a hierarchical link-state interior IP routing protocol designed to overcome the limitations of the distance vector routing protocols. *Open* means that OSPF is a standards-based protocol defined in an RFC. *Hierarchical* means that an OSPF network can be divided into multiple areas. The distance vector protocols, RIP and IGRP, are single-area routing protocols. A single area means all routes in an area are advertised to all routers in the same area. Because there is only one area, all routes are advertised everywhere. As the number of routers in a single area grows, the number of routes advertised grows along with the propagation and convergence times. For large networks, it is desirable to limit the scope of these advertisements by dividing the network into multiple areas.

A multiple-area network is similar to the postal system examined in Chapter 1, "Routing and Switching in Everyday Life." If the postal system used a single area, all post offices would receive information about all destinations. Because this does not scale, the postal system uses a hierarchical structure that controls the information needed at the various levels. A city post office needs only specific information about directly connected streets. A state post office needs only specific information about directly connected cities and states. You can think of the postal system as a multiple-area system with the areas being cities; and states where the areas need only specific information about destinations in their area; and summary information about destinations outside their area. Although an OSPF network can use a single area, using multiple areas has many advantages, as you will see in the next section.

OSPF Areas

A single OSPF area can be used for small networks because the total number of routes advertised is small. In Figure 6-1, the OSPF network has been designed using a single area so all routers know all the specific network prefixes for the entire network.

Figure 6-1   Single Area OSPF Network

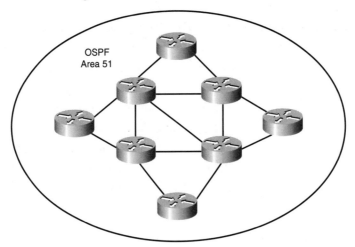

When using a single area, all routing information is advertised or *flooded* by every router to every neighbor router in the area. This is acceptable for small networks, but not for large networks. When a single area is used, the area number can be any number between 0 and 4,294,967,295. This number may look familiar to you. If you convert 4,294,967,295 to dotted decimal, you get 255.255.255.255. This is a 32-bit number that has the same range and format as an IP address. OSPF areas are represented by either a decimal or dotted decimal number. Area 51 and area 0.0.0.51 are equivalent.

Normally, OSPF networks are designed using multiple areas. When a single area is used, summarization is not possible. Using multiple areas allows for a hierarchical and scalable network design. When using multiple OSPF areas, a backbone area, or area 0, must be used. All nonzero OSPF areas must be connected to the backbone, or area 0. In Figure 6-2, the network in Figure 6-1 has been reconfigured to use multiple OSPF areas.

Figure 6-2   Multiple Area OSPF Network

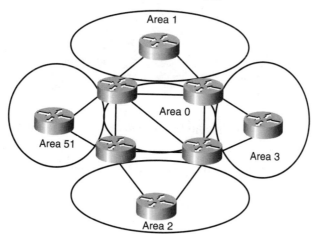

You can think of the routers directly connected to area 0 as the post offices at the state level, and the routers contained within a nonzero area as the city-level post offices.

All nonzero OSPF areas in Figure 6-2 are connected to the backbone, or area 0. Routers are not configured to be in a particular OSPF area. Router interfaces are configured for a particular OSPF area; and nonzero areas are connected to area 0 through a router that has one or more interfaces in area 0, and one or more interfaces in a nonzero area. In Figure 6-3, Router B has an interface in area 0, and an interface in area 51. Area 51 is connected to area 0 through Router B.

Figure 6-3   All Nonzero OSPF Areas Must Be Connected to Area 0

Area 1 is connected to area 0 through Router C. Router C has an interface in area 0, and an interface in area 1. If you rearrange the areas in Figure 6-3, you can produce an invalid OSPF network design because area 51 is no longer connected to area 0. (See Figure 6-4.)

Figure 6-4   Invalid OSPF Network

The network in Figure 6-4 is invalid because area 51 is not connected to area 0 through any router. This situation can arise because of a failure in the network. In Figure 6-5, a link has been added between Routers B and C and has been configured to be in area 0.

Figure 6-5   Valid OSPF Network

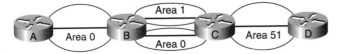

The network in Figure 6-5 is a valid OSPF network because all nonzero OSPF areas are connected to the backbone, or area 0. If the area 0 link between Routers B and C fails, area 51 will be cut off from area 0. There is a way to repair an OSPF network in a situation like this, and this technique is discussed later in this chapter in the section entitled, "OSPF Virtual Links."

Link States

OSPF is a *link-state routing protocol*. How does this compare to the distance vector protocols that you have examined (RIP and IGRP)? A distance vector protocol advertises its routing table to directly connected neighbors. Neighbors add routes to their routing tables based on a simple algorithm. If the received route is not in the routing table, the router adds the route to the routing table. If the received route is in the routing table but the metric is lower, the router replaces the route in the routing table. If the received route is in the routing table but the metric is greater than the route in the routing table, the router adds the route only if the route was received from the neighbor that originally advertised the route. Distance vector protocols advertise prefixes with assumed subnet masks (RIP version 1 and IGRP), or prefixes with a subnet mask (RIP version 2). Distance vector protocols have no knowledge of the network topology or how the routers are interconnected. RIP and IGRP have no way of guaranteeing a loop-free topology. EIGRP, using DUAL, guarantees a loop-free topology but can also assume that some loop-free paths are not loop free.

OSPF does not advertise routes like the distance vector protocols. OSPF advertises link states using **link-state advertisements (LSAs)**. A link is just an interface, such as Ethernet, or serial. Every link has properties that include the OSPF area configured for that link, the bandwidth of the link, and the prefix and subnet mask assigned to the link. The state of the link is whether the link is up or down (functioning or not functioning).

OSPF routers flood, or advertise, their link states to their OSPF neighbors throughout an OSPF area. If a router has interfaces only in one area, that router will maintain one OSPF database for that area. If a router has interfaces in more than one area, the router maintains a separate database for each area. Routers in an area flood their links states until every OSPF router in an area has an identical OSPF database for that area. After the databases in an area agree or are synchronized, each router constructs a graph of the prefixes in an area and the routes to those prefixes. Each router runs a shortest path first (SPF) algorithm to determine the best loop-free path to every destination in the area. The best paths to every destination are then installed in the local IP routing table.

If only one area is used in an OSPF network design, route summarization cannot be used. Before routes can be transferred from the OSPF database to the IP routing table, the databases in an area must agree. If routes could be summarized in an area, some routers would have specific routes and some routers would have summaries. If this were possible, the databases in an area would never agree, and routes would never be placed in the IP routing table. Routes can be summarized between areas, but not within an area. For example, area 1 could have a summary of routes in area 2, and area 2 could have a summary of routes in area 1. However, area 1 cannot have a summary of area 1 routes, and area 2 cannot have a summary of area 2 routes.

In summary, an OSPF network has the following properties:

- One or more OSPF areas.

- If more than one OSPF area is used, a backbone, or area 0, must be configured.

- All nonzero OSPF areas must be connected to area 0.

- For each area configured on an OSPF router, the router maintains an OSPF database for that area.

- Link-state advertisements (LSAs) flood information about a router's interfaces throughout an OSPF area.

- OSPF databases within an area must be identical before a router can calculate the routes that are installed in the IP routing table.

- The Shortest Path First (SPF) algorithm is run on each area database maintained by a router. SPF determines the routes that are installed in the IP routing table.

- Routes can be summarized only between areas, not within an area.

At this point you should have a basic understanding of the concepts of a link-state protocol and the operation and structure of an OSPF network. It's now time to start looking at the details.

OSPF Router ID

Many operations in OSPF are dependent on the OSPF *router ID*. The OSPF router ID is a 32-bit number that identifies an OSPF router. Understanding the determination of the router ID is extremely important.

If only physical interfaces have been configured on a router, the OSPF router ID is the highest IP address assigned to an active physical interface. In Figure 6-6, Router A has four active (up) physical interfaces.

Figure 6-6   OSPF Router ID Using Physical Interfaces

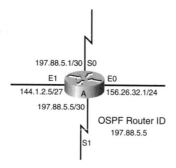

The highest IP address on Router A is the address of interface serial 1 (S1), so the OSPF router ID is 197.88.5.5. If S1 fails, or goes down, the IP address of the failed interface can no longer be used for the OSPF router ID, and the router ID will change to the next highest IP address assigned to an active interface. In this case, the new OSPF router ID becomes 197.88.5.1 when the OSPF process or router is restarted. For stability reasons, you do not want the OSPF router ID to change.

A better approach is to use a virtual, or loopback, interface. A *loopback interface* is a nonphysical, or virtual, interface configured on a router. If a loopback interface is used, OSPF uses the IP address assigned to the loopback interface even if it does not have the highest IP address. In Figure 6-7, a loopback interface has been configured on Router A.

Figure 6-7   Loopback Interface Is the OSPF Router ID

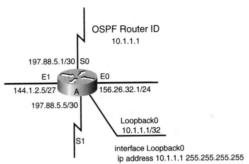

The router ID in Figure 6-7 is now 10.1.1.1. The advantage of using a loopback interface is that a loopback interface never goes down (unless, of course, the router fails). Therefore, the OSPF router ID will be stable if you do not add another loopback interface. If you add another loopback interface with a higher IP address, the first loopback interface changes, followed by a change in the router ID. Actually, the router ID changes only when the OSPF process or the router is restarted. If there was a power failure, or the router is manually restarted, the OSPF router ID changes. (See Figure 6-8.)

Figure 6-8   Two Loopback Interfaces on the Router

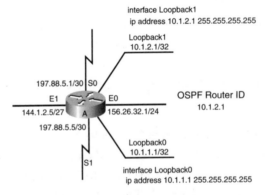

The OSPF router ID changes to 10.1.2.1, which could affect the OSPF configuration. To stabilize the OSPF router ID, the best approach is to use the command **router-id** *ip-address* under the OSPF process configuration (you configure an OSPF process in the next section). The value of the IP address can be any address as long as the address is unique in your network.

Basic OSPF Configuration

This section uses the network in Figure 6-9 to demonstrate the basic configuration of an OSPF network.

Figure 6-9   Basic OSPF Configuration

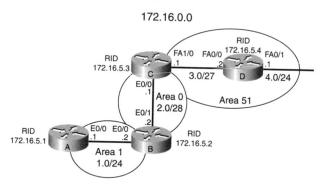

There are more than 100 commands to configure and fine-tune OSPF; but regardless of the complexity of the OSPF configuration, they all start with a basic setup. The steps for configuring a minimum OSPF configuration are

Step 1   Configure a loopback interface on each OSPF router.

Step 2   Configure IP addresses on the physical interfaces.

Step 3   Configure the OSPF process on each router.

Before configuring an OSPF process on a router, configure the loopback interface that will be used as the router ID. For all routers in Figure 6-9, the loopback interface is configured with a 32-bit host address. (See Example 6-1.) A host address uses a 32-bit subnet mask.

Example 6-1 Basic OSPF Configuration

```
Router A
interface Loopback0
 ip address 172.16.5.1 255.255.255.255

Router B
interface Loopback0
 ip address 172.16.5.2 255.255.255.255

Router C
interface Loopback0
 ip address 172.16.5.3 255.255.255.255

Router D
interface Loopback0
 ip address 172.16.5.4 255.255.255.255
```

The next step is to configure the physical interfaces, as shown in Example 6-2.

Example 6-2 Configuring the Physical Interface

```
Router A
interface Ethernet0/0
 ip address 172.16.1.1 255.255.255.0

Router B
interface Ethernet0/0
 ip address 172.16.1.2 255.255.255.0
interface Ethernet0/1
 ip address 172.16.2.2 255.255.255.240

Router C
interface Ethernet0/0
 ip address 172.16.2.1 255.255.255.240
interface FastEthernet1/0
 ip address 172.16.3.1 255.255.255.224

Router D
interface FastEthernet0/0
 ip address 172.16.3.2 255.255.255.224
interface FastEthernet0/1
 ip address 172.16.4.1 255.255.255.0
```

Finally, configure the OSPF process on each router, as shown in Example 6-3.

Example 6-3   Configuring the OSPF Process

```
Router A
router ospf 1
 router-id 172.16.5.1
 network 172.16.1.0 0.0.0.255 area 1
 network 172.16.5.1 0.0.0.0 area 1

Router B
router ospf 1
 router-id 172.16.5.2
 network 172.16.1.0 0.0.0.255 area 1
 network 172.16.2.0 0.0.0.15 area 0
 network 172.16.5.2 0.0.0.0 area 1

Router C
router ospf 1
 router-id 172.16.5.3
 network 172.16.2.0 0.0.0.15 area 0
 network 172.16.3.0 0.0.0.31 area 51
 network 172.16.5.3 0.0.0.0 area 51

Router D
router ospf 1
 router-id 172.16.5.4
 network 172.16.3.0 0.0.0.31 area 51
 network 172.16.4.0 0.0.0.255 area 51
 network 172.16.5.4 0.0.0.0 area 51
```

OSPF, like IGRP and EIGRP, requires a process number or process ID. The *process ID* can be any number between 1 and 65,535, and multiple OSPF processes can be configured on a router. Unlike IGRP and EIGRP, the process number does not need to be the same on all OSPF routers.

The **router-id**command permanently sets the OSPF router ID to the IP address configured for the first loopback interface. Remember, you want a stable OSPF router ID. Using the **router-id**command ensures that the OSPF router ID will not change, even if you add another loopback interface with a higher IP address.

The **network**command in OSPF serves the same purpose as the **network**command in IGRP and EIGRP. A prefix and mask, or OSPF *wildcard bits*, determine the interfaces that will be enabled for OSPF. The wildcard bits are the inverse of the mask used with IGRP and EIGRP. A 0 bit means that the corresponding bit in the prefix must match. A 1 bit means that OSPF does not care what the corresponding bit in the prefix is. For example, the prefix and wildcard bits 172.16.3.0 0.0.0.31 mean that the first three bytes of an interface IP address must exactly match 172.16.3. The last byte of the interface IP address must have the first 3 bits set equal to 0.

The last byte of the mask has a hexadecimal value of 31, 3 zero bits followed by 5 one bits:

31 = 0 0 0 1 1 1 1 1

The last 5 bits have a value of 1 so they are "don't care" bits. So any interface with an IP address between 172.16.3.1 and 172.16.3.30 (.0 and .31 are reserved) will be enabled for OSPF. Every OSPF enabled interface must be configured for an OSPF area. The last part of the **network** command places the interface, or interfaces, into a specific OSPF area.

There are two ways to configure the OSPF **network** command. The first is to use the wildcard bits as shown:

```
network 172.16.3.0 0.0.0.31 area 51.
```

The second method is to use a regular subnet mask, as follows:

```
network 172.16.3.0 255.255.255.224 area 51.
```

If the second method is used, the router converts the bits to the wildcard bits, which is simply the process of changing the 0s to 1s and the 1s to 0s.

After an interface is enabled for OSPF, OSPF discovers neighbors on the interface and advertises the interface and its parameters using LSAs.

There are three methods that can be used when using the **network** command to enable interfaces for OSPF. In Figure 6-10, Router A has four interfaces from the 172.16.0.0 address space and each interface is using a 24-bit subnet mask.

Figure 6-10   **network** Command Enables Router Interfaces for OSPF

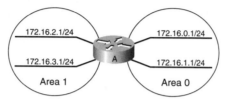

The first method to enable interfaces for OSPF is to use the full 32-bit address of each interface when assigning the interface to an OSPF area, using a 32-bit inverse-mask (0.0.0.0) as follows:

```
network 172.16.0.1 0.0.0.0 area 0
network 172.16.1.1 0.0.0.0 area 0
network 172.16.2.1 0.0.0.0 area 1
network 172.16.3.1 0.0.0.0 area 1
```

This method works fine unless you change the IP address of the interface. If you change 172.16.1.1 to 172.16.1.254, the interface will no longer be enabled for OSPF even though you have used an address from the 172.16.1.0/24 address block.

The second method is to have the OSPF wildcard bits match the inverse of the subnet mask configured on the interface, as follows:

```
network 172.16.0.0 0.0.0.255 area 0
network 172.16.1.0 0.0.0.255 area 0
network 172.16.2.0 0.0.0.255 area 1
network 172.16.3.0 0.0.0.255 area 1
```

This method has the advantage of having a one-to-one correspondence between the interface subnet mask and the OSPF wildcard bits, and makes it easy to spot configuration errors. The disadvantage is that there is one network statement for every OSPF interface. For a router with only a few interfaces, this is not a problem. From an administrative viewpoint, this method requires that the OSPF configuration be updated each time a new interface is configured on the router.

The final method is to summarize the interfaces using the OSPF wildcard bits, as follows:

```
network 172.16.0.1 0.0.1.255 area 0
network 172.16.2.1 0.0.1.255 area 1
```

The first network statement prefix and wildcard bits include both the 172.16.0.0/24 and 172.16.1.0/24 interfaces. The second network statement includes both the 172.16.2.0/24 and 172.16.3.0/24 interfaces. For a router with a few interfaces, this does not have any advantage. Assume you have a router with 64 interfaces that are to be configured in the same OSPF area. (See Figure 6-11.)

Figure 6-11   OSPF Wild Card Bits Can Enable Multiple OSPF Interfaces Using One **network** Command

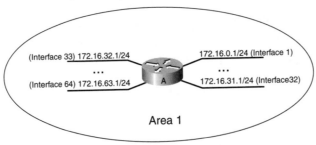

You could use 64 **network**commands to enable the interfaces for OSPF. Or you could use one network statement, as follows, as long as the prefix and wildcard bits include all 64 interfaces:

```
network 172.16.0.0 0.0.63.255 area 1
```

Any of the three methods works. Choose the method that makes sense for your network.

OSPF Neighbor Discovery

When OSPF is enabled on an interface, the router sends a Hello packet on the network for neighbor discovery. (See Figure 6-12.) For a multi-access network (more than one router), a Hello packet is sent every 10 seconds.

Figure 6-12   OSPF Neighbor Discovery and Database Synchronization

The down state signifies that an OSPF router is not sending Hello packets. When OSPF is enabled on the interface, the router transitions to the Init, or initialization, state, and begins sending Hello packets. The initialization state discovers OSPF neighbors on a link. Included in the Hello packet is the router's OSPF router ID. When a router receives a Hello packet from a neighbor, the router places its own router ID in the Hello packet and transmits it on the network. When a router sees its own router ID in a neighbor's Hello packet, the neighbors are in state 2-way.

On a multi-access network, a ***Designated Router (DR)*** and ***Backup Designated Router (BDR)*** are elected. Usually, the router with the highest router ID becomes the DR and the router with the next highest router ID usually becomes the BDR. Regarding the election of the DR and BDR, timing is everything. Assume that Router C in Figure 6-12 is enabled for OSPF before Routers A and B. Router C starts sending Hello packets trying to discover any OSPF neighbors. From Router C's point of view, it is the only OSPF router on the Ethernet network and so it declares itself as the DR. Now Router B is enabled for OSPF and starts sending Hello packets. Routers B and C discover each other, but C remains the designated router even though Router B has a higher router ID. Why? This is a stability mechanism built into OSPF. After a router becomes the DR, it remains the DR until it fails. Therefore, Router B becomes the BDR. When Router A is enabled for OSPF, it discovers that a DR and BDR have already been elected. Even though Router A has the highest router ID; it will not become the DR, or BDR, unless the DR, or BDR, fails. The term for all routers on a multi-access network that are not the DR or BDR is ***DROTHER***.

All OSPF routers must exchange their databases with their neighbors, and ensure that the databases on each router for a particular area are identical. It doesn't make sense for every router on a multi-access network to have to send its database to every other router on the network. Therefore, every router creates a router or type 1 LSA that describes the state of the router's attached interfaces. All routers send their router LSA to the DR and BDR. The DR and BDR create a network or type 2 LSA and send it to every router on the multi-access network. All routers form a full adjacency with the DR and BDR. Being adjacent with the DR and BDR just means that is where the router sends its LSAs. In Figure 6-13, Router C forms a full adjacency with the DR and BDR, but stops in state 2-way with Router D.

Figure 6-13   OSPF Router Designations

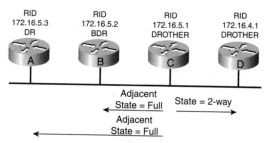

For point-to-point networks there is no concept of a DR and BDR because there can be only two neighbors on a point-to-point link. (See Figure 6-14.) The routers on a point-to-point link form a full adjacency for the exchange of OSPF link-state advertisements.

Figure 6-14   OSPF Neighbors on a Point-to-Point Network Form a Full Adjacency

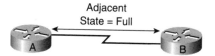

Verifying OSPF neighbor adjacencies is done using the **show ip ospf neighbor** command. (See Example 6-4.)

Example 6-4   Verifying Neighbor Adjacencies with the **show ip ospf neighbor** Command

```
B#show ip ospf neighbor

Neighbor ID     Pri   State          Dead Time   Address       Interface
172.16.5.3      1     FULL/DR        00:00:34    172.16.2.1    Ethernet0/1
172.16.5.1      1     FULL/BDR       00:00:37    172.16.1.1    Ethernet0/0
```

Router B has reached state FULL with Routers A and C; therefore, OSPF is functioning properly. The parameter listed after the neighbor's ID is the OSPF priority of the network interface. The router's OSPF priority on an interface is first used when electing the DR and BDR. The router with the highest interface priority is elected the DR. The OSPF interface priority is 1, by default, so OSPF uses the router ID to determine the DR and BDR. If the priority is set to 0, the router cannot become the DR or BDR for the network. Interface priority is configured on the interface using the **ip ospf priority** command. For example, if you set the interface priority on the Ethernet 0/0 interface on Router A to 2, Router A is elected the designated router on the Ethernet network connecting Routers A and B. (See Example 6-5.)

Example 6-5   Adjusting OSPF Priority to Influence the DR Selection

```
Router A
interface Ethernet0/0
 ip address 172.16.1.1 255.255.255.0
 ip ospf priority 2
```

OSPF Timers

On multi-access networks, the OSPF Hello timer is set to 10 seconds by default. All OSPF routers connected to a common network, whether it is multi-access or point-to-point, will not form an adjacency unless the Hello times are equal. The Hello packets are used for neighbor discovery, but are also used as a keepalive. If a Hello packet is not received from a neighbor for four Hello periods, the neighbor is declared down. This time is referred to as the *dead time*.

After OSPF has reached a full adjacency with the appropriate neighbors and the databases have been synchronized, OSPF transmits only database information if there is a change in the network or if 30 minutes have elapsed. So in a stable network, OSPF is a quiet protocol.

After the initial exchange and synchronization of the databases, OSPF calculates the shortest path to every destination using the SPF algorithm. The SPF algorithm will be run again only if there is a change in the network. Depending on the number of routers in an area and the number of network prefixes in an area, the SPF algorithm could be computationally extensive. If a network is *flapping* (going from up to down to up to down and so on), every time the network changes state, OSPF sends an update, and every router in the area has to recalculate the shortest path. To prevent the router from endlessly calculating the SPF algorithm, an SPF timer is used to set the minimum amount of time that must elapse before the SPF calculation is run again. By default, the SPF timer is set to 10 seconds.

OSPF Metrics

Route costs, or metrics, determine the best path to a destination. The route with the lowest metric is considered to be the best route. The metric, or cost, of a RIP route is a hop count. The metric of an IGRP or EIGRP route is determined from the bandwidth, reliability, load, and delay of an interface. OSPF uses a dimensionless metric based on the bandwidth of an interface. The cost of an OSPF interface is given by the following formula:

Cost = 100,000,000/(Interface Bandwidth)

The OSPF costs for various interfaces are listed in Table 6-1.

Table 6-1   OSPF Costs for Common Network Interfaces

Interface Type	Interface Bandwidth	OSPF Cost
Ethernet	10,000,000	10
Fast Ethernet	100,000,000	1
Gigabit Ethernet	1,000,000,000	1
T1	1,544,000	64
E1	2,048,000	48

Do you see anything strange with the OSPF costs in Table 6-1? Fast Ethernet and Gigabit Ethernet have the same OSPF cost. OSPF cannot differentiate between the two when calculating a shortest path. When OSPF was developed, fast Ethernet was FAST! So the constant that was chosen for the OSPF metric formula seemed like a big enough number. Today, Gigabit Ethernet is becoming popular and the OSPF metric formula has become outdated. This limitation can be overcome. The constant can be changed under the OSPF configuration using the command **auto-cost reference-bandwidth**The value entered is in megabits per second. To set the OSPF metric constant to 1 billion, enter a value of 1000. (See Example 6-6.)

Example 6-6 Modifying the OSPF Metric Constant

```
router ospf 1
 router-id 172.16.5.1
 auto-cost reference-bandwidth 1000
```

Gigabit interfaces now have a cost of 1 and fast Ethernet interfaces have a cost of 10. When using the **auto-cost** command, ensure that all OSPF routers are configured with the same value so they have a consistent view of the network.

OSPF Router Types

There are three general types of routers in an OSPF network:

- Area border router (ABR)

- Autonomous system boundary router (ASBR)

- Internal router

There are specific functions that can only be implemented on a specific OSPF router type, and understanding the router types is essential for understanding OSPF.

A router that has at least one interface configured in area 0 and at least one interface configured in a nonzero area is called an *area border router (ABR)*, as shown in Figure 6-15.

Figure 6-15 OSPF Area Border Router

An ABR maintains an OSPF database for each connected area and must run the SPF algorithm on each database. OSPF routes can be summarized only on an ABR. Routes or prefixes can be summarized from a nonzero area into the backbone, or from the backbone into a nonzero area.

Any router that has been configured for OSPF and is injecting or redistributing static, connected, or routes learned from another routing protocol is called an *autonomous system boundary router (ASBR)* as shown in Figure 6-16.

Figure 6-16 OSPF Autonomous System Boundary Router

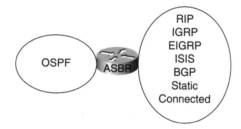

Non-OSPF routes that are redistributed into OSPF can be summarized only on an ASBR. OSPF advertises routes in two cases:

- Prefixes that have been configured on an interface and the interface has been enabled for OSPF.

- Any route that has been learned from an OSPF neighbor.

If interfaces on a router have not been configured for OSPF, any configured static routes, or routes learned from another protocol, OSPF, by default, will not advertise these routes. The only way to advertise non-OSPF routes into the OSPF domain is through route redistribution. ***Route redistribution*** is the process of taking a non-OSPF route and turning it into an OSPF route. In Figure 6-17, an ASBR is attached to two routing domains: RIP and OSPF.

Figure 6-17   Redistributing RIP into OSPF

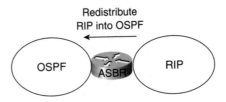

RIP routes have a hop count for their metric, and OSPF routes have a dimensionless metric based on the bandwidth of the interface. Before RIP routes can be turned into OSPF routes, the RIP metric must be replaced with an OSPF metric. On the ASBR, you use the **redistribute** command under the OSPF process and assign an OSPF metric to the redistributed RIP routes. (See Example 6-7.)

Example 6-7   Redistributing RIP Routes into OSPF

```
router ospf 1
  redistribute rip subnets metric 10
```

The **redistribute** command takes routes learned from RIP and converts them to OSPF routes with an OSPF metric of 10 (or whatever metric you care to use). The **subnets** keyword forces OSPF to redistribute all RIP routes. Without the subnets keyword, OSPF redistributes only classful RIP routes. A classful RIP route is a class A prefix with an 8-bit subnet, a class B prefix with a 16-bit subnet, or a class C prefix with a 24-bit subnet.

The final OSPF router type is an ***internal router***. An internal OSPF router has all of its OSPF interfaces configured for the same area. (See Figure 6-18.)

Figure 6-18   OSPF Internal Router

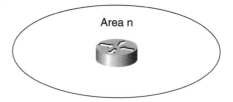

Internal OSPF routers maintain one OSPF database.

OSPF Route Types

This section discusses the following various OSPF route types:

- Intra-area (O)

- Interarea (IA)

- External Type 1 (E1)

- External Type 2 (E2)

The network in Figure 6-19 is running OSPF and a non-OSPF protocol, such as RIP, IGRP, or EIGRP.

Routers A and B are running a non-OSPF protocol and Router A is advertising four IP prefixes to Router B. Routers B, C, and D are running OSPF, therefore Router B has both non-OSPF and OSPF routes in its routing table.

Network 10.1.2.0/24 originates in area 1; so from the perspective of Routers C and D, this is an *OSPF intra-area route* and is designated by an O in the routing tables on Routers C and D. Any router having an interface configured for OSPF area 1 sees this route as an OSPF intra-area route.

Figure 6-19 OSPF Route Types

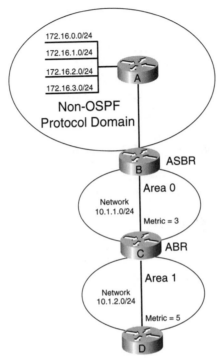

From the perspective of Router B, the 10.1.2.0/24 route is an *OSPF interarea route.* This route is designated by IA in the routing table on Router B because B has no interfaces configured for OSPF area 1. Similarly, Router B sees network 10.1.1.0/24 as an OSPF intra-area route.

Because Router B is running a non-OSPF protocol and OSPF, does this make Router B an ASBR? No, not yet. Router B is learning non-OSPF routes from Router A, and OSPF routes from Router C. But the non-OSPF routes are not automatically being advertised (redistributed) into the OSPF domain. Routers C and D have only OSPF routes in their routing tables because there is no route redistribution on Router B.

Routers C and D have no knowledge of the non-OSPF routes, and without route redistribution these networks are not reachable by Routers C and D. If you want all of the OSPF routers to be able to reach the non-OSPF routes, the non-OSPF routes need to be redistributed into OSPF on Router B. After the non-OSPF routes are redistributed into OSPF, Router B becomes an ASBR.

When a route is redistributed into OSPF, the route becomes an OSPF external route signifying the route was learned from a non-OSPF protocol. Each route redistributed into OSPF needs to be assigned an OSPF metric, and this metric represents the cost to reach the non-OSPF network from the ASBR where the route was redistributed into OSPF. External routes can be redistributed into OSPF as either type 1 or type 2 external routes. By default, the route type is type 2. A type 2 external carries only the metric assigned to the route during redistribution. If a route was redistributed into OSPF with a metric of 5, every OSPF router would have this route in the routing table with a metric of 5. External type 2 routes do not include the cost, or metric, from an OSPF router to the ASBR.

An external type 1 route includes both the redistributed metric and the OSPF cost to reach the ASBR. In Figure 6-19, if the non-OSPF routes are redistributed into OSPF as external type 2 with a metric of 5, every OSPF router will have this route in their routing table as an E2 route with a metric of 5. If the non-OSPF routes are redistributed into OSPF as type 1 external routes, the metric to reach the ASBR is included in the metric. Router B would show a metric of 5; Router C a metric of 8 (3 to reach the ASBR plus 5 to reach the route); and Router D a metric of 13 (5 to reach C plus 3 to reach the ASBR plus 5 to reach the route).

OSPF Area Types

OSPF areas can be configured as different types depending on the goals of the network design. The following areas are discussed in this section:

- Stub area

- Totally stubby area

- Not-so-stubby area (NSSA)

- Totally not-so-stubby area

Stub Area

In Figure 6-19, Router D is learning all the redistributed non-OSPF routes. There-fore, there is an additional route entry for each external route in the routing table on Router D. Does Router D need these specific external routes in its routing tables? No. There is only one exit point for Router D from area 1. For all routes outside of area 1, Router D must send traffic through Router C. Therefore, area 1 can be configured as a *stub area*. In a stub area, external routes are blocked from being advertised into the area and a default route is advertised into the area instead of the specific external routes. The only routes that are advertised into an OSPF stub area are OSPF interarea routes and a default route. Every router in a stub area must have the area configured as a stub. For area 1, additional configuration is required on Routers C and D. (See Example 6-8).

Example 6-8   Configuring an OSPF Stub Area

```
Router C
router ospf 1
 router-id 172.16.5.1
 area 1 stub

Router D
router ospf 1
 router-id 172.16.5.2
 area 1 stub
```

In Figure 6-20, area 1 has been configured as an OSPF stub area. External type 1 and 2 routes will be blocked from entering the area, and a default route will be injected into the stub area.

Figure 6-20   OSPF Stub Area

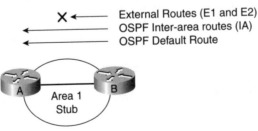

The routing table on Router A no longer contains the specific external routes, but does contain an OSPF default route and OSPF interarea and intra-area routes.

A stub area can have more than one exit point. In Figure 6-21, there are two exit points from the stub area. One exit point is through Router B, and the other exit point is through Router C.

Figure 6-21 OSPF Stub Area with Multiple Exit Points

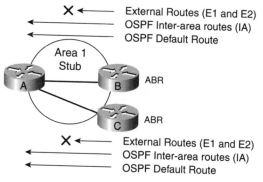

When there is more than one ABR, or exit point, from a stub area, all ABRs inject a default route into the stub area.

Totally Stubby Area

The argument for using a stub area was that the internal routers in a stub area did not need the specific external route information. A default route was sufficient. This argument can also be applied to OSPF interarea routes. The routers in a stub area do not need specific OSPF interarea routes, and a default route is sufficient to enable the routers in the stub area to reach OSPF areas outside the stub area. The difference between a stub area and a *totally stubby area* is that in a totally stubby area, OSPF interarea routes are also blocked as shown in Figure 6-22.

Figure 6-22   An OSPF Totally Stubby Area

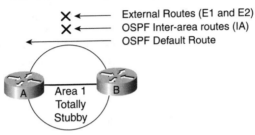

To create a totally stubby area, you need only to use the keyword **no-summary** on the ABRs. (See Example 6-9.)

Example 6-9   Creating a Totally Stubby Area

```
Router B
router ospf 1
 router-id 172.16.5.2
 area 1 stub no-summary
```

The routing table on Router A now contains only OSPF intra-area routes, connected interfaces, and an OSPF default route.

Not-So-Stubby Area (NSSA)

In Figure 6-23, an EIGRP domain has been added to the network. You want to prevent the redistributed RIP routes from Router C from being advertised into areas 1 and 51. In addition, you want to redistribute the EIGRP routes on Router F and advertise them into area 51 and area 0. Can you do this by making area 51 a stub area? The answer is no. External routes are not allowed into an OSPF stub area. If you configure area 51 as a stub area, the redistributed EIGRP routes have nowhere to go. You need a modification of the stub area to allow the EIGRP routes from Router D, but block the RIP routes from Router C.

Figure 6-23   OSPF NSSA

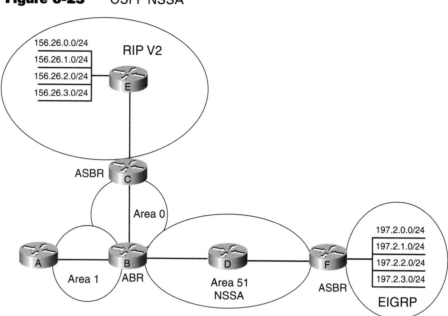

When an area on an ASBR is configured as a NSSA, the routes that are redistributed into OSPF are converted from E1 or E2 routes into N1 or N2 routes. N1 and N2 routes are advertised throughout a NSSA. When the N1 and N2 routes reach the ABR, they are converted back into E1 or E2 routes. For the network in Figure 6-23, Router F is the ASBR for the EIGRP routes. The EIGRP routes are redistributed into OSPF, converted from E1 or E2 routes, and then advertised into area 51 as N1 or N2 routes. When these routes reach the ABR, Router B, they are converted back into E1 and E2 routes. All routers that have an interface in the NSSA must configure the area as a NSSA.   (See Example 6-10.)

Example 6-10   Configuring an OSPF NSSA

```
Router F
router ospf 1
 router-id 197.2.7.1
 area 51 nssa
 redistribute eigrp 1 metric 1 subnets
```

continues

Example 6-10 Configuring an OSPF NSSA (continued)

```
Router D
router ospf 1
 router-id 172.16.5.4
 area 51 nssa

Router B
router ospf 1
 router-id 172.16.5.2
 area 51 nssa
 redistribute rip metric 1 metric-type 1 subnets
```

Router D will have the redistributed EIGRP routes in its routing table as NSSA routes. (See Example 6-11.)

Example 6-11 Routing Table in a NSSA

```
D#show ip route
Codes: C - connected, S - static, I - IGRP, R - RIP, M - mobile, B - BGP
       D - EIGRP, EX - EIGRP external, O - OSPF, IA - OSPF inter area
       N1 - OSPF NSSA external type 1, N2 - OSPF NSSA external type 2
       E1 - OSPF external type 1, E2 - OSPF external type 2, E - EGP
       i - IS-IS, L1 - IS-IS level-1, L2 - IS-IS level-2, ia - IS-IS inter area
       * - candidate default, U - per-user static route, o - ODR
       P - periodic downloaded static route

Gateway of last resort is not set

     156.26.0.0/24 is subnetted, 4 subnets
     172.16.0.0/16 is variably subnetted, 9 subnets, 4 masks
O IA    172.16.5.1/32 [110/22] via 172.16.3.1, 00:10:01, FastEthernet0/0
C       172.16.4.0/24 is directly connected, FastEthernet0/1
O       172.16.5.3/32 [110/2] via 172.16.3.1, 00:10:02, FastEthernet0/0
O IA    172.16.5.2/32 [110/12] via 172.16.3.1, 00:10:02, FastEthernet0/0
O IA    172.16.1.0/24 [110/21] via 172.16.3.1, 00:10:02, FastEthernet0/0
C       172.16.5.4/32 is directly connected, Loopback0
O IA    172.16.2.0/28 [110/11] via 172.16.3.1, 00:10:05, FastEthernet0/0
C       172.16.3.0/27 is directly connected, FastEthernet0/0
O N2 197.2.1.0/24 [110/1] via 172.16.4.2, 00:10:05, FastEthernet0/1
O N2 197.2.0.0/24 [110/1] via 172.16.4.2, 00:10:05, FastEthernet0/1
O N2 197.2.3.0/24 [110/1] via 172.16.4.2, 00:10:05, FastEthernet0/1
O N2 197.2.2.0/24 [110/1] via 172.16.4.2, 00:10:05, FastEthernet0/1
O N2 197.2.5.0/24 [110/1] via 172.16.4.2, 00:10:05, FastEthernet0/1
     197.2.7.0/32 is subnetted, 1 subnets
O       197.2.7.1 [110/2] via 172.16.4.2, 00:10:05, FastEthernet0/1
```

The 197.2.0.0 EIGRP routes are in the routing table as OSPF type N2 routes. On Router C, these routes are type E2 routes because the ABR, Router B, has converted them from NSSA routes to external routes. (See Example 6-12.) In Example 6-12, the command **include E2** displays only the E2 routes.

Example 6-12   Conversion of N2 to E2 routes

```
B#show ip route | include E2
        E1 - OSPF external type 1, E2 - OSPF external type 2, E - EGP
O E2 197.2.1.0/24 [110/1] via 172.16.2.1, 00:13:24, Ethernet0/1
O E2 197.2.0.0/24 [110/1] via 172.16.2.1, 00:13:24, Ethernet0/1
O E2 197.2.3.0/24 [110/1] via 172.16.2.1, 00:13:24, Ethernet0/1
O E2 197.2.2.0/24 [110/1] via 172.16.2.1, 00:13:24, Ethernet0/1
O E2 197.2.5.0/24 [110/1] via 172.16.2.1, 00:13:24, Ethernet0/1
```

Another thing to notice is that the ASBR for the EIGRP routes, Router F, is not injecting a default route into the NSSA. Unlike the stub areas, OSPF does not automatically inject a default route into a NSSA as shown in Figure 6-24.

Figure 6-24   Injecting a Default Route

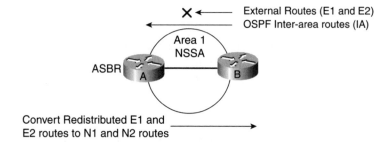

The ABR can be configured to inject a default route into the NSSA. (See Example 6-13.)

Example 6-13   Configuring a NSSA Default Route

```
Router C
router ospf 1
 router-id 172.16.5.3
 area 51 nssa no-redistribution default-information-originate
 redistribute rip metric 1 metric-type 1 subnets
```

Router D now has a default route in the IP routing table. (See Example 6-14.)

Example 6-14 Router D IP Routing Table

```
D#show ip route | include 0.0.0.0
!Output omitted for brevity
O*N2 0.0.0.0/0 [110/1] via 172.16.3.1, 00:00:26, FastEthernet0/0
```

Totally Not-So-Stubby Area

An OSPF stub area was made a totally stubby area by configuring the ABR to block OSPF interarea routes from entering the stub area. An OSPF NSSA can be made a totally NSSA by also blocking the OSPF interarea routes on the ABR. (See Example 6-15.)

Example 6-15 Configuring a Totally NSSA

```
Router C
router ospf 1
 router-id 172.16.5.3
 area 51 nssa no-redistribution no-summary
 redistribute rip metric 1 metric-type 1 subnets
```

When a NSSA is configured with the no-summary option, a default route is automatically injected into the area. (See Figure 6-25.)

Figure 6-25 An OSPF Totally NSSA

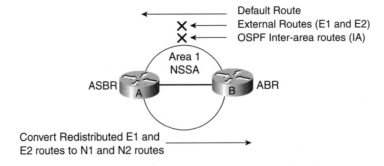

The routing table on Router D now contains the default route, but no OSPF inter-area routes. (See Example 6-16.)

Example 6-16   Verifying the NSSA Default Route

```
D#show ip route | include 0.0.0.0
!Output omitted for brevity
O*IA 0.0.0.0/0 [110/2] via 172.16.3.1, 00:00:17, FastEthernet0/0
```

OSPF External Route Summarization

In the network in Figure 6-26, four specific RIP routes and four specific EIGRP routes are being injected into the OSPF domain.

Figure 6-26   Redistributed Routes Summarized by OSPF on the ASBR

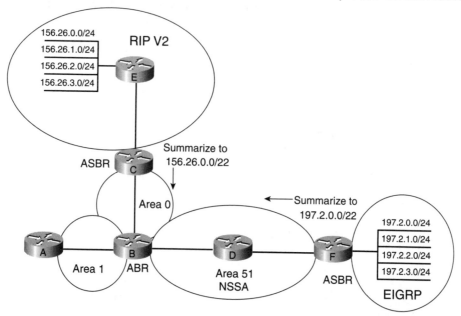

External or redistributed routes can be summarized on the ASBR using the
summary-address command. Without summarization of the external routes, all
eight routes are injected into the OSPF domain. For example, without summarization,
Router B has all the specific external routes in its routing table. (See Example 6-17.)

Example 6-17   Unsummarized External Routes

```
B#show ip route | include O E
O E1    156.26.2.0 [110/11] via 172.16.2.1, 00:45:08, Ethernet0/1
O E1    156.26.3.0 [110/11] via 172.16.2.1, 00:45:08, Ethernet0/1
O E1    156.26.0.0 [110/11] via 172.16.2.1, 00:45:08, Ethernet0/1
O E1    156.26.1.0 [110/11] via 172.16.2.1, 00:45:08, Ethernet0/1
O E2 197.2.1.0/24 [110/1] via 172.16.2.1, 00:45:04, Ethernet0/1
O E2 197.2.0.0/24 [110/1] via 172.16.2.1, 00:45:04, Ethernet0/1
O E2 197.2.3.0/24 [110/1] via 172.16.2.1, 00:45:04, Ethernet0/1
O E2 197.2.2.0/24 [110/1] via 172.16.2.1, 00:45:04, Ethernet0/1
O E2 197.2.5.0/24 [110/1] via 172.16.2.1, 00:45:04, Ethernet0/1
```

After summarization, these eight external routes have been reduced to two.
(See Example 6-18.)

Example 6-18   Summarized Routes

```
Router C
router ospf 1
 router-id 172.16.5.3
 area 51 nssa no-redistribution no-summary
 summary-address 156.26.0.0 255.255.252.0
 redistribute rip metric 1 metric-type 1 subnets

Router F
router ospf 1
 router-id 197.2.7.1
 area 51 nssa
 summary-address 197.2.0.0 255.255.252.0
 redistribute eigrp 1 metric 1 subnets

B#show ip route | include O E
O E1    156.26.0.0 [110/11] via 172.16.2.1, 00:00:58, Ethernet0/1
O E2 197.2.0.0/22 [110/1] via 172.16.2.1, 00:00:42, Ethernet0/1
!Output omitted for brevity
```

OSPF Route Summarization

OSPF routes can be summarized only on an ABR. In Figure 6-27, Router A is advertising four 156.26.0.0 OSPF networks and Router D is advertising four 197.2.1.0 networks.

Figure 6-27   OSPF Routes Can Be Summarized Only on an ABR

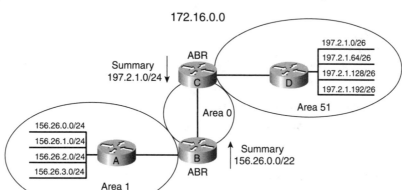

Without OSPF route summarization, Router D will see all four 156.26.0.0 routes and Router A will see all four 197.2.1.0 routes. (See Example 6-19.)

Example 6-19   Router A and Router D Without OSPF Route Summarization

```
A#show ip route | include 197.2.1
     197.2.1.0/26 is subnetted, 4 subnets
O IA    197.2.1.192 [110/22] via 172.16.1.2, 00:05:56, Ethernet0/0
O IA    197.2.1.128 [110/22] via 172.16.1.2, 00:05:56, Ethernet0/0
O IA    197.2.1.64 [110/22] via 172.16.1.2, 00:05:56, Ethernet0/0
O IA    197.2.1.0 [110/22] via 172.16.1.2, 00:05:56, Ethernet0/0

D#show ip route | include 156.26
     156.26.0.0/24 is subnetted, 4 subnets
O IA    156.26.2.0 [110/22] via 172.16.3.1, 00:00:19, FastEthernet0/0
O IA    156.26.3.0 [110/22] via 172.16.3.1, 00:00:04, FastEthernet0/0
O IA    156.26.0.0 [110/22] via 172.16.3.1, 00:10:14, FastEthernet0/0
O IA    156.26.1.0 [110/22] via 172.16.3.1, 00:00:29, FastEthernet0/0
```

OSPF routes are summarized on the ABR using the **area range** command.
(See Example 6-20.)

Example 6-20   Configuring OSPF Route Summarization

```
Router B
router ospf 1
 router-id 172.16.5.2
 area 1 range 156.26.0.0 255.255.252.0

Router C
router ospf 1
 router-id 172.16.5.3
 area 51 range 197.2.1.0 255.255.255.0
```

The routing tables on Routers A and B contain a summary for the 197.2.1.0 networks, and the routing tables on Routers C and D contain a summary for the
156.26.0.0 networks. (See Example 6-21.)

Example 6-21   Results of OSPF Route Summarization

```
A#show ip route | include 197.2.1.0
O IA 197.2.1.0/24 [110/22] via 172.16.1.2, 00:02:49, Ethernet0/0

B#show ip route | include 197.2.1.0
O IA 197.2.1.0/24 [110/12] via 172.16.2.1, 00:04:41, Ethernet0/1

C#show ip route | include 156.26.0.0
O IA    156.26.0.0 [110/21] via 172.16.2.2, 00:05:06, Ethernet0/0

D#show ip route | include 156.26.0.0
O IA    156.26.0.0 [110/22] via 172.16.3.1, 00:05:58, FastEthernet0/0
```

OSPF Virtual Links

In Figure 6-28, the network is a valid OSPF network. All nonzero areas are connected through a router to area 0.

Figure 6-28   Valid OSPF Network Design

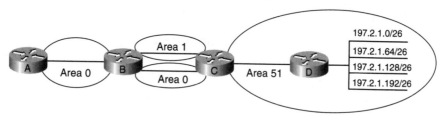

Router A is receiving the 197.2.1.0 routes from area 51, as shown in Example 6-22.

Example 6-22   Verifying OSPF Network Operation

```
A#show ip route | include 197.2
       197.2.1.0/26 is subnetted, 4 subnets
O IA    197.2.1.192 [110/76] via 172.16.1.2, 00:03:42, Ethernet0/0
O IA    197.2.1.128 [110/76] via 172.16.1.2, 00:03:42, Ethernet0/0
O IA    197.2.1.64 [110/76] via 172.16.1.2, 00:03:42, Ethernet0/0
O IA    197.2.1.0 [110/76] via 172.16.1.2, 00:03:42, Ethernet0/0
```

If the area 0 link between Routers B and C fails, area 51 will no longer be connected to area 0. Area 51 will, in effect, be cut off from area 0. (See Figure 6-29.)

Figure 6-29   Invalid OSPF Network Design

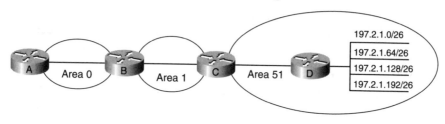

Area 51 is cut off from area 0. Router A will no longer receive routes from area 51. (See Example 6-23.)

Example 6-23   Area 0 is Cut Off from Area 51

```
A#show ip route | include O IA
O IA    172.16.5.2/32 [110/11] via 172.16.1.2, 00:01:20, Ethernet0/0
O IA    172.16.2.0/28 [110/20] via 172.16.1.2, 00:01:20, Ethernet0/0
```

To fix this situation, the best solution is to repair the area 0 link between Routers B and C. Fixing this link could take some time, but you need to get the network functioning NOW! A temporary solution is to use an OSPF virtual link, as shown in Figure 6-30.

Figure 6-30   Using a Virtual Link to Connect a Nonzero OSPF Area to Area 0

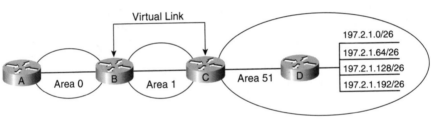

The area 0 link between Routers B and C is a physical connection between the routers. This physical connection was configured to be in area 0, giving you a valid OSPF network. What you need is a virtual connection that gives you the same functionality to temporarily fix the network. A virtual link is automatically considered to be in area 0, but protocol traffic flows through the physical area 1 link between Routers B and C. A virtual link is configured on the endpoints, which in this case are Routers B and C. The format for the virtual link command is

area *transit-area* **virtual-link** *router-id*

The transit area is the area between area 0 and the area that was disconnected from area 0. In this case, the transit area is area 1. The *router-id* is the OSPF router ID of the other end of the link. This is an example of why you need a stable router ID.

If you configure a virtual link and the router ID of one end of the virtual link changes, the virtual link fails.

There are a number of ways to determine the OSPF router ID. One is to look at the OSPF configuration and see if the **router-id**command was used. Another is to use the **show ip ospf neighbor** command to get the router ID of the neighbor. (See Example 6-24.)

Example 6-24   **show ip ospf neighbor** Command Output

```
B#show ip ospf neighbor

Neighbor ID     Pri   State        Dead Time   Address       Interface
172.16.5.1       1    FULL/DR      00:00:35    172.16.1.1    Ethernet0/0
172.16.5.3       1    FULL/BDR     00:00:34    172.16.2.1    Ethernet0/1

C#show ip ospf neighbor

Neighbor ID     Pri   State        Dead Time   Address       Interface
172.16.5.2       1    FULL/DR      00:00:33    172.16.2.2    Ethernet0/0
172.16.5.4       1    FULL/DR      00:00:30    172.16.3.2    FastEthernet1/
```

With the router ID information, you can now configure the virtual link on Routers B and C. (See Example 6-25.)

Example 6-25   Configuring the Virtual Link on Router B and Router C

```
Router B
router ospf 1
 router-id 172.16.5.2
 area 1 virtual-link 172.16.5.3


Router C
router ospf 1
 router-id 172.16.5.3
 area 1 virtual-link 172.16.5.2
```

You can verify the operation of the virtual link using the **show ip ospf virtual-links** command on either Router B or C. (See Example 6-26.)

Example 6-26   Verifying the Virtual Link

```
C#show ip ospf virtual-links | include Virtual
Virtual Link OSPF_VL0 to router 172.16.5.2 is up
```

The network should be fixed and the 197.2.1.0 routes from area 51 should be in the routing table on Router A. (See Example 6-27.)

Example 6-27   Verifying the Operation of the Virtual Link

```
A#show ip route | include 197.2.1
     197.2.1.0/26 is subnetted, 4 subnets
O IA    197.2.1.192 [110/22] via 172.16.1.2, 00:05:16, Ethernet0/0
O IA    197.2.1.128 [110/22] via 172.16.1.2, 00:05:16, Ethernet0/0
O IA    197.2.1.64 [110/22] via 172.16.1.2, 00:05:16, Ethernet0/0
O IA    197.2.1.0 [110/22] via 172.16.1.2, 00:05:16, Ethernet0/0
```

After the area 0 link between Routers B and C is repaired, the virtual link can be removed.

Selecting the Shortest Path

Does OSPF always pick the shortest path between any two networks? That depends on how the shortest path is determined. For intra-area paths where the source and destination networks are in the same OSPF area, the shortest path will be taken. But things can get interesting if the source and destination networks are in different OSPF areas. In Figure 6-31, what is the shortest path between networks 1 and 2 based on OSPF interface metrics?

Figure 6-31 Shortest Path, Based on OSPF Cost Only, Between Networks 1 and 2

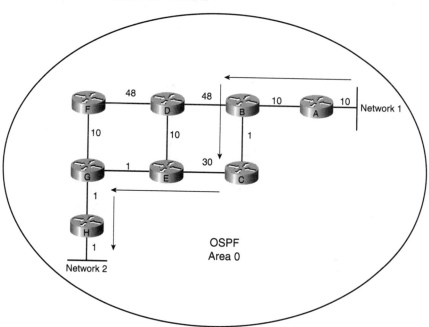

Because a single OSPF area is used, the shortest path as shown in Figure 6-31 is from Router A to B to C to E to G to H with a total metric or cost of 54. Any other path has a higher total OSPF metric or cost. In Figure 6-32, multiple OSPF areas have been configured for the network in Figure 6-31.

What is the shortest path between networks 1 and 2? The path from network 1 to network 2 is now an OSPF interarea path, and OSPF determines the shortest path in three steps.

The first step is to determine the shortest path to a router connected to area 0. Router A has only one path to a router connected to area 0. This path is from network 1 to Router A to Router B.

Figure 6-32   OSPF Shortest Path Between Networks 1 and 2

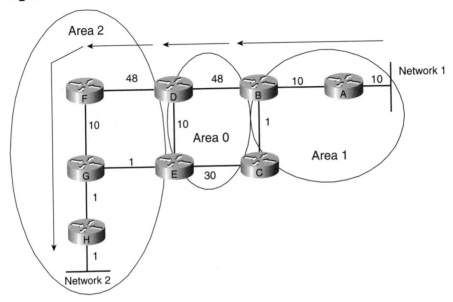

After area 0 has been reached, the next step is to find the shortest path across area 0 to a router that is attached to area 2 without going back through area 1. The link between Routers B and C is in area 1, so OSPF will not consider using this path. The only choice is the link from Router B to Router D. After you have reached a router that is attached to the destination area, you are done with the path across area 0.

The final component is to find the shortest path across area 2 without going back through area 0. The only choice Router D has is through Routers F, G, and H. Therefore, the metric from network 1 to network 2 is 20 (metric to reach area 0) plus 48 (metric to reach area 2 without going back through area 1) plus 60 (metric across area 2 without going back through area 0) for a total metric of 128.

Figure 6-33 shows the path from network 2 to network 1 is not the same path used to go from network 1 to network 2. This is referred to as *asymmetrical routing*. The path from network 2 to a router connected to area 0 is from H to G to E. The shortest path across area 0 to area 1 is E to C. And finally, the shortest path across area 1 to network 1 is C to B to A for a total metric of 54.

Figure 6-33   Asymmetrical Routing in an OSPF Network

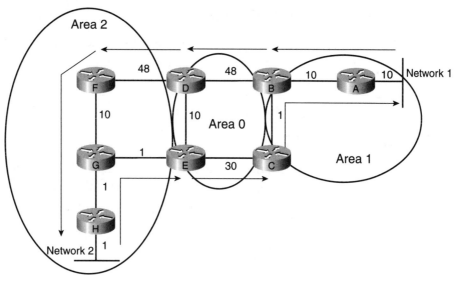

Can this problem be fixed? Yes. If the link between Routers B and C is in area 0 instead of area 1, the shortest path will be taken and routing will be symmetrical. (See Figure 6-34.)

Figure 6-34   Symmetrical OSPF Routing

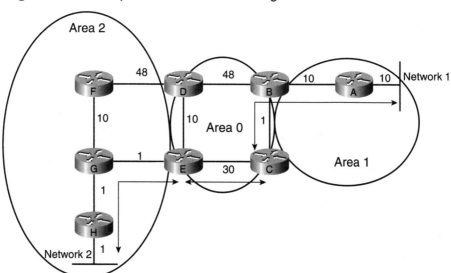

If you trace the path from network 1 to network 2, you see that the shortest path is now being taken and routing is symmetrical.

So, what is the moral of this story? Be careful when assigning interfaces to OSPF areas, and remember how OSPF determines an interarea shortest path.

OSPF LSA Types

In the beginning of this chapter, in the section entitled "Link States," you learned that OSPF routers use LSAs to advertise their networks. You did not need to know the details, or formats, of LSAs to understand the operation of OSPF. But it is useful to know what types of LSAs are used by OSPF and the information they contain. Table 6-2 lists the LSAs used by OSPF.

Table 6-1　　OSPF LSA Types

LSA Type Number	LSA Name
1	Router
2	Network
3	Network Summary
4	ASBR Summary
5	AS External
6	Multicast OSPF
7	NSSA External

Each LSA type is described as follows:

- **Router LSA**—Created for each area that a router is connected to. Describes the cost and state of the router's links in the area. A router LSA is only flooded in its OSPF area.

- **Network LSA**—Created by the DR on a multi-access network and contains information for all routers connected to the multi-access network.

- **Network summary LSA**—Generated by ABRs and contain information about interarea OSPF prefixes. A network summary LSA is flooded into the nonzero OSPF area.

- **ASBR summary LSA**—Generated by ABRs and have the same format as network summary LSAs, but they contain the location of an ASBR and not specific IP prefix information.

- **AS external LSA**—Generated by ASBRs and contain information regarding prefixes that are external to the OSPF domain (type 1 and type 2 external routes).

- **Multicast LSA**—OSPF has been modified to supporting IP multicast using this LSA, but multicast OSPF is not used.

- **NSSA external LSA**—Generated by ASBRs when the area has been configured as a NSSA. These are external routes designated as either N1 or N2, and are only flooded throughout the NSSA. The ABR router converts the N1 and N2 routes to E1 and E2 before advertising them into the OSPF domain.

For a detailed description of the LSA types, see the References section at the end of the chapter.

Summary

OSPF is a complex protocol. The following list summarizes its fundamental properties:

- One or more OSPF areas.

- If more than one OSPF area is used, a backbone, or area 0, must be configured.

- All nonzero OSPF areas must be connected to area 0.

- For each area configured on an OSPF router, the router maintains an OSPF database for that area.

- Link-state advertisements (LSAs) flood information about a router's interfaces throughout an OSPF area.

- OSPF databases within an area must be identical before a router can calculate the routes that are installed in the IP routing table.

- The Shortest Path First (SPF) algorithm is run on each area database maintained by a router. SPF determines the routes that are installed in the IP routing table.

- Routes can be summarized only between areas, not within an area.

- Virtual links temporarily connect a nonzero area to the backbone.

- There are three types of OSPF routers: internal, ABRs, and ASBRs.

- External routes can be summarized only on an ASBR.

- OSPF routes can be summarized only on an ABR.

- The four types of OSPF routes are intra-area, interarea, external, and NSSA.

- OSPF has six area types: backbone or area 0, nonbackbone, stub, totally stubby, NSSA, and totally NSSA.

- An OSPF interarea route has three components: path to area 0, path across area 0, and the path across the destination area.

Chapter Review Questions

You can find the answers to these questions in Appendix A.

1. What are the purposes of areas in an OSPF network?

2. Why are intra-area summary routes not allowed?

3. What types of routes are allowed into a stub area?

4. What types of routes are allowed into a totally stubby area?

5. What types of routes are allowed into a NSSA?

6. What types of routes are allowed into a totally NSSA?

7. What is the difference between an E1 and E2 OSPF route?

8. What are the three types of OSPF routers?

9. What are the six OSPF route types?

10. Where can routes be summarized in an OSPF network?

11. How is the OSPF router ID determined?

12. How does OSPF determine the DR on a multi-access network?

13. How does OSPF determine an interarea shortest path?

14. What is the purpose of an OSPF virtual link?

15. How is the OSPF cost of an interface calculated?

16. The following OSPF routes originate in OSPF area 1:

188.14.19.0/28

188.14.19.16/28

188.14.19.32/28

188.14.19.48/28

What is the command to summarize these routes on the ABR between area 1 and the backbone?

17. How many OSPF databases are on an OSPF router?

18. What is the administrative distance of OSPF routes?

19. If a router learns about the same network prefix through RIP, IGRP, EIGRP, and OSPF, which route will be preferred?

References

RFCs are technical documents that are sometimes difficult to follow. You may want to review the other references listed here first if you are interested in learning more:

- Moy, J. April 1998. RFC 2328, OSPF Version 2.

- Parkhurst, William. 2002. *OSPF Command and Configuration Handbook*. Indianapolis: Cisco Press.

- Cisco Documentation, Cisco.com.

What You Will Learn

After reading this chapter, you should be able to

- ✔ Explain the Intermediate System-to-Intermediate System (IS-IS) routing protocol

- ✔ Understand the concepts, terminology, and operation of IS-IS

- ✔ Compare IS-IS with OSPF

- ✔ Understand the basics of configuring IS-IS on Cisco routers

Intermediate System-to-Intermediate System—Better, Stronger, Faster, and Scarier

IS-IS is a hierarchical link-state interior routing protocol similar to OSPF. The International Organization for Standardization (ISO) originally developed IS-IS to route packets using Network Service Access Point (NSAP) addresses, and not IP addresses.

Comparing IS-IS and IP Networks

In the IP world, the two main entities are hosts and routers. (See Figure 7-1.) An IP protocol is used between routers for the exchange of routing information. A host is usually the source or destination of an IP packet, and a router's job is to deliver the IP packet from the source to the destination. The Address Resolution Protocol (ARP) is used between hosts and routers for determining the mapping between an IP and Ethernet address. An IP host is usually configured with a static route or default gateway that points to the nearest router.

Figure 7-1   In the IP World, Routers Route Packets Between IP Hosts

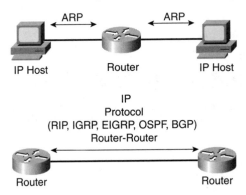

In the ISO world, routers are referred to as ***intermediate systems (IS)*** and hosts as ***end systems (ES)***. In Figure 7-2, a router is the IS between ESs. Thus, the routing protocol that exchanges routing information between ISs is called Intermediate System-to-Intermediate System, or IS-IS. (If you used this same approach in the IP world, you could call all IP routing protocols Router-to-Router [R-R] protocols.) Instead of a static or default route, ISO uses the ES-IS protocol for end stations to discover the nearest router or IS.

Figure 7-2   In the ISO World, ISs Route Packets Between ESs

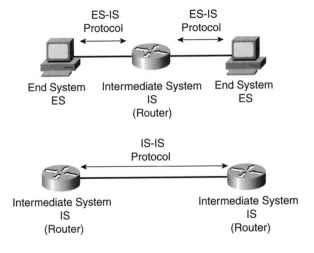

In the early days of networking, the ISO and IP protocols battled to be the adopted standard for the Internet. We know that IP won; there is not an ISO Internet, but an IP Internet. IS-IS was adapted to route IP packets in addition to ISO packets. IS-IS can be configured to route NSAP packets only, IP packets only, or both. Typically, you find IS-IS routing both and this form of the protocol is called ***Integrated IS-IS***. Why do you need to route both if there is not an ISO Internet? Although Integrated IS-IS routes IP, it still uses NSAP addresses for neighbor discovery. Therefore, it is important to understand the structure of NSAP addresses and how they create a hierarchical multi-area network.

Having to work with two addressing formats, NSAP and IP, is what tends to make IS-IS a scary protocol. You may be comfortable with IP addresses, but not with NSAP addresses. What you need to understand about NSAP addresses in relationship to IS-IS, however, is relatively straightforward. After a discussion of the structure and use of NSAP addresses, and a few examples, you should have no problems using them with IS-IS.

Figure 7-3 shows the formats of IP and NSAP addresses. An NSAP address can be 8 to 20 bytes in length and has three components:

- Area ID

- System ID

- NSAP selector (NSEL)

Figure 7-3   IP and NSAP Address Formats

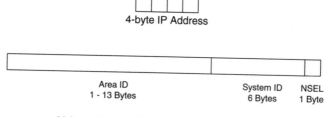

4-byte IP Address

Area ID
1 - 13 Bytes

System ID
6 Bytes

NSEL
1 Byte

20-byte Network Service Access Point Address
Format (NSAP)

The area ID can be 1 to 13 bytes in length. The area ID determines a router's IS-IS area. This is similar to the area IDs used by OSPF. An OSPF area ID is a 32-bit number while an IS-IS area ID is 1 to 13 bytes, or 8 to 104 bits in length.

The system ID identifies a router. The system ID can be any hexadecimal value that fits into six bytes. When configuring a router for IS-IS, you are free to choose the system ID. For example, if you have three IS-IS routers, you can use the following system IDs:

- 111111111111 for router 1

- 222222222222 for router 2

- 333333333333 for router 3

Another approach is to use the IP address of a router's loopback interface for the system ID. An IP address is 4 bytes and when written in the dotted decimal format, each byte can have a value between 0 and 255. If you write the dotted decimal format for an IP address and use 3 decimal digits for each byte, the dotted decimal representation will have 12 digits as shown in Figure 7-4.

Figure 7-4   Converting an IP Address to an IS-IS System ID

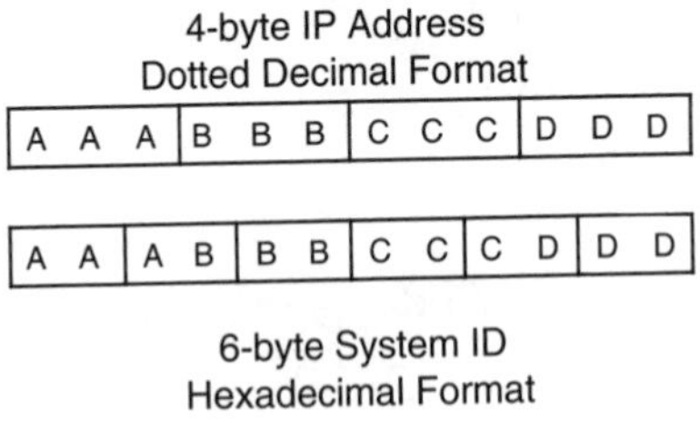

4-byte IP Address
Dotted Decimal Format

| A A A | B B B | C C C | D D D |

| A A | A B | B B | C C | C D | D D |

6-byte System ID
Hexadecimal Format

For example, IP address 172.16.1.23 can be written as 172.016.001.023. If you rewrite the IP address as 6 hexadecimal digits, you get 17.20.16.00.10.23.

The third component of the NSAP address is the NSAP selector (NSEL). The NSEL specifies a network layer service similar to a port number in TCP/IP. For example, in TCP/IP, a port number identified the application the IP packet should be sent to on the receiving host. Because NSAP addresses are not used for routing, the NSEL is not used to select the destination application (IP is used for this function), so the NSEL value is set to 0. Therefore, a selector value of 0 identifies a router. A router that is configured for IS-IS area 1 with a loopback address of 10.1.2.3 has an NSAP address of 01.01.00.01.00.20.03.00, assuming you are using the loopback IP address to determine the IS-IS system ID.

IS-IS Areas

An IS-IS network can be configured as a single or multiple area network. When using a single area, the area number can be any number that fits into 13 bytes. (See Figure 7-5).

Figure 7-5   Single Area IS-IS Network

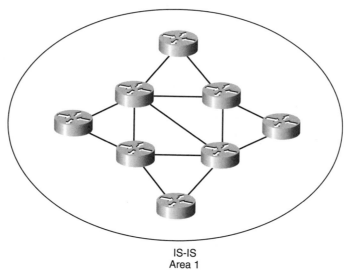

IS-IS
Area 1

Normally, IS-IS networks are designed using multiple areas. When a single area is used, summarization is not possible. Using multiple areas allows for a hierarchical and scalable network design.

There are two types of routing in an IS-IS network. Routing within an area is called **Level 1 routing**. Routing between IS-IS areas is called **Level 2 routing**. Level 1 IS-IS routers only maintain a database of intra-area routes. Level 2 IS-IS routers maintain a database of inter-area routes. In OSPF, Level 1 routing is referred to as *intra-area routing* and Level 2 routing as *interarea routing*.

When multiple areas are used in a network design, OSPF requires a backbone area, or area 0. All nonzero OSPF areas must be connected to the backbone, or area 0, through an Area Border Router (ABR). IS-IS also has a backbone, but not a backbone area. An IS-IS backbone is a contiguous chain of Level 2 capable routers. If you can trace a continuous line through level-2 capable IS-IS routers to or through every IS-IS area, you have a valid IS-IS network design. Figure 7-6 is a multiple area IS-IS network and each router, except for Router G, is designated as either a Level 1, Level 2, or Level 1-2 router.

Figure 7-6   Multiple Area IS-IS Network

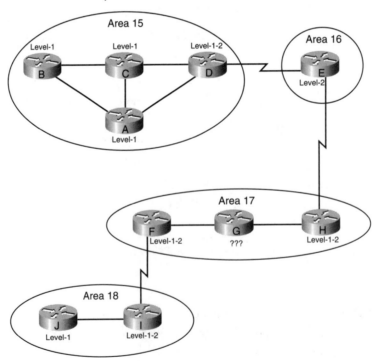

A Level 1 router is a router that maintains one IS-IS link-state database. A Level 1 IS-IS link-state database contains routing information for routing within an area. Level 1 IS-IS routers are equivalent to OSPF internal routers. A Level 1-2 capable IS-IS router maintains two *link-state databases*. The Level 1 database contains routing information for the area. The Level 2 database contains routing information for interarea routing. Level 1-2 IS-IS routers are equivalent to OSPF ABRs. IS-IS Level 2 capable routers maintain only a Level 2 database, and they are responsible for routing between areas and not within an area. There is no OSPF counterpart for an IS-IS Level 2 router. IS-IS and OSPF router types are listed in Table 7-1.

Table 7-1   IS-IS and OSPF Router Types

IS-IS Router Type	OSPF Router Type	Description
Level 1	Internal	Intra-area routing
Level 1-2	Area Border Router	Intra- and interarea routing
Level 2	None	Interarea routing

In Figure 7-6, Routers A, B, C, and J are Level 1 IS-IS routers, and they maintain one link-state database for routes within their area. Routers D, F, H, and I are Level 1-2 routers because they need to route within their areas and between areas. Router E is a Level 2 only router. The function of Router E is to route only between IS-IS areas. What about Router G? If this were an OSPF network, Router G would be an internal router—because all of the router interfaces are in the same area. If you make Router G a Level 1 only router, you would have a broken IS-IS network—because there would not be a contiguous backbone connecting areas 15, 16, 17, and 18. (See Figure 7-7.) Remember that an IS-IS backbone is a contiguous chain of Level 2 capable routers used to connect all IS-IS areas.

Figure 7-7   IS-IS Backbone Must Be a Contiguous Chain of Level 2
Capable Routers

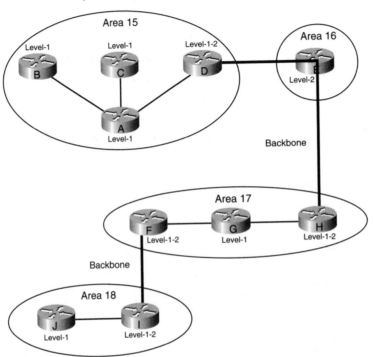

Router G must be configured as a Level 1-2 router to have a contiguous backbone connecting all IS-IS areas. (See Figure 7-8).

An IS-IS backbone is more flexible and scalable than an OSPF backbone, or area 0. For example, if you want to merge two OSPF networks, you have to ensure that every nonzero area is connected to area 0. In Figure 7-9, all nonzero areas must be connected to the backbone or area 0. With OSPF, ensuring that all nonzero areas are physically connected to the backbone can be difficult.

Figure 7-8   For a Contiguous IS-IS Backbone, Router G Must Be
Configured as a Level 1-2 Capable Router

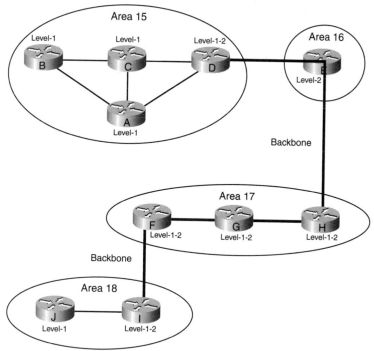

Figure 7-9   All Nonzero OSPF Areas Must Connect to Area 0

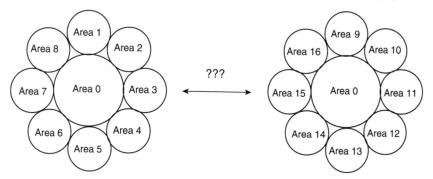

If these were IS-IS networks, what would you have to do to merge them? The solution is easy. Add a link between the two IS-IS networks and make the border routers Level 2 capable so you have a contiguous backbone. (See Figure 7-10.)

Figure 7-10   Merging Two IS-IS Networks Requires a Level 2 Capable Link Between the Networks

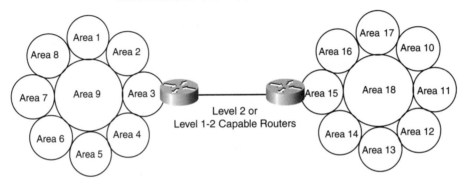

IS-IS Link States

IS-IS is a link-state routing protocol. IS-IS does not advertise routes like the distance vector protocols. IS-IS advertises link states using *link-state packets (LSPs)*. IS-IS routers flood, or advertise, their link states to their IS-IS neighbors throughout an IS-IS area. If a router is configured only as a Level 1 IS-IS router, that router will maintain one IS-IS database for that area. If a router has been configured as a Level 1-2 router, the router maintains a separate database for intra-area and interarea routes. A Level 2 IS-IS router maintains one interarea database. Routers in an area flood their link states until every IS-IS router in an area has an identical IS-IS database for that area. After the databases in an area agree, or are synchronized, each router constructs a graph of the prefixes in an area and the routes to those prefixes. Each router runs a shortest path first (SPF) algorithm to determine the best path to every destination in the area. The best paths to every destination are then installed in the local IP routing table.

As with OSPF, route summarization cannot be used if one area is only used in an IS-IS network design. Before routes can be transferred from the IS-IS database to the IP routing table, the databases in an area must agree. If routes could be summarized in an area, some routers would have specific routes and some routers would have summaries. If this were possible, the databases in an area would never agree and routes would never be placed in the IP routing table. Routes can be summarized between areas, but not within an area. For example, area 1 could have a summary of routes in area 2 and area 2 could have a summary of routes in area 1. But area 1 cannot have a summary of area 1 routes and area 2 cannot have a summary of area 2 routes. In summary, an IS-IS network has the following properties:

- One or more IS-IS areas.

- If more than one IS-IS area is used, a contiguous backbone must be configured that connects all areas. An IS-IS backbone is a contiguous chain of Level 2 capable routers.

- Level 1 routers maintain a link-state database for their area. Level 2, or backbone, routers maintain a link-state database for interarea routes.

- LSPs flood information about a router's interfaces throughout an IS-IS area.

- IS-IS databases within an area must be identical before a router can calculate the routes that are installed in the IP routing table.

- The SPF algorithm is run on each area database maintained by a router. SPF determines the routes that are installed in the IP routing table.

- Routes can only be summarized between areas, not within an area.

At this point, you should have a basic understanding of the concepts of the IS-IS routing protocol and the operation and structure of an IS-IS network. The next section looks at the basic configuration of IS-IS on Cisco routers, and compares the IS-IS configuration to an OSPF configuration.

Basic Single Area IS-IS Configuration

This section examines the process of configuring a single IS-IS area using the network in Figure 7-11.

Figure 7-11   Single Area IS-IS Network

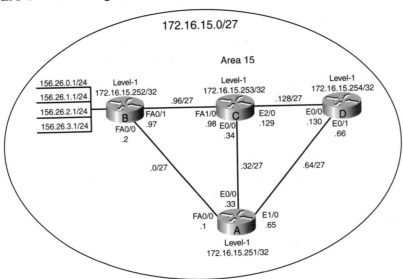

The steps for a basic single area IS-IS configuration are as follows:

Step 1   Configure a loopback interface on each OSPF router.

Step 2   Configure IP addresses on the physical interfaces.

Step 3   Configure the IS-IS process on each router.

Step 4   Enable IS-IS on the router interfaces.

The loopback addresses, IS-IS system IDs, and router NSAP addresses are listed in Table 7-2. The system IDs and NSAP addresses are derived from the loopback addresses.

Table 7-2   Loopback and System IDs for Figure 7-11

Router	Loopback	System ID	NSAP
A	172.16.15.251/32	17.20.16.01.52.51	15.17.20.16.01.52.51.00
B	172.16.15.252/32	17.20.16.01.52.52	15.17.20.16.01.52.52.00
C	172.16.15.253/32	17.20.16.01.52.53	15.17.20.16.01.52.53.00
D	172.16.15.254/32	17.20.16.01.52.54	15.17.20.16.01.52.54.00

The loopback interfaces on Routers A, B, C, and D are configured first because they are being used for the router's NSAP address. (See Example 7-1.)

Example 7-1   Loopback Interface Configurations

```
Router A
interface Loopback0
 ip address 172.16.15.251 255.255.255.255

Router B
interface Loopback0
 ip address 172.16.15.252 255.255.255.255

Router C
interface Loopback0
 ip address 172.16.15.253 255.255.255.255

Router D
interface Loopback0
 ip address 172.16.15.254 255.255.255.255
```

Four additional loopback interfaces are configured on Router B, so you have some networks to advertise. Loopback interfaces can be used to create virtual networks, so you can experiment with some of the properties of IS-IS. (See Example 7-2.)

Example 7-2 Using Loopback Interfaces to Simulate Physical Networks

```
Router B
interface Loopback1
 ip address 156.26.0.1 255.255.255.0

interface Loopback2
 ip address 156.26.1.1 255.255.255.0

interface Loopback3
 ip address 156.26.2.1 255.255.255.0

interface Loopback4
 ip address 156.26.3.1 255.255.255.0
```

After the loopback and physical interfaces have been configured, the next step is to enable the IS-IS routing process on each router. (See Example 7-3). When an OSPF process is configured, the router ID is taken from one of the IP addresses configured on an interface with loopback addresses having precedence. For IS-IS, the ID of the router is configured under the IS-IS router process, and is referred to as the network entity title (NET).

Example 7-3 IS-IS Process Configuration

```
Router A
router isis
 net 15.1720.1601.5251.00
 is-type level-1

Router B
router isis
 net 15.1720.1601.5252.00
 is-type level-1

Router C
router isis
 net 15.1720.1601.5253.00
 is-type level-1

Router D
router isis
 net 15.1720.1601.5254.00
 is-type level-1
```

By default, an IS-IS router is a Level 1-2 router. The command **is-type level-1** forces the routers to be Level 1 capable only.

With the loopback interfaces configured and the IS-IS process enabled, the next step is to enable interfaces for IS-IS. Similar to the other interior routing protocols you have learned about, once an interface is enabled for a protocol, the prefix and mask configured on the interface will be advertised. In addition, EIGRP, OSPF, and IS-IS try to discover neighbor routers on these interfaces using hello packets. With RIP, IGRP, EIGRP, and OSPF, interfaces are enabled under the routing process. With IS-IS, interfaces are enabled using the interface command **ip router isis** as shown for Router A in Example 7-4. The configurations for Routers B, C, and D are the same as for Router A.

Example 7-4   Enabling Router A Interfaces for IS-IS

```
Router A
interface Loopback0
 ip address 172.16.15.251 255.255.255.255
 ip router isis

interface FastEthernet0/0
 ip address 172.16.15.1 255.255.255.224
 ip router isis

interface Ethernet1/0
 ip address 172.16.15.65 255.255.255.224
 ip router isis

interface Ethernet0/0

 ip address 172.16.15.33 255.255.255.224
 ip router isis
```

Examples 7-1 through 7-4 are the minimum configurations you need to enable IS-IS for the network in Figure 7-11. All IS-IS routes should now be in the routing tables on all IS-IS routers. The IS-IS routes are verified using the **show ip route** command as shown in Example 7-5.

Example 7-5 Verifying Advertising of IS-IS Routes

```
D#show ip route
Codes: C - connected, S - static, I - IGRP, R - RIP, M - mobile, B - BGP
       D - EIGRP, EX - EIGRP external, O - OSPF, IA - OSPF inter area
       N1 - OSPF NSSA external type 1, N2 - OSPF NSSA external type 2
       E1 - OSPF external type 1, E2 - OSPF external type 2, E - EGP
       i - IS-IS, L1 - IS-IS level-1, L2 - IS-IS level-2, ia - IS-IS inter area
       * - candidate default, U - per-user static route, o - ODR
       P - periodic downloaded static route

Gateway of last resort is not set

      156.26.0.0/24 is subnetted, 4 subnets
i L1     156.26.2.0 [115/30] via 172.16.15.129, Ethernet0/0
i L1     156.26.3.0 [115/30] via 172.16.15.129, Ethernet0/0
i L1     156.26.0.0 [115/30] via 172.16.15.129, Ethernet0/0
i L1     156.26.1.0 [115/30] via 172.16.15.129, Ethernet0/0
      172.16.0.0/16 is variably subnetted, 9 subnets, 2 masks
C        172.16.15.128/27 is directly connected, Ethernet0/0
i L1     172.16.15.251/32 [115/20] via 172.16.15.65, Ethernet0/1
C        172.16.15.254/32 is directly connected, Loopback0
i L1     172.16.15.253/32 [115/20] via 172.16.15.129, Ethernet0/0
i L1     172.16.15.252/32 [115/30] via 172.16.15.129, Ethernet0/0
i L1     172.16.15.32/27 [115/20] via 172.16.15.65, Ethernet0/1
i L1     172.16.15.0/27 [115/20] via 172.16.15.65, Ethernet0/1
i L1     172.16.15.96/27 [115/20] via 172.16.15.129, Ethernet0/0
C        172.16.15.64/27 is directly connected, Ethernet0/1
```

To determine if all IS-IS neighbors have been discovered, use the command **show isis topology.**(See Example 7-6.)

Example 7-6 Verifying IS-IS Neighbors

```
D#show isis topology

IS-IS paths to level-1 routers
System Id      Metric  Next-Hop      Interface     SNPA
A              10      A             Et0/1         0003.6cb3.ac1c
B              20      C             Et0/0         0004.c109.1dc0
                       A             Et0/1         0003.6cb3.ac1c
C              10      C             Et0/0         0004.c109.1dc0
D              --
```

The output of the **show isis topology** command lists the system ID of the neighbor in the first column. The system ID is symbolic, and does not show the neighbor's

NSAP address. To verify a neighbor's NSAP address, use the command **show isis hostname**, as shown in Example 7-7.

Example 7-7   Displaying IS-IS Router System IDs

```
D#show isis hostname
Level  System ID        Dynamic Hostname  (notag)
 1       1720.1601.5252 B
 1       1720.1601.5253 C
 1       1720.1601.5251 A
         * 1720.1601.5254 D
```

In the second and third columns, the output of the **show isis topology**command lists the metric—or distance—to the neighbor, the next hop router to reach the neighbor, and the interface used to reach the neighbor. The last column lists the Ethernet address of the neighbor router's interface.

At this point you have an understanding of how to configure and verify a basic single area IS-IS network. Before moving on to a multiple area IS-IS network, you will learn about IS-IS metrics.

IS-IS Metrics

All IP routing protocols use interface costs or metrics to determine the best path to a destination. RIP uses a hop count that does not take into account the speed or bandwidth of the interface. IGRP and EIGRP use a four-component metric that consists of delay, bandwidth, reliability, and load. By default, only the delay and bandwidth parameters calculate an IGRP or EIGRP metric. An OSPF metric is calculated from the bandwidth of the network interface. The default IS-IS metric is probably the least useful. With IS-IS, by default, all interfaces have a cost or metric of 10. This can be seen from the IP routing table, or from the output of the **show isis topology**command from Example 7-6.

If you look in the routing table on Router D and inspect the route to the loopback interface on Router C, the cost to reach this network is 20. (See Example 7-8.)

Example 7-8 IS-IS Route Metric from Router D to Router C

```
D#show ip route | include 172.16.15.253
i L1     172.16.15.253/32 [115/20] via 172.16.15.129, Ethernet0/0
```

The cost from Router D to Router C across the Ethernet interface is 10, and the cost from Router C to its loopback address is also 10. This gives a total cost of 20.

The cost from Router C to reach the first loopback interface on Router B is also 20, as shown in Example 7-9.

Example 7-9 IS-IS Route Metric from Router C to Router B

```
C#show ip route | include 172.16.15.252
i L1     172.16.15.252/32 [115/20] via 172.16.15.97, FastEthernet1/0
```

From an IS-IS point of view, the cost from Router D to Router C is the same as the cost from Router C to Router B. IS-IS does account for the fact that the fast Ethernet network is 10 times faster than the Ethernet network. This is because of using a default metric, or cost, of 10 for every interface. The default IS-IS metric is referred to as an *IS-IS narrow metric*.

You can help IS-IS by modifying the metric of each interface. If you use the same calculation as OSPF, an Ethernet interface has a cost of 10—and a fast Ethernet interface has a cost of 1. IS-IS interface metrics are modified using the **isis metric** interface command. On Routers A, B, and C, the IS-IS cost of the fast Ethernet interfaces is changed to be 1 instead of 10—as shown in Example 7-10 for the fast Ethernet interface on Router A. Routers B and C have similar configurations.

Example 7-10 Modifying the IS-IS Interface Metric

```
Router A
interface FastEthernet0/0
 ip address 172.16.15.1 255.255.255.224
 ip router isis
 isis metric 1
```

You should now see a difference in the cost from Router D to C as compared to the cost to go from Router C to B. (See Example 7-11.)

Example 7-11 Verifying the New IS-IS Route Metrics

```
D#show ip route | include 172.16.15.253
i L1    172.16.15.253/32 [115/20] via 172.16.15.129, Ethernet0/0

C#show ip route | include 172.16.15.252
i L1    172.16.15.252/32 [115/11] via 172.16.15.97, FastEthernet1/0
```

For IS-IS to calculate a true shortest path, the metrics of all the interfaces need to be changed to reflect the difference in interface bandwidths. This can be done easily, but if you have a large network, this process is prone to error. Metrics in IGRP, EIGRP, and OSPF are more convenient because the metrics are automatically calculated based on the interface parameters.

Another limitation of using default IS-IS metrics is that only 6 bits are used for Level 1 routes and 10 bits for Level 2 routes. For Level 1 routes, there are 2^6-1, or 63, different metric values. This may not be sufficient depending on the mix of interfaces in the network. For example, if you have a gigabit Ethernet interface as the fastest interface in the network, you can set the IS-IS metric to 1. Fast Ethernet has one-tenth the bandwidth, so you can set the IS-IS metric to 10. Ethernet would then have a metric of 100 but the largest IS-IS metric is 63. Therefore, you cannot adequately represent a mix of high- and low-speed interfaces in an IS-IS network using the default metric size.

To overcome the problems with the default metric size, IS-IS can be configured to use a larger or wider metric that uses 24 bits for intra-area routes and 32 bits for interarea routes. IS-IS can be enabled to use *IS-IS wide metrics* using the **metric-style wide** command under the IS-IS router configuration as shown for Router A in Example 7-12.

Example 7-12 Configuring IS-IS for Wide Metrics

```
Router A
router isis
 net 15.1720.1601.5251.00
 is-type level-1
 metric-style wide
```

Interface metrics can now be configured with a value in the range of 1 to 16,777,214. This new range is sufficient to handle any mix of interface speeds, but you still need to manually configure a metric on every IS-IS interface. When using wide metrics, the default interface metric is still 10.

IS-IS Multiple Area Configuration

This section uses the network in Figure 7-12 to investigate the properties of a multiple area IS-IS network. The loopback addresses, system IDs, and NSAP addresses for the routers in area 17 are listed in Table 7-3.

Figure 7-12   Multiple Area IS-IS Network

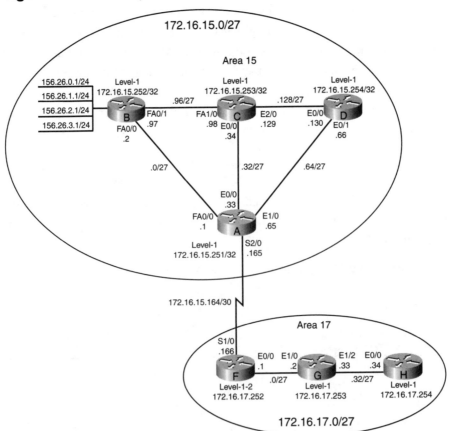

Table 7-3   Additional Loopback and System IDs for Figure 7-12

Router	Loopback	System ID	NSAP
F	172.16.17.252/32	17.20.16.01.72.52	17.17.20.16.01.72.52.00
G	172.16.17.253/32	17.20.16.01.72.53	17.17.20.16.01.72.53.00
H	172.16.17.254/32	17.20.16.01.72.54	17.17.20.16.01.72.54.00

Router A now has a connection to area 17 through Router F. Both Routers A and F need to be configured as Level 1-2 capable routers. Routers G and H do not have any connections to another area, so they can be configured as Level 1 only capable routers. (See Example 7-13.) The link between Routers A and F also needs to be enabled for IS-IS.

Example 7-13   Configuring IS-IS Link Types

```
Router A
router isis
 net 15.1720.1601.5251.00
 is-type level-1-2
 metric-style wide

Router F
interface Loopback0
 ip address 172.16.17.252 255.255.255.255
 ip router isis
router isis
 net 17.1720.1601.7252.00
 is-type level-1-2
 metric-style wide

Router G
interface Loopback0
 ip address 172.16.17.253 255.255.255.255
 ip router isis

router isis
 net 17.1720.1601.7253.00
 is-type level-1
 metric-style wide

Router H
interface Loopback0
```

Example 7-13 Configuring IS-IS Link Types (continued)

```
ip address 172.16.17.254 255.255.255.255
ip router isis

router isis
net 17.1720.1601.7254.00
is-type level-1
metric-style wide
```

If you list the configurations, there is no **is-type**command shown in the configurations for Routers A and F. Level 1-2 is the default, so this command does not appear in the configurations.

Routers A and F have a Level 2 neighbor relationship because they are configured for different areas, as shown in Example 7-14.

Example 7-14 Verifying IS-IS Level 2 Capability

```
A#show isis topology level-2
IS-IS paths to level-2 routers
System Id          Metric  Next-Hop          Interface    SNPA
A                    - -
F                    10      F                Se2/0        *HDLC*

F#show isis topology level-2
IS-IS paths to level-2 routers
System Id       Metric  Next-Hop      Interface     SNPA
A                10      A             Se1/0         *HDLC*
F                - -
```

All IS-IS routes should be in the routing tables on all the routers as shown in Example 7-15 for Router F.

Example 7-15 IP Routing Table for Router F

```
F#show ip route
Codes: C - connected, S - static, I - IGRP, R - RIP, M - mobile, B - BGP
       D - EIGRP, EX - EIGRP external, O - OSPF, IA - OSPF inter area
       N1 - OSPF NSSA external type 1, N2 - OSPF NSSA external type 2
       E1 - OSPF external type 1, E2 - OSPF external type 2, E - EGP
       i - IS-IS, L1 - IS-IS level-1, L2 - IS-IS level-2, ia - IS-IS inter area
       * - candidate default, U - per-user static route, o - ODR
       P - periodic downloaded static route
```

Example 7-15 IP Routing Table for Router F

```
Gateway of last resort is not set

       156.26.0.0/24 is subnetted, 4 subnets
i L2     156.26.2.0 [115/21] via 172.16.15.165, Serial1/0
i L2     156.26.3.0 [115/21] via 172.16.15.165, Serial1/0
i L2     156.26.0.0 [115/21] via 172.16.15.165, Serial1/0
i L2     156.26.1.0 [115/21] via 172.16.15.165, Serial1/0
       172.16.0.0/16 is variably subnetted, 16 subnets, 3 masks
i L1     172.16.16.164/30 [115/30] via 172.16.17.2, Ethernet0/0
C        172.16.15.164/30 is directly connected, Serial1/0
i L2     172.16.15.128/27 [115/22] via 172.16.15.165, Serial1/0
i L2     172.16.15.251/32 [115/20] via 172.16.15.165, Serial1/0
i L2     172.16.15.254/32 [115/30] via 172.16.15.165, Serial1/0
i L2     172.16.15.253/32 [115/22] via 172.16.15.165, Serial1/0
i L2     172.16.15.252/32 [115/21] via 172.16.15.165, Serial1/0
i L1     172.16.17.253/32 [115/20] via 172.16.17.2, Ethernet0/0
C        172.16.17.252/32 is directly connected, Loopback0
i L1     172.16.17.254/32 [115/30] via 172.16.17.2, Ethernet0/0
i L1     172.16.17.32/27 [115/20] via 172.16.17.2, Ethernet0/0
i L2     172.16.15.32/27 [115/20] via 172.16.15.165, Serial1/0
C        172.16.17.0/27 is directly connected, Ethernet0/0
i L2     172.16.15.0/27 [115/11] via 172.16.15.165, Serial1/0
i L2     172.16.15.96/27 [115/12] via 172.16.15.165, Serial1/0
i L2     172.16.15.64/27 [115/20] via 172.16.15.165, Serial1/0
```

The routing table on Router F contains both Level 1 and Level 2 routes. The Level 1 routes are those that originate in area 17. The Level 2 routes are those that originate in area 15. The Level 1 only routers have only routes from their own area as shown in Example 7-16 for Router G.

Example 7-16 IP Routing Table for Router G

```
G#show ip route
Codes: C - connected, S - static, I - IGRP, R - RIP, M - mobile, B - BGP
       D - EIGRP, EX - EIGRP external, O - OSPF, IA - OSPF inter area
       N1 - OSPF NSSA external type 1, N2 - OSPF NSSA external type 2
       E1 - OSPF external type 1, E2 - OSPF external type 2, E - EGP
       i - IS-IS, L1 - IS-IS level-1, L2 - IS-IS level-2, ia - IS-IS inter area
       * - candidate default, U - per-user static route, o - ODR
       P - periodic downloaded static route

Gateway of last resort is 172.16.17.1 to network 0.0.0.0

       172.16.0.0/16 is variably subnetted, 6 subnets, 3 masks
i L1     172.16.16.164/30 [115/20] via 172.16.17.34, Ethernet1/2
```

continues

Example 7-16 IP Routing Table for Router G (continued)

```
C       172.16.17.253/32 is directly connected, Loopback0
i L1    172.16.17.252/32 [115/20] via 172.16.17.1, Ethernet1/0
i L1    172.16.17.254/32 [115/20] via 172.16.17.34, Ethernet1/2
C       172.16.17.32/27 is directly connected, Ethernet1/2
C       172.16.17.0/27 is directly connected, Ethernet1/0
i*L1 0.0.0.0/0 [115/10] via 172.16.17.1, Ethernet1/0
```

The Level 1 only routers in area 15 have specific routes from area 15 but no specific routes from area 17. The Level 1 only routers in area 17 have specific routes from area 17 but no specific routes from area 15. The Level 1 only routers do have a default route that points to the border router, either A or F. You have seen this behavior in Chapter 6, "Open Shortest Path First—Better, Stronger, Faster," for OSPF stub areas where a default route is advertised into the stub area.

When using a basic OSPF configuration, all routes appear on all routers. Every OSPF router's IP routing table contains all specific intra-area, interarea, and external routes. You could configure an OSPF area as a stub area, blocking the external routes from being advertised into an area. You could further configure an OSPF area as a totally stubby area. In a totally stubby area, both OSPF interarea and external routes are blocked from being advertised into the area. By default, IS-IS treats all areas as totally stubby areas. IS-IS interarea routes are not advertised to Level 1 only routers. The border routers automatically advertise a default route into the area as shown in the routing tables for Router B in Example 7-17.

Example 7-17 IP Routing Table for Router B

```
B#show ip route | include 0.0.0.0
Gateway of last resort is 172.16.15.1 to network 0.0.0.0
i*L1 0.0.0.0/0 [115/1] via 172.16.15.1, FastEthernet0/0
```

If the serial link between Routers A and F in Figure 7-12 fails, areas 15 and 17 will be cut off from each other. For redundancy, a Level 2 capable router is installed so you have another path between the two areas. (See Figure 7-13.)

Figure 7-13   Router E Provides a Redundant Path Between Areas 15 and 16

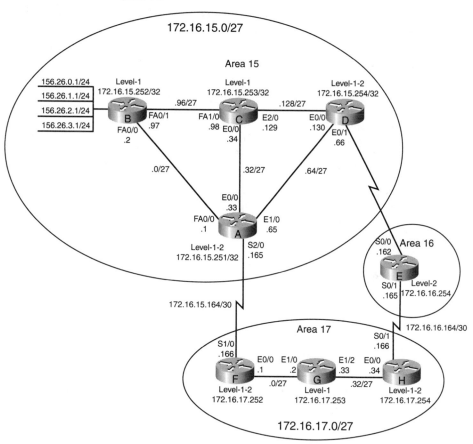

Router H is reconfigured as a Level 1-2 capable router. Does Router G need to be a Level 1-2 router? For the network in Figure 7-13, the answer is no. If the link between Routers A and F fails, Routers G and F will have a default route to Router H. Router G does not need to be a Level 2 capable router because the current IS-IS backbone is contiguous and it connects all IS-IS areas.

IS-IS Route Summarization

The Level 2 capable routers in Figure 7-13 contain all the specific routes in their IP routing tables. For example, Router E has 18 specific routes in Example 7-18.

Example 7-18 IS-IS Routes in the IP Routing Table of Router E

```
E#show ip route | include L2
      i - IS-IS, L1 - IS-IS level-1, L2 - IS-IS level-2, ia - IS-IS inter area
i L2   156.26.2.0 [115/31] via 172.16.15.161, Serial0/0
i L2   156.26.3.0 [115/31] via 172.16.15.161, Serial0/0
i L2   156.26.0.0 [115/31] via 172.16.15.161, Serial0/0
i L2   156.26.1.0 [115/31] via 172.16.15.161, Serial0/0
i L2   172.16.15.128/27 [115/20] via 172.16.15.161, Serial0/0
i L2   172.16.15.251/32 [115/30] via 172.16.15.161, Serial0/0
i L2   172.16.15.254/32 [115/20] via 172.16.15.161, Serial0/0
i L2   172.16.15.253/32 [115/30] via 172.16.15.161, Serial0/0
i L2   172.16.15.252/32 [115/31] via 172.16.15.161, Serial0/0
i L2   172.16.17.253/32 [115/30] via 172.16.16.166, Serial0/1
i L2   172.16.17.252/32 [115/40] via 172.16.16.166, Serial0/1
i L2   172.16.17.254/32 [115/20] via 172.16.16.166, Serial0/1
i L2   172.16.17.32/27 [115/20] via 172.16.16.166, Serial0/1
i L2   172.16.15.32/27 [115/30] via 172.16.15.161, Serial0/0
i L2   172.16.17.0/27 [115/30] via 172.16.16.166, Serial0/1
i L2   172.16.15.0/27 [115/21] via 172.16.15.161, Serial0/0
i L2   172.16.15.96/27 [115/21] via 172.16.15.161, Serial0/0
i L2   172.16.15.64/27 [115/20] via 172.16.15.161, Serial0/0
```

Does Router E need all the specific routes in the IP routing table? No. All 172.16.15.0/24 routes belong to area 15. All 172.16.17.0/24 routes belong to area 17. The 156.26.0.0 routes in area 15 can be summarized into one route. As with OSPF, route summarization is configured on the border routers. For the network in Figure 7-13, the border routers are Routers A, D, F, and H. Routers A and D summarize the 172.16.15.0 and 156.26.0.0 routes and Routers F and H summarize the 172.16.17.0 routes. The configuration for route summarization on the border routers is shown in Example 7-19.

Example 7-19 Configuring IS-IS Route Summarization

```
Router A
router isis
  summary-address 156.26.0.0 255.255.252.0
  summary-address 172.16.15.0 255.255.255.0
  net 15.1720.1601.5251.00
  metric-style wide

Router D
router isis
  summary-address 156.26.0.0 255.255.252.0
  summary-address 172.16.15.0 255.255.255.0
  net 15.1720.1601.5254.00
  metric-style wide

Router F
router isis
  summary-address 172.16.17.0 255.255.255.0
  net 17.1720.1601.7252.00
  metric-style wide

Router H
router isis
  summary-address 172.16.17.0 255.255.255.0
  net 17.1720.1601.7254.00
  metric-style wide
```

The routing tables on the Level 2 capable routers have been significantly reduced, as shown in Example 7-20 for Router A.

Example 7-20 Results for IS-IS Route Summarization

```
A#show ip route | include L2
      i - IS-IS, L1 - IS-IS level-1, L2 - IS-IS level-2, ia - IS-IS inter area
i L2    172.16.16.164/30 [115/30] via 172.16.15.66, Ethernet1/0
i L2    172.16.16.254/32 [115/30] via 172.16.15.66, Ethernet1/0
i L2    172.16.17.0/24 [115/40] via 172.16.15.66, Ethernet1/0
```

OSPF has two separate commands for route summarization. The **area range** command summarizes OSPF routes and the **summary-address** command summarizes external routes. With IS-IS, the **summary-address** command is used for all route summarization.

Route Leaking

Router G has two default routes in its IP routing table. One default route is from Router F and one is from Router H, as shown in Example 7-21.

Example 7-21   IS-IS Default Routes

```
G#show ip route
     172.16.0.0/16 is variably subnetted, 6 subnets, 3 masks
i L1    172.16.16.164/30 [115/20] via 172.16.17.34, Ethernet1/2
C       172.16.17.253/32 is directly connected, Loopback0
i L1    172.16.17.252/32 [115/20] via 172.16.17.1, Ethernet1/0
i L1    172.16.17.254/32 [115/20] via 172.16.17.34, Ethernet1/2
C       172.16.17.32/27 is directly connected, Ethernet1/2
C       172.16.17.0/27 is directly connected, Ethernet1/0
i*L1 0.0.0.0/0 [115/10] via 172.16.17.34, Ethernet1/2
                [115/10] via 172.16.17.1, Ethernet1/0
```

What is the shortest path from Router G to one of the 156.26 networks in area 15? The shortest path is through Router F to Router A. Router G does not know this is the shortest path. Both default routes in the routing table on Router G have the same IS-IS cost. You would like Router G to use the path through Router F to reach the 156.26 networks. This can be accomplished by leaking specific Level 2 routes into area 17. *Route leaking* is the process of redistributing selected Level 2 routes into an area as Level 1 routes. (See Example 7-22).

Example 7-22   Configuring Route Leaking on Router F

```
Router F
router isis
 summary-address 172.16.17.0 255.255.255.0
 redistribute isis ip level-2 into level-1 distribute-list 100
 net 17.1720.1601.7252.00
 metric-style wide

access-list 100 permit ip 156.26.0.0 0.0.255.255 any
```

The access-list identifies the routes that are allowed to be leaked into the area as Level 1 routes. In this case, you are only allowing 156.26 routes. The routing table on Router G now contains a specific route to the 156.26 networks. (See Example 7-23.)

Example 7-23   Results of IS-IS Route Leaking

```
G#show ip route
Codes: C - connected, S - static, I - IGRP, R - RIP, M - mobile, B - BGP
       D - EIGRP, EX - EIGRP external, O - OSPF, IA - OSPF inter area
       N1 - OSPF NSSA external type 1, N2 - OSPF NSSA external type 2
       E1 - OSPF external type 1, E2 - OSPF external type 2, E - EGP
       i - IS-IS, L1 - IS-IS level-1, L2 - IS-IS level-2, ia - IS-IS inter area
       * - candidate default, U - per-user static route, o - ODR
       P - periodic downloaded static route

Gateway of last resort is 172.16.17.34 to network 0.0.0.0

     156.26.0.0/22 is subnetted, 1 subnets
i ia    156.26.0.0 [115/31] via 172.16.17.1, Ethernet1/0
     172.16.0.0/16 is variably subnetted, 6 subnets, 3 masks
i L1    172.16.16.164/30 [115/20] via 172.16.17.34, Ethernet1/2
C       172.16.17.253/32 is directly connected, Loopback0
i L1    172.16.17.252/32 [115/20] via 172.16.17.1, Ethernet1/0
i L1    172.16.17.254/32 [115/20] via 172.16.17.34, Ethernet1/2
C       172.16.17.32/27 is directly connected, Ethernet1/2
C       172.16.17.0/27 is directly connected, Ethernet1/0
i*L1 0.0.0.0/0 [115/10] via 172.16.17.34, Ethernet1/2
                [115/10] via 172.16.17.1, Ethernet1/0
```

Router G will choose the specific 156.26.0.0 route over the default route because of the longest match property of IP routing.

Comparing IS-IS and OSPF

IS-IS and OSPF are similar protocols. Both are hierarchical link-state interior routing protocols. Table 7-4 is a comparison of the major properties of IS-IS and OSPF.

Both IS-IS and OSPF are widely used in networks today. Usually IS-IS is deployed by Internet service providers (ISPs), whereas OSPF is typically used in enterprise networks.

Table 7-4   IS-IS and OSPF Comparison

	IS-IS	OSPF
Protocol Type	Link State	Link State
Routing Types	Interarea Intra Area	Level 1 Level 2
Routes	IP, ISO	IP Only
Backbone	Contiguous chain of L2 routers	Area 0
Area Significance	Router	Interface
Router ID	System ID	IP Address
Default Area Type	Totally Stubby	All routes in all areas
Router Types	Level 1 Level 2 Level 1-2	Internal No counterpart ABR, ASBR
Default Metric	10	Based on the interface bandwidth Metric = 100,000,000/bandwidth

Summary

Like OSPF, IS-IS has many complexities. The following list summarizes the fundamental properties of IS-IS:

- One or more IS-IS areas.

- If more than one IS-IS area is used, a backbone must be configured. An IS-IS backbone consists of a contiguous line of Level 2 capable IS-IS routers.

- Level 1 only routers maintain one database for their area. A default route is used to reach the nearest Level 2 router.

- Level 2 capable routers maintain a database for routes to reach all IS-IS areas.

- Link-state packets (LSPs) flood information about a router's interfaces throughout an IS-IS area.

- IS-IS databases within an area must be identical before a router can calculate the routes that are installed in the IP routing table.

- The Shortest Path First (SPF) algorithm is run on each area database maintained by a router. SPF determines the routes that are installed in the IP routing table.

- Routes can be summarized only between areas, not within an area.

- There are three types of IS-IS routers: Level 1 only, Level 2 only, and Level 1-2 capable.

- External routes can be summarized only on an ASBR.

- IS-IS routes can be summarized only on an IS-IS border router.

Chapter Review Questions

You can find the answers to these questions in Appendix A.

1. Describe the structure and format of an NSAP address.

2. Assume a router has a loopback address of 135.77.9.254. Convert the loopback address to an IS-IS system ID.

3. Describe the difference between an OSPF and IS-IS backbone.

4. In IS-IS, what does Level 1 routing mean?

5. What is the OSPF counterpart to Level 1 routing?

6. In IS-IS, what is the function of a Level 1-2 router?

7. What is the OSPF counterpart to a Level 1-2 IS-IS router?

8. What is the difference between the types of routes allowed by default into IS-IS and OSPF areas?

9. What is route leaking?

10. Compare IS-IS metrics with OSPF metrics.

11. What is the difference between an IS-IS narrow and wide metric?

References

Use the following references to learn more about the concepts described in this chapter:

- Martey, Abe. 2002. *IS-IS Network Design Solutions*. Indianapolis: Cisco Press.

- Cisco documentation, Cisco.com.

What You Will Learn

After reading this chapter, you should be able to

- ✔ Explain the Border Gateway Protocol (BGP)

- ✔ Understand the concepts, terminology, and operation of BGP

- ✔ Configure basic BGP on Cisco routers

CHAPTER 8

Border Gateway Protocol— The Glue That Holds the Internet Together

In 1991, the first website was developed for the Stanford Linear Accelerator Center. By 1993 there were approximately 600 websites. The number of websites grew to 10,000 by 1994, 100,000 by 1995, and more than 1 million by 1997. The number of websites continues to grow at a phenomenal rate, and today there are millions of websites accessible through the Internet. Millions of websites means there are millions of IP addresses— and a scalable IP routing protocol is needed to tie them all together to form the World Wide Web.

In Chapter 1, "Routing and Switching in Everyday Life," one of the systems you examined was the highway system. If you consider a house to be a website, and a city to be a company containing one or more websites, the highway system is what ties them all together. You used an interstate highway map to get to a particular city, and then used a city map to get to a specific location. The city map is analogous to using an interior routing protocol (RIP, IGRP, EIGRP, OSPF, or IS-IS) to determine a route within a specific organization. The interstate highway map is analogous to an exterior gateway protocol (EGP) used for Internet routing. The Border Gateway Protocol (BGP) is the protocol used today for Internet routing, and this chapter discusses the concepts and operation of BGP and how BGP is used spin the web that is the Internet.

Understanding the Need for BGP

When you get home from work, school, or play, many of you connect to the Internet. You may check your e-mail, see how your investments did that day, or just surf the Internet. Have you ever wondered how your e-mail gets to your computer or how your favorite website appears on your screen? If you have read the first seven chapters of this book, your answer should be "IP routing takes care of getting information to my computer." The interior gateway protocols (RIP, IGRP, EIGRP, OSPF, and IS-IS) cannot scale to the number of IP prefixes existing on the Internet. The interior protocols were designed for use within an organization, and their best path algorithms cannot handle the number of routes required for Internet routing. BGP uses a simple algorithm for determining the best path to a destination; using new properties of routes in addition to the network prefix and subnet mask. These new properties, or route attributes, along with BGP route summarization, allow BGP to scale to the number of routes required for Internet routing.

Figure 8-1 shows a simplified representation of the structure of the Internet. Service providers, such as your cable company, own a block or blocks of IP addresses. These IP addresses are assigned to enterprise customers such as businesses, universities, or individual users. There are many service providers around the world and each is assigned a unique autonomous system (AS) number, the use of which you will soon learn about in the later section entitled, "Autonomous System—AS-PATH." For example, the service provider assigned AS 1 owns the 156.26.0.0 Class B address space (156.26.0.0/24 to 156.26.255.0/24). The service provider is free to subnet this IP address block and assign subnets to customers. For the customers of AS 1 to reach any IP destination on the Internet, the entire world needs to know how to route an IP packet to the customers of this service provider; and the customers of AS 1 need to know how to route an IP packet from their networks to anywhere in the world. For Internet routing, you can eliminate interior routing protocols RIP version 1 (RIPv1) and IGRP because these protocols have too many limitations to use in an enterprise network, and there is no way you would use them for Internet routing. RIPv2 improves on RIPv1, but it has the limitations of a maximum hop count of 15 and a slow convergence time. A maximum hop count of 15 eliminates RIP from consideration for Internet routing. EIGRP, OSPF, and IS-IS are the recommended routing protocols to use in an enterprise network. They all have faster convergence time, and are able to determine a loop-free routing topology. The amount of time and computer resources a router needs to exchange routes and determine a loop-free topology depends on the number of network

prefixes that have to be dealt with. A protocol for Internet routing must be able to handle a large number of routes as shown in Example 8-1.

Figure 8-1   Simplified Representation of the Structure of the Internet

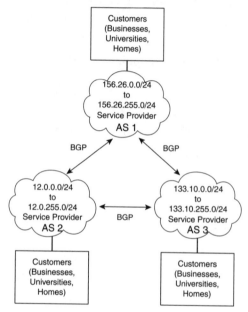

The output shown in Example 8-1 is from one of AT&T's Internet routers, and shows the number of Internet routes on the day I wrote this chapter (the number of routes increases everyday).

Example 8-1   Routing Table on an Internet Router

```
*******************************************************
        AT&T Enhanced Network Services
            (CERFnet)
            route-server
```

continues

Example 8-1 Routing Table on an Internet Router (continued)

```
**************************************************

route-server>show ip bgp summary | include network entries
127990 network entries and 383407 paths using 29796898 bytes of memory
```

As highlighted in the output, there are 127,990 network prefixes and 383,407 paths to reach these prefixes from this router. EIGRP, OSPF, and IS-IS would self-destruct if they were asked to handle this many prefixes. Why are there more paths than network prefixes? For redundancy and reliability, there are multiple paths that can be taken between any two endpoints on the Internet.

You need a simple and robust protocol that can handle the number of routes that exist on the Internet. That protocol is the *Border Gateway Protocol (BGP)*. Before you learn about the operation of BGP, you need to become familiar with BGP terminology and how BGP determines the best path to a network prefix.

BGP Attributes

The Interior Gateway Routing Protocols (IGRPs) that you have learned advertised a network prefix with a metric, or cost, for each prefix (RIPv1 and IGRP). In addition, RIPv2, EIGRP, OSPF, and IS-IS include subnet mask information along with the advertised network prefix. If there are multiple paths from a router to the same destination, the best path is the one with the total lowest cost or metric. Each of the interior protocols uses a different metric, and each protocol considers the route with the lowest total cost to be the best path.

BGP also advertises prefix and mask information to a neighboring BGP router; but these advertisements include other parameters, or attributes, BGP can use to determine a best path. There are four types of BGP attributes:

- **Well-known mandatory**—An attribute that must be advertised to and understood by all BGP neighbors.

- **Well-known discretionary**–An optional attribute that is not required to be advertised to a BGP neighbor.

- **Optional transitive**–If a BGP neighbor receives an attribute it does not understand, the attribute is passed on to other BGP neighbors.

- **Optional nontransitive**–If a BGP neighbor receives an attribute it does not understand, the attribute is not passed on to other BGP neighbors.

Table 8-1 lists the basic BGP attributes discussed in this chapter and their type. Table 8-1 is not a complete list of the BGP attributes. Additional BGP attributes and their use can be found in the references at the end of this chapter. The attributes listed in Table 8-1 can be used to determine a best path to a destination as discussed in the following sections.

Table 8-1 BGP Attributes and Their Attribute Type

Attribute Name	Attribute Type	Description
AS_PATH	Well-known mandatory	An ordered list of each AS that a BGP route advertisement has passed through
WEIGHT	Cisco defined attribute	Used to select a path from a router
LOCAL_PREF	Well-known discretionary	Used to select an exit path from the local AS
MULTI_EXIT_DISC	Optional nontransitive	Used to select a path into the local AS
ORIGIN	Well-known mandatory	Indicates how BGP learned the route IGP—Network statement EGP—Learned from an EBGP neighbor Incomplete—Learned through redistribution

continues

Table 8-1   BGP Attributes and Their Attribute Type (continued)

Attribute Name	Attribute Type	Description
NEXT_HOP	Well-known mandatory	EBGP—Set to the address of the interface used to communicate with an external neighbor IBGP—EBGP next hop is sent unchanged to IBGP neighbors
Community	Optional transitive	A number used to group routes so a policy can be applied to the group

Autonomous System Path Attribute—AS_PATH

The AS_PATH attribute is used by BGP for best path selection and routing loop detection. Every service provider is assigned a unique *autonomous system (AS)* number in the range 1 to 64,511. These AS numbers are registered and assigned in the same way that unique IP address blocks are assigned. Service providers can also use private AS numbers in the range 64,512 to 65,534, but the private AS numbers cannot be advertised on the Internet and are for internal use only. The private AS numbers are similar to the private IP address blocks such as the 10.0.0.0/8 private IP address space.

In Figure 8-2, there are four service providers with assigned AS numbers of 1, 2, 3, and 4. The service provider with AS number 1 is advertising the network prefix and mask of 156.26.32.0/24 to the service provider with AS number 2. Before the prefix and mask from AS 1 is advertised, the AS_PATH attribute is set to the value 1.

Figure 8-2   AS_PATH Attribute

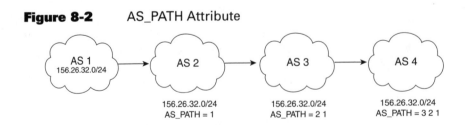

When the advertisement is received by AS 2, AS 2 knows the prefix originated in AS 1 because the last and only AS number in the AS_PATH attribute is equal to 1. AS 2 also knows that the prefix originated in AS 1 because there is only one AS number listed in the AS_PATH attribute. When AS 2 advertises the 156.26.32.0/24 prefix to AS 3, AS 2 will prepend, or put at the beginning, its own AS number in the AS_PATH attribute. When AS 3 receives the advertisement, the AS_PATH attribute now has a value of 2 1 with a space between the AS numbers. AS 3 knows the prefix originated in AS 1 (the last number in the attribute is 1), and the prefix has passed through AS 2. Finally, AS 3 prepends its AS number to the AS_PATH attribute, and advertises the prefix to AS 4. AS 4 receives an AS_PATH attribute of 3 2 1 for the 156.26.32.0/24 prefix.

If all the other BGP attributes are equal, the router with the shortest AS path is considered to be the best path. In Figure 8-2, there is only one advertisement for network 156.26.32.0/24. By default, it has to be the best path. If there are multiple paths, the AS_PATH attribute is used to select the best path. In Figure 8-3, AS 4 is now receiving two advertisements for network 156.26.32.0/24. The advertisement from AS 3 has an AS path length of 3, and the route from AS 5 has a path length of 2. Therefore, AS 4 considers the route through AS 5 to be the best route, and this is the route installed in the IP routing table.

Figure 8-3   Route with the Shortest AS Path Attribute Is the Best Path

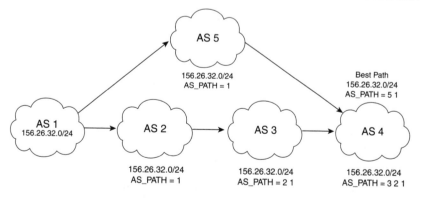

An AS path is an ordered list of the number of autonomous systems the advertisement has passed through. This is similar to the hop count used by RIP because an AS number in the path can be considered to be a hop toward the destination.

In addition to using the AS path to determine the best path to a particular IP prefix if there is more than one path, BGP also uses the AS_PATH attribute for loop detection.

In Figure 8-4, AS 4 is advertising the best path for 156.26.32.0/24 to AS 6. AS 6 advertises this prefix to AS 1 with an AS_PATH attribute of 6 4 5 1. When AS 1 receives the advertisement from AS 6, this route will be rejected because AS 1 is contained in the AS_PATH attribute. BGP routers reject any advertisement containing their own AS number.

Figure 8-4   BGP Loop Detection

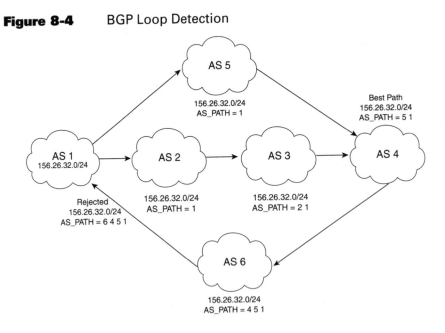

As mentioned earlier in this section, all things being equal, the AS_PATH attribute is used to select the best path. "All things" refer to other BGP attributes that can also influence the selection of the best path.

WEIGHT Attribute

The WEIGHT attribute is not defined in the BGP specification. Cisco has defined the WEIGHT attribute as another option that can be used for determining a best path to a destination. In Figure 8-5, AS 2 is receiving two advertisements for prefix 156.26.32.0/24. The advertisement from AS 3 has an AS path length of 3, and the advertisement from AS 1 has an AS path length of 2. By default, the weight attribute of all received BGP routes is 0, so AS 2 selects the route through AS 1 because it has the shortest AS_PATH attribute.

Figure 8-5   AS 2 Selects the Path to 156.26.32.0/24 Through AS 1 Because It Has the Shortest AS_PATH Attribute

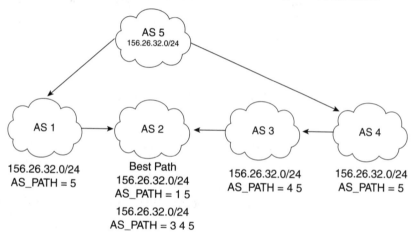

If you want a router in AS 2 to prefer the path through AS 3 instead of the path through AS 1, you can manipulate the WEIGHT attribute. The WEIGHT attribute is a 16-bit number having a value between 0 and 65,535, with a higher weight value taking precedence over a lower weight value. The WEIGHT attribute takes precedence over the AS_PATH attribute, and is used to influence the best path selection when there is more than one path to a particular destination. In Figure 8-6, a router in AS 2 has manipulated the WEIGHT attribute for the route received from AS 3. This path, although it has a longer AS_PATH attribute, will be considered the best path because of the higher WEIGHT attribute of the path.

Figure 8-6   WEIGHT Attribute

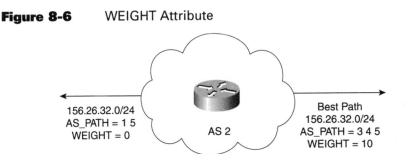

156.26.32.0/24
AS_PATH = 1 5
WEIGHT = 0

AS 2

Best Path
156.26.32.0/24
AS_PATH = 3 4 5
WEIGHT = 10

The WEIGHT attribute has only local significance. This means a router does not advertise the WEIGHT attribute to neighboring BGP routers. When a router receives a BGP prefix, the WEIGHT attribute is set to 0. Any BGP route originated by a router has a default weight attribute of 32,768.

Local Preference Attribute—LOCAL_PREF

The LOCAL_PREF attribute is similar to the WEIGHT attribute. When there is more than one route to a destination, the route with the highest LOCAL_PREF is preferred only if the WEIGHT attributes for the paths are the same. WEIGHT takes precedence over LOCAL_PREF and LOCAL_PREF takes precedence over the AS_PATH attribute. By default, the LOCAL_PREF attribute has a value of 100 and a higher value is preferred over a lower value. LOCAL_PREF is a 32-bit number with a value in the range of 0 to 4,294,967,295.

In Figure 8-7, Routers A and B have two paths to network 156.26.32.0/24. Router A is using the default LOCAL_PREF value of 100 for both paths. Router B has set the LOCAL_PREF attribute for the path shown to 200. Therefore, Router B prefers the path through AS 3. Unlike the WEIGHT attribute, the LOCAL_PREF attribute is advertised throughout the local AS. Router A receives an advertisement for prefix 156.26.32.0/24 from Router B with a LOCAL_PREF of 200. Therefore, Router A also prefers the path through AS 3 to reach the network prefix 156.26.32.0/24.

Figure 8-7   LOCAL_PREF Attribute

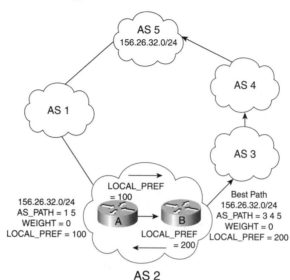

Metric or MULTI_EXIT_DISC (MED) Attribute

The WEIGHT attribute is used to prefer a path from a particular router. The
LOCAL_PREF attribute is used to prefer a path leaving a particular AS. The metric, or MULTI_EXIT_DISC (multi-exit discriminator or MED), is used to prefer a
path into an AS. MED is a 32-bit number having a value between 0 and
4,294,967,295 with a lower value being preferred over a higher value.

In Figure 8-8, AS 5 owns the network prefix 156.26.32.0/24 and there are two
paths to reach this prefix from AS 1. AS 5 wants AS 1 to use the path on the right
for traffic from AS 1 to AS 5. AS 5 sets the MED on the left to any value higher
than the default value of 0 and advertises this value to AS 1.

Figure 8-8 MED Attribute

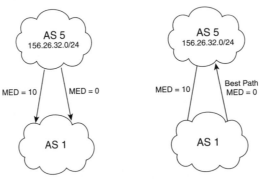

If the other BGP attributes are equal, AS 1 prefers the path on the right to AS 5 because of the lower value of the MED for this path. For the attributes you have seen so far, WEIGHT takes preference over LOACL_PREF, and LOCAL_PREF takes precedence over the shortest AS path. If WEIGHT, LOCAL_PREF, and the AS_PATH attributes are the same for the paths, MED is used to make a best path determination.

ORIGIN Attribute

The ORIGIN attribute indicates one of the three sources of a route in the BGP routing table. The three ways BGP can learn a route are

- Using the **network** statement
- From an EBGP neighbor
- Through redistribution

The **network** statement is used to cause BGP to advertise a route in the local IP routing table to a BGP neighbor. Routes injected into BGP through the **network** statement have their ORIGIN attribute set to IGP, indicating the route is interior to the originating AS.

There are two types of BGP connections. One is a connection between BGP routers in the same AS. This type of connection is referred to as *Internal BGP (IBGP)*. A connection between routers in different autonomous systems is called *External BGP (EBGP)*, and it is the second type of BGP connection. (See Figure 8-9.)

Figure 8-9   IBGP and EBGP

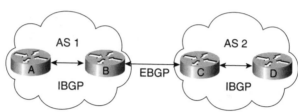

Routes learned from an EBGP neighbor have an ORIGIN attribute of EGP. Any routes that are redistributed into BGP have an ORIGIN attribute of incomplete. In order of preference, IGP routes are preferred over EGP routes and EGP routes are preferred over incomplete routes. EBGP routes are preferred over IBGP routes.

NEXT_HOP Attribute

When a router advertises a prefix to an EBGP neighbor, the NEXT_HOP attribute is set to the IP address of the interface used to connect to the neighbor. When a BGP router advertises a route learned through EBGP to an IBGP neighbor, the NEXT_HOP attribute is not modified. (See Figure 8-10.)

When a router receives a route from a BGP neighbor, the first attribute that is checked is the NEXT_HOP attribute. If the NEXT_HOP is not reachable (not in the local IP routing table), the route is rejected. EBGP neighbors are usually directly connected by a physical interface, so the NEXT_HOP will be in the IP routing table as a connected interface. IBGP neighbors do not have to be directly connected. In Figure 8-10, Router B accepts the route from Router A because the NEXT_HOP network is a directly connected network. Router C will accept the route from Router B if the NEXT_HOP network is in the IP routing table on Router C.

Figure 8-10   NEXT_HOP Attribute

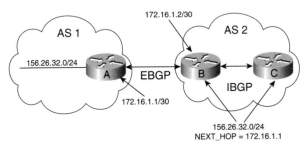

Community Attribute

A router has the ability to manipulate routes sent to or received from a neighbor. All routing protocols can perform route filtering on sent or received routes. With output route filtering, a router can prevent specific routes from being advertised to a neighbor. With input route filtering, a router can reject, or filter out, routes received from a neighbor. For protocols other than BGP, route filtering is based on a prefix and mask. The router is configured with one or more conditions consisting of a prefix and a mask, and any routes that match one of the conditions will be filtered. For example, the condition using the prefix mask combination 156.26.32.0/24 can filter any route that matches 156.26.32.0/24, or is a subnet of this IP address block.

Input and output route filtering can also be used with BGP, but BGP has additional route attributes that can be used to identify the routes to be filtered or manipulated. Instead of simply filtering a route, you may want to manipulate one or more of the attributes associated with a BGP route. In Figure 8-11, AS 1 is receiving 11 routes from three different autonomous systems. Assume AS 1 wants to either filter out (reject) the boxed routes in Figure 8-11, or modify one or more of the same attributes of the indicated routes. You can accomplish this by using four conditions that identify the prefix/mask pairs that you are interested in filtering or manipulating.

Figure 8-11   Filtering Using Prefix and Mask Pairs

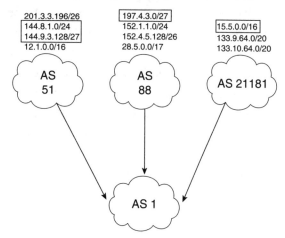

You need to check for the following conditions:

- Does the route match 144.8.1.0/24?

- Does the route match 144.9.3.128/27?

- Does the route match 197.4.3.0/27?

- Does the route match 15.5.0.0/16?

If a received route matches one of the four conditions, filter or manipulate the selected parameters of the route. If the received route does not match one of the four conditions, accept the route as is.

For this example, you did not have to worry about too many conditions; there are only four. But there are more than 100,000 BGP routes in the Internet routing table, and if you want to apply the same filter to a large number of routes, your list of conditions could grow to a size that would be difficult to manage.

Although you can filter or manipulate BGP routes based on prefix/mask combinations, you can use another technique to reduce the number of conditions the router needs to check to determine if a particular route is a candidate for filtering or manipulation. You could contact your friends in AS 51, 88, and 21181, and ask them to do you a favor. That favor is to attach a number to the routes you are interested in manipulating. The number you pick is 4, and you ask your friends to send only the number 4 with the routes you have identified. In BGP, this extra number is called a ***community attribute,*** and it is used to group routes so a common policy can be applied to all routes belonging to the same community. (See Figure 8-12.) Therefore, instead of having to configure 4 conditions, or 400 conditions, you need only to configure one condition. That condition is to match any route that has a particular community value. For this example, that community value is 4.

Figure 8-12   BGP Community Attribute

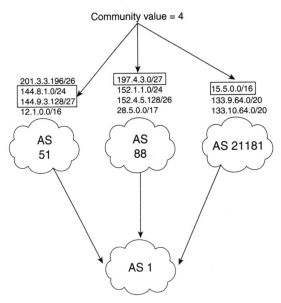

Basic BGP Configuration—EBGP

External BGP (EBGP) neighbors are usually directly connected. In Figure 8-13, you configure EBGP between Routers A and B and investigate the operation and configuration of EBGP neighbors.

Figure 8-13   Configuring EBGP

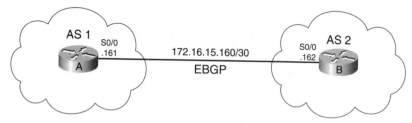

The first step in configuring EBGP is to configure a loopback interface on Routers A and B. (See Example 8-2.) As with OSPF, the IP address assigned to the loopback interface is used as the BGP router ID.

Example 8-2   Configuring Loopback Interfaces on Routers A and B

```
Router A
interface Loopback0
 ip address 172.16.15.254 255.255.255.255

Router B
interface Loopback0
 ip address 172.16.16.254 255.255.255.255
```

The next step is to enable the BGP process on both routers. (See Example 8-3.)

Example 8-3   Enabling the BGP Process on the Routers

```
Router A
router bgp 1
 neighbor 172.16.15.162 remote-as 2

Router B
router bgp 2
 neighbor 172.16.15.161 remote-as 1
```

The general form of the command to enable the BGP process is **router bgp** *as-number. as-number* is the number that has been assigned to the AS. Only one AS number can be assigned to a service provider, so there can be only one BGP process configured on a router. The command **neighbor** *neighbor-ip-address* enables BGP on an interface. The interface that is enabled for BGP is determined from the

IP routing table. The IP routing table determines the interface used to reach the neighbor's IP address. For EBGP, the neighbors are usually directly connected, so the interface used is the one directly connected to the neighbor. For the configuration in Figure 8-13, that interface is serial 0/0 on both Routers A and B. This differs from the interior routing protocols.

The protocols RIP, IGRP, EIGRP, and OSPF use a **network** statement under the routing process configuration to determine the interfaces that are enabled for a protocol, and which prefixes and masks are advertised. The enabled interfaces for the interior routing protocols are also used for neighbor discovery (EIGRP, OSPF, and IS-IS). Interfaces are enabled for IS-IS under the interface configuration using the **ip router isis** command. With EBGP you don't need to discover EBGP neighbors because you already know the interface used to reach the neighbor. Therefore, you can form an EBGP neighbor relationship without advertising any routes. When EBGP is enabled on an interface, the routers attempt to form a BGP relationship by progressing through the following states:

- **Idle State**—Initialize a TCP connection with the BGP neighbor.

- **Connect State**—Wait for a TCP connection to be established with the BGP neighbor. If a TCP connection is established, send an OPEN message and transition to the OpenSent State. If a connection timeout occurs, transition to the Active State.

- **Active State**—Wait for a TCP connection to be established with the BGP neighbor. If a TCP connection is established, transition to the Connect State.

- **OpenSent State**—Wait for an OPEN message from the BGP neighbor. If errors occur, transition to the Idle State. If an OPEN message is received from the BGP neighbor, transition to the OpenConfirm State.

- **OpenConfirm State**—Wait for a KEEPALIVE message from the BGP neighbor. When a KEEPALIVE is received, transition to the Established State.

- **Established State**—Exchange routing information.

In the Connect State, a BGP router sends an OPEN message to each neighbor. The OPEN message identifies a router to a neighbor, and is used for parameter exchange. The parameters exchanged in the OPEN message follow:

- Version number (the current BGP version number is 4)

- AS number

- Hold time (the time a BGP router will wait before declaring a neighbor down)

- BGP router ID

After a BGP router sends an OPEN message to a neighbor, the router transitions to the OpenSent State, and waits to receive an OPEN message from the neighbor. When the OPEN message is received from the neighbor, the routers transition to the OpenConfirm State, and wait for a KEEPALIVE message. By default, KEEPALIVE messages are sent every 60 seconds, and are used to verify the neighbor is still there. After the neighbors have received a KEEPALIVE message, the routers transition to the Established State, and exchange KEEPALIVE, UPDATE, and NOTIFICATION messages.

An UPDATE message advertises or withdraws network prefixes. An UPDATE message advertises the following:

- IP prefixes and subnet mask lengths; also referred to as Network Layer Reachability Information (NLRI)

- BGP attributes

- Withdrawn routes

A NOTIFICATION message is used when an error occurs that causes the BGP session to be shut down.

If the BGP neighbors do not reach the Established State, there is a problem. The problem could be as simple as one of the BGP neighbors has not yet been configured. For this case, the configured neighbor will be in the Active State waiting to create a TCP connection with the neighbor. There could be errors in the BGP configuration. Even for the most basic BGP configuration there can be up to six errors. The BGP AS numbers may be wrong (two errors), the neighbor's IP address may be wrong (two errors), or the neighbor's remote-AS number may be wrong (two errors). If the configuration parameters are correct, the EBGP neighbors should reach the Established State as shown in the partial listing in Example 8-4.

Example 8-4   Verifying the BGP Connection

```
A#show ip bgp neighbors
BGP neighbor is 172.16.15.162,  remote AS 2, external link
  BGP version 4, remote router ID 172.16.16.254
  BGP state = Established, up for 02:02:11
!Output omitted for brevity
```

The EBGP neighbor for Router A is 172.16.15.162. This is the IP address used in the **neighbor** command on Router A. The neighbor's AS number is 2 and this is an external link because Router A is in AS 1. The BGP version number is 4, which is the current version in use today. The BGP state is Established, and any other state indicates either the routers are still transitioning to the Established State or there are configuration errors. The remote router ID is the BGP router ID of the neighbor. In this case, the router ID is taken from the address of the loopback interface, similar to OSPF. Finally, the keepalive interval is 60 seconds. If a KEEPALIVE message is not received from a neighbor within the holdtime (180 seconds), the neighbor is declared down.

Advertising IP Prefixes

The EBGP neighbors are in the Established State, but neither router is advertising routing information. This is in contrast to the interior routing protocols where neighbor discovery and route advertisement are both tied to the use of the **network** statement. With BGP, there are three ways IP prefixes can be injected into the BGP routing table, as follows:

- **network** command
- Route redistribution
- From a BGP neighbor

Figure 8-14 illustrates the three methods.

Figure 8-14 Prefixes Enter the Local BGP Routing Table Using the **network** Command, Route Redistribution, or from a BGP Neighbor

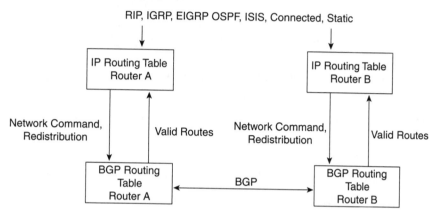

Using the network Command to Inject Routes

The first way to enter prefixes into the BGP routing table is using the **network** command under the BGP configuration. The **network** command is used to transfer prefixes from the IP routing table to the BGP routing table as BGP routes. Prefixes in the IP routing table are learned from a dynamic interior routing protocol (RIP, IGRP, EIGRP, OSPF, or IS-IS), by configuring static routes, or from the IP address and mask assigned to a directly connected interface. The IP routing table on Router A contains only connected routes because no other IP routing protocols have been configured, as shown in Example 8-5.

Example 8-5 Router A Contains Only Connected Routes

```
A#show ip route
Codes: C - connected, S - static, I - IGRP, R - RIP, M - mobile, B - BGP
       D - EIGRP, EX - EIGRP external, O - OSPF, IA - OSPF inter area
       N1 - OSPF NSSA external type 1, N2 - OSPF NSSA external type 2
       E1 - OSPF external type 1, E2 - OSPF external type 2, E - EGP
       i - IS-IS, L1 - IS-IS level-1, L2 - IS-IS level-2, ia - IS-IS inter area
       * - candidate default, U - per-user static route, o - ODR
       P - periodic downloaded static route
```

continues

Example 8-5 Router A Contains Only Connected Routes (continued)

```
Gateway of last resort is not set

     172.16.0.0/16 is variably subnetted, 4 subnets, 3 masks
C        172.16.15.160/30 is directly connected, Serial0/0
C        172.16.15.128/27 is directly connected, Ethernet0/0
C        172.16.15.254/32 is directly connected, Loopback0
C        172.16.15.64/27 is directly connected, Ethernet0/1
```

The operation of the **network**command depends on the state of autosummariza-tion configured under the BGP routing process. By default, autosummarization is enabled, so we examine this case first. The format of the network command is

network*prefix* **mask** *subnet-mask*

The *subnet-mask* parameter is optional. If the *subnet-mask* parameter is not used, BGP assumes a classful prefix. With autosummarization enabled, the **network** command can be used to inject a classful prefix into the BGP routing table. For this operation to be successful, there must exist at least one subnet of the classful prefix in the IP routing table. The routing table on Router A contains subnets of 172.16.0.0/16. Therefore, you can inject the classful prefix 172.16.0.0/16 using the following form of the **network**command:

```
router bgp 1
network 172.16.0.0
 neighbor 172.16.15.162 remote-as 2
```

You should see this classful prefix in the BGP routing table on Router A. (See Example 8-6.)

Example 8-6 BGP Routing Table on Router A

```
A#show ip bgp
BGP table version is 8, local router ID is 172.16.15.254
Status codes: s suppressed, d damped, h history, * valid, > best, i - internal
Origin codes: i - IGP, e - EGP, ? - incomplete

   Network          Next Hop          Metric LocPrf Weight Path
*> 172.16.0.0       0.0.0.0                0           32768 i
```

In Example 8-6, a next hop of 0.0.0.0 and a blank AS path attribute indicate that 172.16.0.0 originates on Router A. You can also see that the Metric, or MED, is 0 and the WEIGHT is 32768 (default values). After a valid route is injected into the BGP routing table, the route will be advertised to Router B as shown in Example 8-7.

Example 8-7   BGP Routing Table on Router B

```
B#show ip bgp
BGP table version is 4, local router ID is 172.16.16.254
Status codes: s suppressed, d damped, h history, * valid, > best, i - internal
Origin codes: i - IGP, e - EGP, ? - incomplete

   Network          Next Hop          Metric LocPrf Weight Path
*> 172.16.0.0       172.16.15.161          0           0 1 i
```

In Example 8-7, the 172.16.0.0/16 prefix has been successfully advertised to Router B. Notice that the NEXT_HOP attribute is equal to the IP address used to reach Router B, the AS path attribute is 1, and the Metric and WEIGHT attributes have a value of 0. This BGP route is a valid route and is transferred to the IP routing table on Router B, as shown in Example 8-8.

Example 8-8   IP Routing Table on Router B

```
B#show ip route
Codes: C - connected, S - static, I - IGRP, R - RIP, M - mobile, B - BGP
       D - EIGRP, EX - EIGRP external, O - OSPF, IA - OSPF inter area
       N1 - OSPF NSSA external type 1, N2 - OSPF NSSA external type 2
       E1 - OSPF external type 1, E2 - OSPF external type 2, E - EGP
       i - IS-IS, L1 - IS-IS level-1, L2 - IS-IS level-2, ia - IS-IS inter area
       * - candidate default, U - per-user static route, o - ODR
       P - periodic downloaded static route

Gateway of last resort is not set

     172.16.0.0/16 is variably subnetted, 4 subnets, 3 masks
C       172.16.16.164/30 is directly connected, Serial0/1
C       172.16.15.160/30 is directly connected, Serial0/0
C       172.16.16.254/32 is directly connected, Loopback0
B       172.16.0.0/16 [20/0] via 172.16.15.161, 00:09:41
```

You have successfully advertised your first BGP route. From the routing table, you see the administrative distance of EBGP is 20 and the cost or metric for the

BGP route is 0. BGP does not use a cost to determine the best path but instead uses the BGP attributes of WEIGHT, LOCAL_PREF, AS_PATH, MED, and ORIGIN.

Cisco recommends that you disable autosummarization when using BGP. This is accomplished using the **no auto-summary** command under the BGP configuration, as shown in Example 8-9.

Example 8-9   Disabling Autosummarization

```
Router A
router bgp 1
 network 172.16.0.0
 neighbor 172.16.15.162 remote-as 2
 no auto-summary

Router B
router bgp 2

 neighbor 172.16.15.161 remote-as 1
 no auto-summary
```

What happens when you disable autosummarization on the BGP routers? Will network 172.16.0.0/16 be advertised? If you examine the BGP table on Routers A and B and the IP routing table on Router B, you see that this prefix is no longer being advertised. (See Example 8-10.)

Example 8-10   Routing Tables on Routers A and B

```
A#show ip bgp
!no output

B#show ip bgp
!no output

B#show ip route
     172.16.0.0/16 is variably subnetted, 3 subnets, 2 masks
C       172.16.16.164/30 is directly connected, Serial0/1
C       172.16.15.160/30 is directly connected, Serial0/0
C       172.16.16.254/32 is directly connected, Loopback0
```

When autosummarization is disabled, this changes the operation of the **network** command. The new rule is that the prefix and mask used with the **network** command must exactly match a prefix and mask in the IP routing table. If there is not an exact match, the route will not be transferred to the BGP routing table. The command used was **network 172.16.0.0** and the router now looks for an exact match in the IP routing table. There are subnets of 172.16.0.0 in the IP routing table on Router A, but not the specific 172.16.0.0/16 route. To inject the connected networks on Router A into the BGP routing table, you must use the exact prefix and mask with the **network** command. Router A has four directly connected networks that you want to turn into BGP routes. (See Example 8-11.)

Example 8-11 Router A's Directly Connected Routes

```
A#show ip route | include directly connected
C        172.16.15.160/30 is directly connected, Serial0/0
C        172.16.15.128/27 is directly connected, Ethernet0/0
C        172.16.15.254/32 is directly connected, Loopback0
C        172.16.15.64/27 is directly connected, Ethernet0/1
```

The **network** commands needed to inject these prefixes into BGP are shown in Example 8-12.

Example 8-12 Required **network** Commands When Autosummary Is
Disabled

```
Router A
router bgp 1
 network 172.16.15.64 mask 255.255.255.224
 network 172.16.15.128 mask 255.255.255.224
 network 172.16.15.160 mask 255.255.255.252
 network 172.16.15.254 mask 255.255.255.255
 neighbor 172.16.15.162 remote-as 2
 no auto-summary
```

You should now see four prefixes in the BGP routing tables on Routers A and B. (See Example 8-13.)

Example 8-13 Four Prefixes in Router A and B Routing
Tables

```
A#show ip bgp
BGP table version is 13, local router ID is 172.16.15.254
Status codes: s suppressed, d damped, h history, * valid, > best, i - internal
Origin codes: i - IGP, e - EGP, ? - incomplete

   Network          Next Hop            Metric LocPrf Weight Path
*> 172.16.15.64/27  0.0.0.0                  0         32768 i
```

continues

Example 8-13 Four Prefixes in Router A and B Routing
Tables (continued)

```
*> 172.16.15.128/27 0.0.0.0               0           32768 i
*> 172.16.15.160/30 0.0.0.0               0           32768 i
*> 172.16.15.254/32 0.0.0.0               0           32768 I


B#show ip bgp
BGP table version is 9, local router ID is 172.16.16.254
Status codes: s suppressed, d damped, h history, * valid, > best, i - internal
Origin codes: i - IGP, e - EGP, ? - incomplete

   Network          Next Hop         Metric LocPrf Weight Path
*> 172.16.15.64/27   172.16.15.161         0             0 1 i
*> 172.16.15.128/27 172.16.15.161          0             0 1 i
*> 172.16.15.160/30 172.16.15.161          0             0 1 i
*> 172.16.15.254/32 172.16.15.161          0             0 1 i
```

Example 8-14 verifies the BGP routes have been transferred to the IP routing table
on Router B.

Example 8-14 IP Routing Table on Router B

```
B#show ip route
     172.16.0.0/16 is variably subnetted, 6 subnets, 3 masks
C       172.16.16.164/30 is directly connected, Serial0/1
C       172.16.15.160/30 is directly connected, Serial0/0
B       172.16.15.128/27 [20/0] via 172.16.15.161, 00:02:36
B       172.16.15.254/32 [20/0] via 172.16.15.161, 00:02:36
C       172.16.16.254/32 is directly connected, Loopback0
B       172.16.15.64/27 [20/0] via 172.16.15.161, 00:02:36
```

There are four prefixes in the BGP routing table on Router B, but only three BGP
learned prefixes in the IP routing table. Router A is advertising network
172.16.15.160/30 to Router B via BGP. This is a directly connected network on
Router B, so it is in the IP routing table as a connected network and not a BGP
learned prefix. (See Example 8-15.)

Example 8-15   Network Between Routers A and B Is Directly Connected

```
B#show ip route
        172.16.0.0/16 is variably subnetted, 6 subnets, 3 masks
C          172.16.16.164/30 is directly connected, Serial0/1
C          172.16.15.160/30 is directly connected, Serial0/0
B          172.16.15.128/27 [20/0] via 172.16.15.161, 00:02:36
B          172.16.15.254/32 [20/0] via 172.16.15.161, 00:02:36
C          172.16.16.254/32 is directly connected, Loopback0
B          172.16.15.64/27 [20/0] via 172.16.15.161, 00:02:36
```

Using Redistribution to Inject Routes

The second method for injecting routes into the BGP routing table is to use redistribution. On Router A, re-enable autosummarization using the **auto-summary** command, and delete the network statements using the **no** form of the **network** command. (See Example 8-16.)

Example 8-16   Removing Commands from the Configuration

```
Router A
router bgp 1
 no network 172.16.15.64 mask 255.255.255.224
 no network 172.16.15.128 mask 255.255.255.224
 no network 172.16.15.160 mask 255.255.255.252
 no network 172.16.15.254 mask 255.255.255.255
 neighbor 172.16.15.162 remote-as 2
 auto-summary
```

Configure Router A to inject the connected networks into BGP using redistribution, as shown in Example 8-17.

Example 8-17   Configuring Redistribution

```
Router A
router bgp 1
 redistribute connected
 neighbor 172.16.15.162 remote-as 2
```

The connected routes should now be in the BGP routing table on Router A, as shown in Example 8-18.

Example 8-18 Connected Routes in Router A's BGP Routing Table

```
A#show ip bgp
BGP table version is 2, local router ID is 172.16.15.254
Status codes: s suppressed, d damped, h history, * valid, > best, i - internal
Origin codes: i - IGP, e - EGP, ? - incomplete

   Network          Next Hop          Metric LocPrf Weight Path
*> 172.16.0.0       0.0.0.0                0            32768 ?
```

Notice that the BGP routing table has just one route. When autosummarization is enabled, BGP automatically summarizes redistributed routes to a classful boundary. All of the connected interfaces on Router A are subnets of the Class B address block 172.16.0.0/16 so Router A automatically summarizes the connected networks. Disable autosummarization on Router A so the specific prefixes assigned to the connected interfaces are injected into BGP. (See Example 8-19.)

Example 8-19 Disabling Autosummarization on Router A

```
Router A
router bgp 1
 redistribute connected
 neighbor 172.16.15.162 remote-as 2
 no auto-summary
```

The specific prefixes and masks for the connected networks should now be in the BGP routing tables on Routers A and B, and in the IP routing table on Router B. (See Example 8-20.)

Example 8-20 Verifying the Redistributed Routes

```
A#show ip bgp
BGP table version is 7, local router ID is 172.16.15.254
Status codes: s suppressed, d damped, h history, * valid, > best, i - internal
Origin codes: i - IGP, e - EGP, ? - incomplete

   Network            Next Hop        Metric LocPrf Weight Path
*> 172.16.15.64/27    0.0.0.0              0            32768 ?
*> 172.16.15.128/27   0.0.0.0              0            32768 ?
*> 172.16.15.160/30   0.0.0.0              0            32768 ?
*> 172.16.15.254/32   0.0.0.0              0            32768 ?
```

Example 8-20 Verifying the Redistributed Routes (continued)

```
B#show ip bgp
BGP table version is 21, local router ID is 172.16.16.254
Status codes: s suppressed, d damped, h history, * valid, > best, i - internal
Origin codes: i - IGP, e - EGP, ? - incomplete

   Network          Next Hop        Metric LocPrf Weight Path
*> 172.16.15.64/27  172.16.15.161        0          0 1 ?
*> 172.16.15.128/27 172.16.15.161        0          0 1 ?
*> 172.16.15.160/30 172.16.15.161        0          0 1 ?
*> 172.16.15.254/32 172.16.15.161        0          0 1 ?

B#show ip route
     172.16.0.0/16 is variably subnetted, 6 subnets, 3 masks
C       172.16.16.164/30 is directly connected, Serial0/1
C       172.16.15.160/30 is directly connected, Serial0/0
B       172.16.15.128/27 [20/0] via 172.16.15.161, 00:01:44
B       172.16.15.254/32 [20/0] via 172.16.15.161, 00:01:44
C       172.16.16.254/32 is directly connected, Loopback0
B       172.16.15.64/27 [20/0] via 172.16.15.161, 00:01:44
```

You can see from the BGP routing tables on Routers A and B that the redistributed routes have an origin of ? or incomplete.

Using BGP to Inject Routes

The final method of injecting routes into the BGP routing table is through BGP itself. You have seen this on Router B because the routes in Router B's BGP routing table were learned through EBGP from Router A.

The network in Figure 8-15 demonstrates additional EBGP properties, and illustrates the BGP AS_PATH attribute. An additional AS has been added as a BGP neighbor to Router B. The BGP configuration on Router B contains the new neighbor in AS 3. (See Example 8-21.)

Figure 8-15 EBGP Route Advertisement

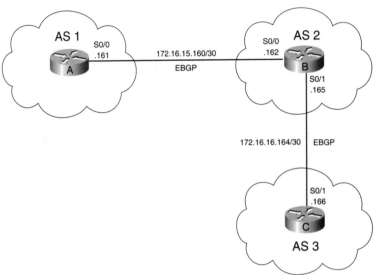

Example 8-21 New Neighbor for Router B

```
Router B
router bgp 2
 neighbor 172.16.15.161 remote-as 1
 neighbor 172.16.16.166 remote-as 3
 no auto-summary

Router C
router bgp 3

 neighbor 172.16.16.165 remote-as 2
```

Router B in AS 2 advertises the prefixes learned through EBGP from Router A to Router C. (See Example 8-22.)

Example 8-22 BGP and IP Routing Tables on Router C

```
C#show ip bgp
BGP table version is 5, local router ID is 172.16.17.254
Status codes: s suppressed, d damped, h history, * valid, > best, i - internal
Origin codes: i - IGP, e - EGP, ? - incomplete

  Network          Next Hop           Metric LocPrf Weight Path
```

Example 8-22 BGP and IP Routing Tables on Router C (continued)

```
*> 172.16.15.64/27   172.16.16.165                          0 2 1 ?
*> 172.16.15.128/27  172.16.16.165                          0 2 1 ?
*> 172.16.15.160/30  172.16.16.165                          0 2 1 ?
*> 172.16.15.254/32  172.16.16.165                          0 2 1 ?

C#show ip route
     172.16.0.0/16 is variably subnetted, 7 subnets, 3 masks
C       172.16.16.164/30 is directly connected, Serial0/1
B       172.16.15.160/30 [20/0] via 172.16.16.165, 00:12:21
B       172.16.15.128/27 [20/0] via 172.16.16.165, 00:12:21
B       172.16.15.254/32 [20/0] via 172.16.16.165, 00:12:21
C       172.16.17.254/32 is directly connected, Loopback0
C       172.16.17.32/27 is directly connected, Ethernet0/0
B       172.16.15.64/27 [20/0] via 172.16.16.165, 00:12:21
```

The AS_PATH attribute on Router C has a value of 2 1, as expected. One of the main points of this exercise was to demonstrate that an EBGP router advertises routes learned from one EBGP neighbor to another EBGP neighbor. The other main point is Router B sets the NEXT_HOP attribute to the IP address of the interface it is using to communicate with Router C. In the next section, you learn this is not the case when using internal or IBGP.

Basic BGP Configuration—IBGP

The network in Figure 8-16 will be used to investigate the configuration and operation of Internal BGP (IBGP). Router D has an EBGP connection to AS 2 and IBGP connections to the routers in AS 1.

Figure 8-16 IBGP and EBGP Connections

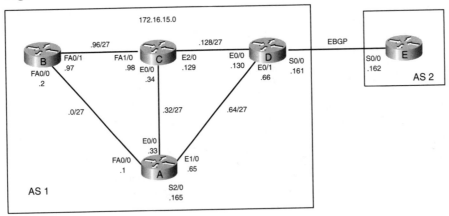

EBGP and IBGP use the same set of configuration commands for enabling the BGP process and for advertising network prefixes. The differences between EBGP and IBGP are in their operation, and not in their configuration. To begin, EBGP is configured between Routers D and E with Router E advertising its directly connected interfaces using route redistribution. (See Example 8-23.)

Example 8-23 Configuring EBGP Between Routers D and E

```
Router D
router bgp 1

 neighbor 172.16.15.162 remote-as 2
 no auto-summary

Router E
router bgp 2
 redistribute connected
 neighbor 172.16.15.161 remote-as 1
 no auto-summary
```

Router D should have the prefixes advertised by Router E in both the BGP and IP routing tables. (See Example 8-24.)

Example 8-24   Router D BGP and IP Routing Tables

```
D#show ip bgp
BGP table version is 4, local router ID is 172.16.15.254
Status codes: s suppressed, d damped, h history, * valid, > best, i - internal
Origin codes: i - IGP, e - EGP, ? - incomplete

   Network          Next Hop          Metric LocPrf Weight Path
*> 172.16.15.160/30 172.16.15.162         0             0 2 ?
*> 172.16.16.164/30 172.16.15.162         0             0 2 ?
*> 172.16.16.254/32 172.16.15.162         0             0 2 ?

D#show ip route
     172.16.0.0/16 is variably subnetted, 6 subnets, 3 masks
B       172.16.16.164/30 [20/0] via 172.16.15.162, 00:27:23
C       172.16.15.160/30 is directly connected, Serial0/0
C       172.16.15.128/27 is directly connected, Ethernet0/0
C       172.16.15.254/32 is directly connected, Loopback0
B       172.16.16.254/32 [20/0] via 172.16.15.162, 00:27:23
C       172.16.15.64/27 is directly connected, Ethernet0/1
```

Configuring IBGP between Routers C and D is no different than configuring
EBGP except the AS numbers on Routers C and D are the same. (See Example 8-25.)

Example 8-25   Configuring IBGP Between Routers C and Router D

```
Router C
router bgp 1
 neighbor 172.16.15.130 remote-as 1
 no auto-summary

Router D
router bgp 1
 neighbor 172.16.15.129 remote-as 1
 neighbor 172.16.15.162 remote-as 2
 no auto-summary
```

After the IBGP processes and neighbors are configured, check to see if the neighbors have established a BGP neighbor relationship. (See Example 8-26.). If you
use the **show ip bgp neighbors,** the router displays all BGP neighbors. To use the
command to display one neighbor, use the neighbor's IP address.

Example 8-26   Verifying a Specific BGP Neighbor

```
D#show ip bgp neighbors 172.16.15.129
BGP neighbor is 172.16.15.129,  remote AS 1, internal link
  BGP version 4, remote router ID 172.16.15.253
  BGP state = Established, up for 00:28:24
  Last read 00:00:24, hold time is 180, keepalive interval is 60 seconds
!Output omitted for brevity
```

Routers C and D have established an IBGP neighbor relationship indicated by "internal link" displayed in the output in Example 8-26. Router D should be advertising the prefixes received from Router E to Router C as shown in Example 8-27.

Example 8-27   BGP Routing Table on Router C

```
C#show ip bgp
BGP table version is 1, local router ID is 172.16.15.253
Status codes: s suppressed, d damped, h history, * valid, > best, i - internal
Origin codes: i - IGP, e - EGP, ? - incomplete

   Network          Next Hop        Metric LocPrf Weight Path
* i172.16.15.160/30 172.16.15.162        0    100      0 2 ?
* i172.16.16.164/30 172.16.15.162        0    100      0 2 ?
* i172.16.16.254/32 172.16.15.162        0    100      0 2 ?
```

Verify that the BGP routes have been transferred to the IP routing table on Router C. (See Example 8-28.)

Example 8-28   IP Routing Table on Router C

```
C#show ip route
      172.16.0.0/16 is variably subnetted, 5 subnets, 3 masks
C        172.16.15.128/27 is directly connected, Ethernet2/0
C        172.16.15.253/32 is directly connected, Loopback0
C        172.16.15.32/27 is directly connected, Ethernet0/0
C        172.16.9.0/30 is directly connected, Serial0/1
C        172.16.15.96/27 is directly connected, FastEthernet1/0
```

The routes have not been transferred from the BGP routing table to the IP routing table on Router C. Any idea what the problem is? If you look at one of the entries in the BGP routing table on Routers C and D, you will notice a slight difference, as highlighted in Example 8-29.

Example 8-29 NEXT_HOP Attribute Is Unchanged by IBGP

```
Router D
*> 172.16.15.160/30 172.16.15.162            0            0 2 ?
Router C
*  i172.16.15.160/30 172.16.15.162           0    100      0 2 ?
```

Both routers have the same next hop for network 172.16.15.160/30, but Router D
considers the route valid (*>) and Router C considers the route valid (*), but there
is not a best path to the prefix. The specifics of the route can be checked using the
show ip bgp*ip-prefix* command on Router C. (See Example 8-30.)

Example 8-30 The NEXT_HOP Is Unknown to Router C

```
C#show ip bgp 172.16.15.160
BGP routing table entry for 172.16.15.160/30, version 0
Paths: (1 available, no best path)
  Not advertised to any peer
  2
    172.16.15.162 (inaccessible) from 172.16.15.130 (172.16.15.254)
      Origin incomplete, metric 0, localpref 100, valid, internal, not
        synchronized
```

The prefix 172.16.15.160 and the other prefixes received from Router D are
inaccessible. This means Router C does not know how to reach the NEXT_HOP.
Recall BGP does not change the NEXT_HOP information received from an EBGP
peer when the prefix is advertised to an IBGP peer. Router D does not change the
NEXT_HOP of 172.16.15.162 when the prefixes are advertised to Router C.
These routes are considered inaccessible because there is not a route in the IP
routing table for prefix 172.16.15.160/30. One way to overcome this problem is to
run an IGP in AS 1 and advertise not only the next-hop network but also all net-
works belonging to AS 1. For this exercise, use single-area OSPF on Routers A,
B, C, and D. The OSPF configurations are identical for all routers in AS 1.
(See Example 8-31.)

Example 8-31 OSPF Configuration for Routers in AS 1

```
router ospf 1
 network 172.16.0.0 0.0.255.255 area 51
```

The network connecting Routers D and E is now being advertised by OSPF making the BGP next hop advertised by Router D accessible. (See Example 8-32.)

Example 8-32   Verifying the Next Hop Is Being Advertised in AS 1

```
C#show ip route | include 172.16.15.160
O       172.16.15.160/30 [110/74] via 172.16.15.130, 00:05:45, Ethernet2/0

C#show ip bgp 172.16.15.160
BGP routing table entry for 172.16.15.160/30, version 2
Paths: (1 available, best #1, table Default-IP-Routing-Table)
  Not advertised to any peer
  2
    172.16.15.162 (metric 74) from 172.16.15.130 (172.16.15.254)
      Origin incomplete, metric 0, localpref 100, valid, internal, synchronized,
      best
```

The BGP routes should now be in the IP routing table on Router C, as shown in Example 8-33.

Example 8-33   Router C IP Routing Table

```
C#show ip route
     172.16.0.0/16 is variably subnetted, 12 subnets, 3 masks
O       172.16.15.160/30 [110/74] via 172.16.15.130, 00:08:45, Ethernet2/0
O       172.16.15.164/30 [110/50] via 172.16.15.97, 00:08:45, FastEthernet1/0
C       172.16.15.128/27 is directly connected, Ethernet2/0
O       172.16.15.251/32 [110/3] via 172.16.15.97, 00:08:45, FastEthernet1/0
O       172.16.15.254/32 [110/11] via 172.16.15.130, 00:08:45, Ethernet2/0
C       172.16.15.253/32 is directly connected, Loopback0
O       172.16.15.252/32 [110/2] via 172.16.15.97, 00:08:46, FastEthernet1/0
C       172.16.15.32/27 is directly connected, Ethernet0/0
O       172.16.15.0/27 [110/2] via 172.16.15.97, 00:08:46, FastEthernet1/0
C       172.16.9.0/30 is directly connected, Serial0/1
C       172.16.15.96/27 is directly connected, FastEthernet1/0
O       172.16.15.64/27 [110/12] via 172.16.15.97, 00:08:46, FastEthernet1/0
```

Prefix 172.16.15.160 is in the IP routing table as an OSPF route. Why is this prefix not an IBGP route? Router C is learning about prefix 172.16.15.160 through OSPF and IBGP. OSPF has an administrative distance of 110, and IBGP has an administrative distance of 200. Therefore, the OSPF route is preferred over the IBGP route.

No BGP routes appear in the IP routing table. Looking at the BGP routing table
on Router C uncovers yet another problem. (See Example 8-34.)

Example 8-34   Router C BGP Routing Table

```
C#show ip bgp
BGP table version is 2, local router ID is 172.16.15.253
Status codes: s suppressed, d damped, h history, * valid, > best, i - internal
Origin codes: i - IGP, e - EGP, ? - incomplete

   Network          Next Hop          Metric LocPrf Weight Path
*>i172.16.15.160/30 172.16.15.162          0    100      0 2 ?
*  i172.16.16.164/30 172.16.15.162         0    100      0 2 ?
*  i172.16.16.254/32 172.16.15.162         0    100      0 2 ?
```

Prefix 172.16.15.160 is valid, but prefixes 172.16.16.164 and 172.16.16.254 do
not have a best path. Checking one of the specific routes uncovers another problem. (See Example 8-35.)

Example 8-35   Prefix in AS 1 Is Not Synchronized

```
C#show ip bgp 172.16.16.164
BGP routing table entry for 172.16.16.164/30, version 0
Paths: (1 available, no best path)
  Not advertised to any peer
  2
    172.16.15.162 (metric 74) from 172.16.15.130 (172.16.15.254)
      Origin incomplete, metric 0, localpref 100, valid, internal,
        not synchronized
```

The two invalid BGP routes are not synchronized. Synchronization is a property
of IBGP. A BGP prefix received from an IBGP neighbor is not considered valid
unless the prefix is already in the IP routing table.

The BGP prefix 172.16.15.160 is synchronized because this prefix is in the IP
routing table as an OSPF route. The BGP prefixes 172.16.16.164 and 172.16.16.254
are not in the IP routing table, therefore, they are not synchronized. The reason for
synchronization can be explained using the network in Figure 8-17.

Figure 8-17 IBGP Synchronization

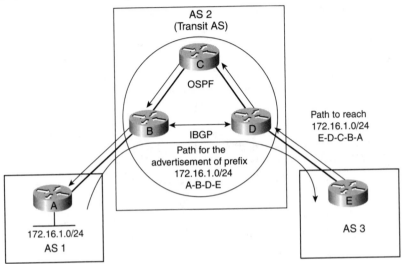

Routers A and B have established an EBGP connection and Router A is advertising prefix 172.16.1.0/24 to Router B. In AS 2, the physical path between Routers B and D is through Router C. A physical connection between IBGP routers is not required, and Routers B and D have established an IBGP connection. BGP packets exchanged between Routers B and D physically pass through Router C, but Router C has no knowledge of their contents.

Routers B and D need to know how to reach each other through IP so AS 2 is running OSPF and advertising all networks internal to AS 2. All that is required to establish an IBGP connection is an IP path between the two routers. Assume synchronization is not a property of IBGP and trace the chain of events in Figure 8-17:

1. Router A advertises prefix 172.16.1.0/24 to Router B through EBGP.

2. Router B accepts the route because the next hop is known (it's a directly connected network), and the prefix is placed in the routing table on Router B.

3. Router B advertises the prefix to Router D through IBGP without changing the next hop information.

4. Router D accepts the route because the next hop is known through OSPF.

5. Router D advertises 172.16.1.0/24 to Router E in AS 3.

6. Router E accepts the prefix because the next hop is known, and the prefix is placed in the IP routing table on Router E.

7. Assume a host in AS 3 sends a packet to a host on network 172.16.1.0/24. The host sends the packet to Router E, and Router E forwards the packet to Router D after consulting the IP routing table.

8. Router D receives the packet and looks at the destination IP address to make a forwarding decision. The next hop is Router C, and the packet is forwarded to Router C.

9. Router C has no knowledge of network 172.16.1.0/24 because this prefix was not learned through OSPF or BGP, so Router C drops the packet.

Synchronization can be disabled using the **no synchronization** command. With synchronization disabled on Router C in Figure 8-16, the BGP routes advertised by Router D are transferred to the IP routing table on Router C. (See Example 8-36.)

Example 8-36 Disabling Synchronization

```
Router C
router bgp 1
 no synchronization
 neighbor 172.16.15.130 remote-as 1
 no auto-summary
```

With synchronization disabled, the routes in the BGP table on Router C are now valid and the BGP routes are transferred to the IP routing table. (See Example 8-37.)

Example 8-37 Transferring BGP Routes to the IP Routing Table

```
C#show ip bgp
BGP table version is 4, local router ID is 172.16.15.253
Status codes: s suppressed, d damped, h history, * valid, > best, i - internal
Origin codes: i - IGP, e - EGP, ? - incomplete

   Network          Next Hop            Metric LocPrf Weight Path
*>i172.16.15.160/30 172.16.15.162            0    100      0 2 ?
*>i172.16.16.164/30 172.16.15.162            0    100      0 2 ?
*>i172.16.16.254/32 172.16.15.162            0    100      0 2 ?

C#show ip route | i B
B       172.16.16.164/30 [200/0] via 172.16.15.162, 00:02:28
B       172.16.16.254/32 [200/0] via 172.16.15.162, 00:02:28
```

Now our problem is solved. Or is it? Router C has routes to the EBGP routes, but Router E does not have a route to Router C. A static route can be used on Router E to reach all the networks in AS 1. (See Example 8-38.)

Example 8-38 Static Route on Router E

```
Router E
ip route 172.16.15.0 255.255.255.0 172.16.15.161
```

The main point of this exercise is that simply turning off synchronization does not solve our problem. We have to ensure that any routes injected into the IP routing table can be reached by the router.

With synchronization enabled, routes learned through IBGP are not considered valid unless the routes are already in the IP routing table. If the routes are already in the IP routing table, why do we need BGP? In Figure 8-17, AS 2 is a BGP transit system between AS 1 and AS 3. You could redistribute the BGP routes into OSPF on Router B, advertise the redistributed routes to Routers C and D through OSPF, and redistribute the routes back into BGP on Router D. This works and routing will be complete, but you lose the BGP attributes when the routes are redistributed into OSPF. The problem in Figure 8-17 is that all the routers in the physical path between AS 1 and AS 3 are not running IBGP. If you configure IBGP on Router C, synchronization can be disabled in AS 2 as long as the next hop advertised by the IBGP routers is reachable.

In Figure 8-16, IBGP is configured between Routers B and C. What BGP routes does Router C advertise to Router B? (See Example 8-39.)

Example 8-39 Routes Advertised from Router C to Router B

```
Router C
router bgp 1
 no synchronization
 neighbor 172.16.15.97 remote-as 1
 neighbor 172.16.15.130 remote-as 1
 no auto-summary

Router B
router bgp 1
 neighbor 172.16.15.98 remote-as 1
```

Before inspecting the BGP routing table on Router B, check to see if a BGP neighbor relationship has been established. (See Example 8-40.)

Example 8-40 Verifying the BGP Neighbor Relationship

```
B#show ip bgp neighbors 172.16.15.98 | include Established
  BGP state = Established, up for 00:04:22
```

To answer the question of which routes Router C is advertising, display the contents of the BGP routing table on Router B.

Example 8-41 BGP Routing Table on Router B

```
B#show ip bgp
!no output
```

Router C has not advertised any BGP routes to Router B. This illustrates another property of IBGP that differs from the operation of EBGP. All IBGP routes have the same AS number so the AS path attribute cannot be used for loop detection. Therefore, an IBGP router will not advertise routes learned from one IBGP neighbor to another IBGP neighbor. This restriction means that IBGP routers have to be fully meshed. In other words, all IBGP routers in an AS must have an IBGP connection to all other IBGP routers. In Figure 8-16, each router must have an IBGP connection to all other routers in the AS. This requires three IBGP connections on Routers A, B, C, and D, for a total of six IBGP connections. (See Example 8-42.) Because this is IBGP, the routers do not have to be physically connected.

Example 8-42 Configuring a Full IBGP Mesh

```
Router A
router bgp 1
 no synchronization
 neighbor 172.16.15.2 remote-as 1
 neighbor 172.16.15.34 remote-as 1
 neighbor 172.16.15.66 remote-as 1

Router B
router bgp 1
 no synchronization
 neighbor 172.16.15.1 remote-as 1
 neighbor 172.16.15.98 remote-as 1
 neighbor 172.16.15.130 remote-as 1
```

Example 8-42 Configuring a Full IBGP Mesh (continued)

```
Router C
router bgp 1
 no synchronization
 neighbor 172.16.15.33 remote-as 1
 neighbor 172.16.15.97 remote-as 1
 neighbor 172.16.15.130 remote-as 1

Router D
router bgp 1
 no synchronization
 neighbor 172.16.15.65 remote-as 1
 neighbor 172.16.15.97 remote-as 1
 neighbor 172.16.15.129 remote-as 1
 neighbor 172.16.15.162 remote-as 2
```

IBGP neighbors do not need a physical connection between them to form a neighbor relationship. All that is required is an IP path between the IBGP neighbors. The configurations in this section used the IP address of a physical interface in the neighbor configuration statements. If the physical interface of the neighbor fails, the BGP connection fails—even though there may be another IP path to another physical interface available. The next section examines a technique to form an IBGP neighbor relationship without specifying a physical interface.

IBGP and Loopback Interfaces

The IBGP configurations on the routers in AS 1 use a physical address in the neighbor commands. What happens if the physical address in the **neighbor** command is no longer available due to a network failure? In Figure 8-18, Router D has three paths to Router C that can be used to form an IBGP connection. If the physical address that is used in the **neighbor** command is unavailable, the other paths will not be used because the route to the physical address is gone.

Figure 8-18   IBGP Does Not Require a Physical Connection Between Neighbors

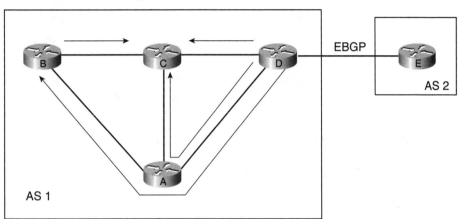

Instead of using a physical address in the **neighbor** command, you can use a router's loopback address. In Figure 8-18, the best path from Router D to Router C's loopback address is through the direct connection between Routers C and D. If this connection fails, the IGP, in this case OSPF, converges and Router D uses the path through Router A to Router C. If the link between A and C fails, OSPF converges again and Router D uses the path through A and B to reach C. Before you start using loopback addresses in the neighbor commands, you need to be aware of how these addresses are used by IBGP.

The **neighbor** commands used to establish the IBGP connection between Routers C and D use physical addresses. (See Example 8-43.)

Example 8-43   Establishing the IBGP Connection

```
Router C
router bgp 1
 neighbor 172.16.15.130 remote-as 1
Router D
router bgp 1
 neighbor 172.16.15.129 remote-as 1
```

When Router C sends a BGP protocol packet to Router D, the destination IP address is set to the address used in the **neighbor** command on Router C or

172.16.15.130. The source IP address used by Router C is the IP address of the interface used to reach Router D or 172.16.15.129. Router D uses a destination IP address of 172.16.15.129 and a source address of 172.16.15.130. The source address used by Router C must match the destination address used by Router D. The source address used by Router D must match the destination address used by Router C. If you use the loopback address in the **neighbor** commands on Routers C and D, the source IP address must be set to the loopback address on each router—and not the physical address of the interface used to reach the router. The new configurations for Routers A, B, C, and D are shown in Example 8-44.

Example 8-44   New Configurations for
Routers A, B, C, and D

```
Router A
router bgp 1
 no synchronization
 neighbor 172.16.15.252 remote-as 1
 neighbor 172.16.15.252 update-source Loopback0
 neighbor 172.16.15.253 remote-as 1
 neighbor 172.16.15.253 update-source Loopback0
 neighbor 172.16.15.254 remote-as 1
 neighbor 172.16.15.254 update-source Loopback0
 no auto-summary

Router B
router bgp 1
 no synchronization
 neighbor 172.16.15.251 remote-as 1
 neighbor 172.16.15.251 update-source Loopback0
 neighbor 172.16.15.253 remote-as 1
 neighbor 172.16.15.253 update-source Loopback0
 neighbor 172.16.15.254 remote-as 1
 neighbor 172.16.15.254 update-source Loopback0
 no auto-summary

Router C
router bgp 1
 no synchronization
 neighbor 172.16.15.251 remote-as 1
 neighbor 172.16.15.251 update-source Loopback0
 neighbor 172.16.15.252 remote-as 1
 neighbor 172.16.15.252 update-source Loopback0
 neighbor 172.16.15.254 remote-as 1
 neighbor 172.16.15.254 update-source Loopback0
 no auto-summary

Router D
router bgp 1
```

Example 8-44   New Configurations for
                   Routers A, B, C, and D (continued)

```
no synchronization
neighbor 172.16.15.162 remote-as 2
neighbor 172.16.15.251 remote-as 1
neighbor 172.16.15.251 update-source Loopback0
neighbor 172.16.15.252 remote-as 1
neighbor 172.16.15.252 update-source Loopback0
neighbor 172.16.15.253 remote-as 1
neighbor 172.16.15.253 update-source Loopback0
no auto-summary
```

The command **update-source Loopback0** causes BGP to set the IP source
address in BGP protocol packets to the IP address assigned to the loopback interface. The source IP address will now match the destination IP address used by the
other routers in the AS. As long as there is an IP path between any two routers, the
BGP connection will be active.

Scaling IBGP

IBGP requires a *full mesh* between IBGP routers. The number of logical IBGP
connections required for 2 to 10 routers is listed in Table 8-2.

Table 8-2   Number of IBGP Connections Required for a Full Mesh of
                2 to 10 Routers

Number of Routers	Number of IBGP Connections
2	1
3	3
4	6
5	10
6	15
7	21
8	28
9	36
10	45

The number of IBGP connections required for a full mesh based on the number of IBGP routers is given by the following formula where n = number of IBGP routers:

Connections = [(n)(n – 1)]/2

The number of required IBGP connections grows as the square of the number of routers. For 20 IBGP routers, the number of required connections is 190. The following sections look at techniques—route reflector and confederation—for reducing the number of connections for an IBGP network.

Route Reflector

A *route reflector* can reduce the number of required IBGP connections from [(n)(n-1)]/2 to n – 1. In Figure 8-19, Router C is a route reflector for Routers A, B, and D. Routers A, B, and D are referred to as clients of the route reflector and establish only an IBGP connection with the route reflector.

Figure 8-19   Route Reflector Reduces the Required Number of IBGP Connections to n - 1

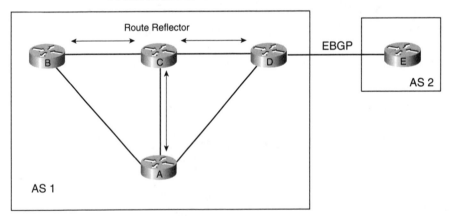

Routers A, B, and D *peer* (form a neighbor connection) only with Router C. The configuration on Router C designates Routers A, B, and D as route reflector clients. (See Example 8-45.) This is the same network used in Figure 8-16, but with Router C as the route reflector.

Example 8-45 Routers A, B, D as Route Reflector Clients

```
Router A
router bgp 1
 no synchronization
 neighbor 172.16.15.253 remote-as 1
 neighbor 172.16.15.253 update-source Loopback0
 no auto-summary

Router B
router bgp 1
 no synchronization
 neighbor 172.16.15.253 remote-as 1
 neighbor 172.16.15.253 update-source Loopback0
 no auto-summary

Router D
router bgp 1
 no synchronization
 neighbor 172.16.15.162 remote-as 2
 neighbor 172.16.15.253 remote-as 1
 neighbor 172.16.15.253 update-source Loopback0
 no auto-summary

Router C
router bgp 1
 no synchronization
 neighbor 172.16.15.251 remote-as 1
 neighbor 172.16.15.251 update-source Loopback0
 neighbor 172.16.15.251 route-reflector-client
 neighbor 172.16.15.252 remote-as 1
 neighbor 172.16.15.252 update-source Loopback0
 neighbor 172.16.15.252 route-reflector-client
 neighbor 172.16.15.254 remote-as 1
 neighbor 172.16.15.254 update-source Loopback0
 neighbor 172.16.15.254 route-reflector-client
 no auto-summary
```

A route reflector advertises, or reflects, prefixes learned from a client to all other clients.

Confederations

Another technique to reduce the number of IBGP connections is called ***confederations***. The AS is divided into two or more subautonomous systems and the subautonomous systems are usually assigned a private AS number in the range of 64,512 to 65,534. In Figure 8-20, Routers B and C are in sub-AS 64555, and Routers A and D are in sub-AS 64556.

Figure 8-20   BGP Confederation

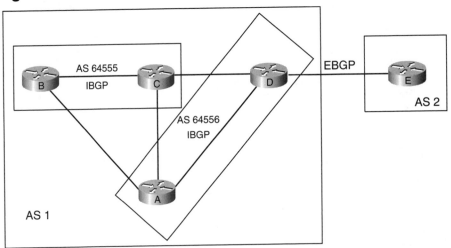

Configuring a confederation is more complicated than configuring a route reflector as seen in Example 8-46.

Example 8-46   Configuring a Confederation

```
Router A
router bgp 64556
 no synchronization
 bgp confederation peers 64555
 neighbor 172.16.15.34 remote-as 64555
 neighbor 172.16.15.254 remote-as 64556
 neighbor 172.16.15.254 update-source Loopback0
 no auto-summary

Router B
router bgp 64555
 no synchronization
 neighbor 172.16.15.253 remote-as 64555
 neighbor 172.16.15.253 update-source Loopback0
 no auto-summary
```

Example 8-46 Configuring a Confederation (continued)

```
Router C
router bgp 64555
 no synchronization
 bgp confederation peers 64556
 neighbor 172.16.15.33 remote-as 64556
 neighbor 172.16.15.252 remote-as 64555
 neighbor 172.16.15.252 update-source Loopback0
 no auto-summary

Router D
router bgp 64556
 no synchronization
 bgp confederation identifier 1
 neighbor 172.16.15.162 remote-as 2
 neighbor 172.16.15.251 remote-as 64556
 neighbor 172.16.15.251 update-source Loopback0
 no auto-summary
```

The private sub-AS number is used to configure the BGP process and neighbor statements. The **bgp confederation peers**command is used on a router having a neighbor in a different sub-AS. Router E should see Router D in AS 1 because this is the assigned AS number. The command **bgp confederation identifier**sets the AS number advertised to an external BGP peer.

Route reflectors and confederations can be combined to further reduce the number of IBGP connections. The AS in Figure 8-21 uses two subautonomous systems, and two route reflectors to reduce the number of IBGP connections from 28 to 7.

Figure 8-21 Route Reflectors and Confederations Used Together

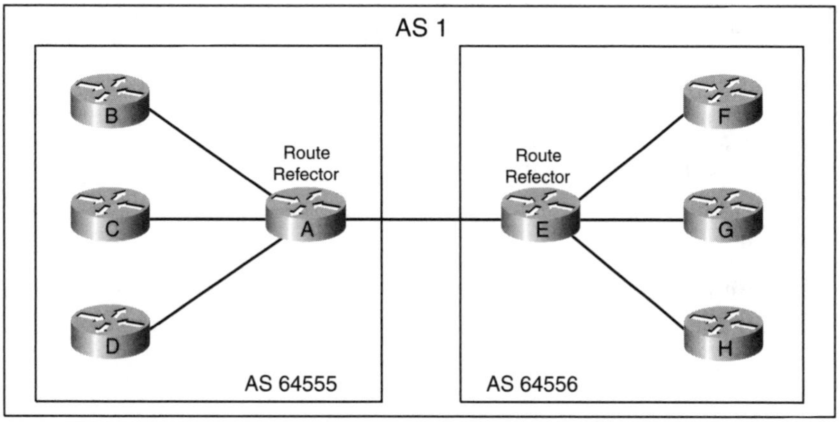

BGP Route Summarization

In Figure 8-22, Router A is advertising four prefixes to Router B through EBGP, and Router B advertises these prefixes to Router C.

Figure 8-22   BGP Route Summarization

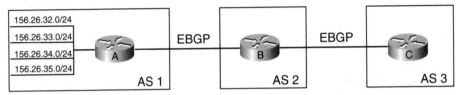

The AS path attribute for the 156.26.0.0 prefixes on Router B equals 1, and on Router C the AS path attribute is 2 1. (See Example 8-47.)

Example 8-47   AS_PATH Attributes on Routers B and C

```
B#show ip bgp
BGP table version is 5, local router ID is 172.16.15.252
Status codes: s suppressed, d damped, h history, * valid, > best, i - internal
Origin codes: i - IGP, e - EGP, ? - incomplete

   Network          Next Hop          Metric LocPrf Weight Path
*> 156.26.32.0/24   172.16.15.1            0             0 1 i
*> 156.26.33.0/24   172.16.15.1            0             0 1 i
*> 156.26.34.0/24   172.16.15.1            0             0 1 i
*> 156.26.35.0/24   172.16.15.1            0             0 1 I


C#show ip bgp
BGP table version is 5, local router ID is 172.16.15.253
Status codes: s suppressed, d damped, h history, * valid, > best, i - internal
Origin codes: i - IGP, e - EGP, ? - incomplete

   Network          Next Hop          Metric LocPrf Weight Path
*> 156.26.32.0/24   172.16.15.97                        0 2 1 i
*> 156.26.33.0/24   172.16.15.97                        0 2 1 i
*> 156.26.34.0/24   172.16.15.97                        0 2 1 i
*> 156.26.35.0/24   172.16.15.97                        0 2 1 i
```

The reason for pointing out the value of the AS_PATH attribute is so you can see what happens to this attribute when you create a BGP summary address. A BGP

summary address is configured using the command **aggregate-address**under the
BGP router configuration. BGP can only summarize the addresses in the BGP
routing table. (See Figure 8-23.)

Figure 8-23   BGP Can Summarize Routes in the BGP Routing Table

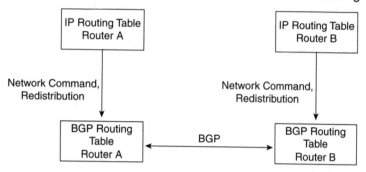

A summary address is created on Router B and includes only the four subnets
advertised by Router A. (See Example 8-48.)

Example 8-48   Summary Address on Router B

```
Router B
router bgp 2
 aggregate-address 156.26.32.0 255.255.252.0
 neighbor 172.16.15.1 remote-as 1
 neighbor 172.16.15.98 remote-as 3
```

The BGP routing table on Router B contains the aggregate and specific prefixes of
156.26.32.0. (See Example 8-49.)

Example 8-49   BGP Routing Table on Router B

```
B#show ip bgp
BGP table version is 6, local router ID is 172.16.15.252
Status codes: s suppressed, d damped, h history, * valid, > best, i - internal
Origin codes: i - IGP, e - EGP, ? - incomplete

   Network          Next Hop          Metric LocPrf Weight Path
*> 156.26.32.0/24   172.16.15.1            0             0 1 i
*> 156.26.32.0/22   0.0.0.0                          32768 i
*> 156.26.33.0/24   172.16.15.1            0             0 1 i
*> 156.26.34.0/24   172.16.15.1            0             0 1 i
*> 156.26.35.0/24   172.16.15.1            0             0 1 i
```

The aggregate prefix has a next hop of 0.0.0.0 because the prefix originates on Router B and is referred to as a *locally originated route*. Also, the AS path attribute for the aggregate prefix has been initialized to an empty string. Router B advertises the aggregate prefix to both Routers A and C. (See Example 8-50.)

Example 8-50   Summarized Route as Seen by Router A

```
A#show ip bgp
BGP table version is 6, local router ID is 172.16.15.251
Status codes: s suppressed, d damped, h history, * valid, > best, i - internal
Origin codes: i - IGP, e - EGP, ? - incomplete

   Network          Next Hop          Metric LocPrf Weight Path
*> 156.26.32.0/24   0.0.0.0                0            32768 i
*> 156.26.32.0/22   172.16.15.2                         0 2 i
*> 156.26.33.0/24   0.0.0.0                0            32768 i
*> 156.26.34.0/24   0.0.0.0                0            32768 i
*> 156.26.35.0/24   0.0.0.0                0            32768 I


C#show ip bgp
BGP table version is 6, local router ID is 172.16.15.253
Status codes: s suppressed, d damped, h history, * valid, > best, i - internal
Origin codes: i - IGP, e - EGP, ? - incomplete

   Network          Next Hop          Metric LocPrf Weight Path
*> 156.26.32.0/24   172.16.15.97                        0 2 1 i
*> 156.26.32.0/22   172.16.15.97                        0 2 i
*> 156.26.33.0/24   172.16.15.97                        0 2 1 i
*> 156.26.34.0/24   172.16.15.97                        0 2 1 i
*> 156.26.35.0/24   172.16.15.97                        0 2 1 i
```

The summary address created by Router B does not include the path information of the specific prefixes that are part of the summary. The specific prefixes originated in AS 1, but the only AS number in the AS path attribute for the prefix is 2.

The AS path attribute for the aggregate route on Routers A and C has a value of 2, indicating this route originated in AS 2. The four specific prefixes are in the BGP routing table on Router A because these prefixes are originated by Router A. Why are the four specific prefixes in the routing table on Router C? When a summary address was created with EIGRP, OSPF, or IS-IS, the specific prefixes making up the summary were not advertised—only the summary address was advertised. By default, BGP advertises the aggregate address and all the prefixes contained within the aggregate address block. To prevent the specific prefixes from being advertised, use the **summary-only** option with the **aggregate-address** command. (See Example 8-51.)

Example 8-51   Suppressing the More Specific Prefixes

```
Router B
router bgp 2
 aggregate-address 156.26.32.0 255.255.252.0 summary-only
 neighbor 172.16.15.1 remote-as 1
 neighbor 172.16.15.98 remote-as 3
```

The BGP routing table on Router B now shows the specific routes as being suppressed. (See Example 8-52.) A suppressed route is a route that is not advertised by BGP.

Example 8-52   Router B BGP Routing Table

```
B#show ip bgp
BGP table version is 10, local router ID is 172.16.15.252
Status codes: s suppressed, d damped, h history, * valid, > best, i - internal
Origin codes: i - IGP, e - EGP, ? - incomplete

   Network          Next Hop          Metric LocPrf Weight Path
s> 156.26.32.0/24   172.16.15.1            0            0 1 i
*> 156.26.32.0/22   0.0.0.0                         32768 i
s> 156.26.33.0/24   172.16.15.1            0            0 1 i
s> 156.26.34.0/24   172.16.15.1            0            0 1 i
s> 156.26.35.0/24   172.16.15.1            0            0 1 i
```

Router C should have only the aggregate prefix in its BGP routing table. (See Example 8-53.)

Example 8-53   Aggregate Prefix in Router C's BGP Routing Table

```
C#show ip bgp
BGP table version is 10, local router ID is 172.16.15.253
Status codes: s suppressed, d damped, h history, * valid, > best, i - internal
Origin codes: i - IGP, e - EGP, ? - incomplete

   Network          Next Hop          Metric LocPrf Weight Path
*> 156.26.32.0/22   172.16.15.97                      0 2 i
```

Additional options are available for the manipulation of BGP aggregate addresses. You can choose to suppress only a subset of the specific prefixes. You can also, on a neighbor-by-neighbor basis, unsuppress routes that have been suppressed using the **aggregate-address**command. In fact, there are more than 100 BGP configuration commands that can be used to fine-tune a BGP configuration. For specific information regarding these additional commands, see the references at the end of this chapter.

BGP Decision Process

For every prefix a BGP router receives, the first thing checked is the NEXT_HOP attribute. If the next hop is not accessible (not in the IP routing table), the prefix is rejected. For routes received from an IBGP peer, the next check after the next hop check is to see if the routes are synchronized. Unsynchronized routes are rejected only if synchronization is enabled. The following steps in the BGP decision process apply only if there is more than one route to a particular prefix:

1. Prefer the path with the highest weight

2. Prefer the path with the highest local preference

3. Prefer locally originated routes (Next Hop = 0.0.0.0)

4. Prefer the path with the shortest AS path

5. Prefer the path with the lowest origin type: IGP is lower than EGP, and EGP is lower than INCOMPLETE

6. Prefer the path with the lowest metric or MED

7. Prefer EBGP routes over IBGP routes

8. Prefer the lowest IGP metric to the next hop

9. Prefer the path from the router with the lowest router ID

Summary

BGP is an exterior gateway protocol (EGP) used to route between the autonomous systems that make up the Internet. The best path algorithms of the interior routing protocols (RIP, IGRP, EIGRP, OSPF, and IS-IS) do not scale to the number of IP prefixes required for Internet routing. The BGP best path algorithm is a simple and elegant mechanism that can handle well over 100,000 routes.

In addition to advertising network prefixes and subnet masks, BGP uses a set of attributes in the best path decision process. These attributes are: AS_PATH, WEIGHT, LOCAL_PREF, ORIGIN, and MULTI_EXIT_DISC. The BGP attributes give BGP the flexibility to make a best path decision based on any, or all, of the attributes.

Although the BGP decision algorithm is relatively simple, the configuration and mastery of BGP is not. This chapter covered the basic concepts, operation, and configuration of BGP, and has provided a foundation for exploring BGP further.

Chapter Review Questions

You can find the answers to these questions in Appendix A.

1. Describe four differences between the operation of IBGP and EBGP.

2. What is the purpose of the AS_PATH attribute?

3. What is the purpose of the WEIGHT attribute?

4. What is the scope of the WEIGHT attribute?

5. What is the purpose of the LOCAL_PREF attribute?

6. What is the scope of the LOCAL_PREF attribute?

7. What is the purpose of the metric or MULTI_EXIT_DISC attribute?

8. What is the order of preference for the BGP attributes AS_PATH, LOCAL_PREF, MED, and WEIGHT?

9. Name all the ways for installing a prefix in the BGP routing table.

10. What is the first thing that BGP checks to determine if a prefix is accessible?

11. What is synchronization?

12. Name two methods for reducing the number of IBGP connections.

13. Why does IBGP require a full mesh?

14. What is the major difference between BGP and IGP route summarization?

15. Why is BGP a better choice for Internet routing than the IGPs?

16. What are the four general types of BGP attributes?

References

Use the following references to learn more about the concepts described in this chapter:

- Doyle, J. and J.D. Carroll. 2001. *Routing TCP/IP,* Volume II. Indianapolis: Cisco Press.

- Halabi, Sam. *Internet Routing Architectures*, Second Edition. 2000. Indianapolis: Cisco Press.

- Parkhurst, William. *Cisco BGP-4 Command and Configuration Handbook.* 2001. Indianapolis: Cisco Press.

- Rekhter, Y. and T. Li. March 1995. RFC 1771, A Border Gateway Protocol 4 (BGP-4).

- Cisco Documentation, Cisco.com.

What You Will Learn

After reading this chapter, you should be able to

- ✔ Explain the Class D or multicast address space

- ✔ Understand the concepts, terminology, and operation of Cisco IP multicast routing protocols (Protocol Independent Multicast[PIM] dense and sparse modes)

- ✔ Comprehend the basics of configuring multicast on Cisco routers

CHAPTER 9

Multicast—What the Post Office Can't Do

If you want to send a greeting card, a wedding invitation, a birth announcement, or your favorite joke to all of your friends and family, you need to address and send a card for each recipient. A more convenient way would be to send one card and have the post office make a copy for each recipient. But the post office cannot do this because they use only unicast addresses—an address that identifies only one destination.

In the world of IP routing, one packet can be sent to multiple recipients with the routers making copies along the way. This process is called *multicasting* and is the subject of this chapter. You will learn the concepts of multicast and the protocols used for implementing a multicast capable network.

Comparing Unicast and Multicast Routing

The previous chapters examined unicast routing and unicast IP routing protocols. With unicast IP routing, the destination IP address is either a Class A, B, or C address identifying one particular host on the Internet. The purpose of the unicast IP routing protocols is to route IP packets from one specific IP source to one specific IP destination. Assume you have a situation where you want multiple hosts to receive IP packets sent by a specific host. In Figure 9-1, the source host is sending packets that need to be received by the six hosts shown.

Figure 9-1   Unicast Delivery to Multiple Hosts

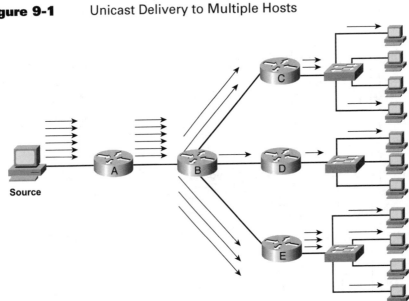

If the source uses the unicast IP address of the destination hosts, the source must send the same packet six times, one for each host. This might not seem like much of a problem, but what happens if hundreds or thousands of hosts want to receive the same information from the source? As the number of destination hosts increases, the number of individual unicast IP packets the source must send also increases. It would not take long for the source and the network to become over-loaded with a large number of identical packets that must be routed from the source to each individual host. Another problem is determining how the multicast source determines the address of the hosts wanting to receive the packets.

Assume you have a magical address that can be used when multiple hosts want to receive the same information. The source sends all the packets to this magical address and the hosts listen for packets addressed to this address as shown in Figure 9-2. Because one packet is being sent to multiple hosts, call this address a *multicast address*.

Figure 9-2 Multicast Delivery to Multiple Hosts

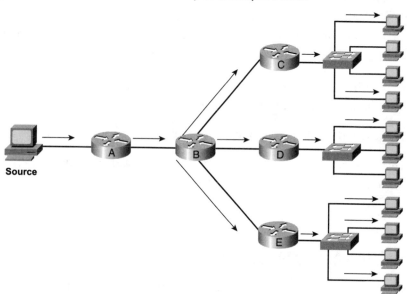

These magical multicast addresses are another class of IP addresses used when there is more than one recipient for information sent from a source. In Figure 9-3, the familiar Class A, B, and C unicast addresses are shown along with a new set of addresses—called Class D addresses—used for multicast.

Figure 9-3 IP Address Classes

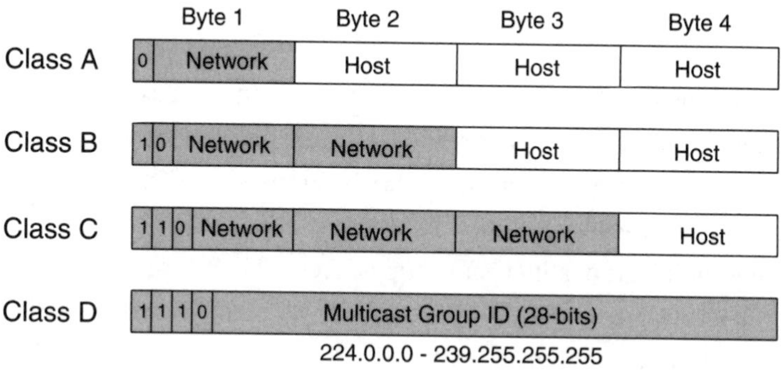

	Byte 1	Byte 2	Byte 3	Byte 4
Class A	0 Network	Host	Host	Host
Class B	1 0 Network	Network	Host	Host
Class C	1 1 0 Network	Network	Network	Host
Class D	1 1 1 0	Multicast Group ID (28-bits)		

224.0.0.0 - 239.255.255.255

Every Class D multicast IP address has the first four bits set to 1 1 1 0. This gives a range of addresses from 224.0.0.0 to 239.255.255.255. Multicast is an elegant solution to enable one source to communicate with multiple hosts. This chapter examines the following components of IP multicast:

- How switches and routers know which hosts want to receive multicast traffic being sent to a particular IP multicast group

- The protocols routers use to forward multicast traffic

- The protocol hosts use to indicate they want to receive multicast traffic for a particular multicast group

Multicast Switching

Unicast IP packets are delivered to a host using the hardware address of the host. This hardware address is typically an Ethernet address. When a router receives a packet, the router removes the hardware address and inspects the destination IP address to determine the interface to use to send the packet toward the host. If the router is attached to the network containing the host, the router uses the address resolution protocol to request the Ethernet address of the host having the destination IP address specified in the packet. The router adds the Ethernet address of the host to the packet and sends the packet to the switch. The switch has a switching table containing a list of the Ethernet addresses of directly attached hosts and the switch port used to reach the host.

The pairing of a host's IP and Ethernet addresses is for unicast IP. Each host has unique unicast IP and Ethernet addresses, and this pairing cannot be used for multicast packet delivery. Because multiple hosts on the same network might need to receive the same multicast packets, this implies they are listening for IP packets with the same multicast destination group address. Therefore, the receiving hosts need a multicast Ethernet address that can be used by the router to deliver multicast IP packets to multiple hosts.

A multicast Ethernet address is formed from the multicast IP address as shown in Figure 9-4. To determine the multicast Ethernet address for the multicast IP address 231.155.25.66, first convert the dotted decimal IP address to hex and then to binary. Add the last 23 bits of the multicast IP address to the Ethernet base address of 01 00 5E 00 00 00 to obtain 01 00 5E 1B 19 42. This is the address a router and a switch would use to deliver a multicast packet to a host.

Figure 9-4   Determining the Multicast Ethernet Address—Method 1

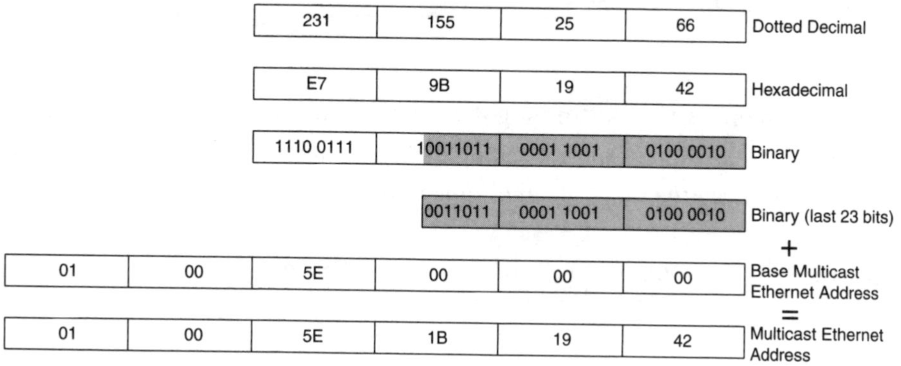

231	155	25	66	Dotted Decimal

E7	9B	19	42	Hexadecimal

1110 0111	10011011	0001 1001	0100 0010	Binary

0011011	0001 1001	0100 0010	Binary (last 23 bits)

+

01	00	5E	00	00	00	Base Multicast Ethernet Address

=

01	00	5E	1B	19	42	Multicast Ethernet Address

An easier way to convert a multicast IP address to a multicast Ethernet address exists. (See Figure 9-5.) The first byte of the multicast IP address is not used to form the multicast Ethernet address. Bytes three and four of the multicast IP address are transferred unchanged to the Ethernet address. The most significant bit of the second byte is not used and is always set to zero. If the second byte has a value larger than 127, subtract 128 from the second byte and transfer to the Ethernet address.

Figure 9-5   Determining the Multicast Ethernet Address—Method 2

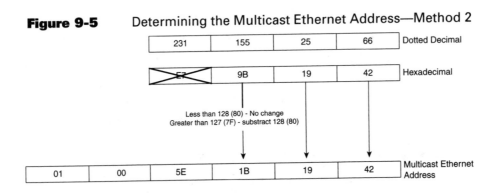

There is one more way of performing the conversion. (See Figure 9-6.) If the upper hexadecimal digit of the second byte of the IP address is greater than 7, subtract 8. Throw away the first byte and transfer everything else.

Figure 9-6   Determining the Multicast Ethernet Address—Method 3

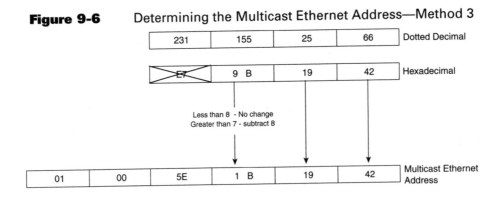

For example, the multicast IP address 229.27.25.66 has the hexadecimal value E5.1B.19.42. The second byte is less than 80_{16} so the multicast Ethernet address is 01 00 5E 1B 19 42. But this is the same Ethernet address for the multicast IP address 231.155.25.66. Can this be correct? If you examine the first 9 bits of any IP multicast address, the first 4 bits are always 1 1 1 0 (Class D address). The next 5 bits are not used to form the multicast Ethernet address– it does not matter what they are. Thirty-two combinations use 5 bits, so 32 IP multicast addresses map to the same multicast Ethernet address. Four of the 32 multicast addresses that map to the Ethernet address 01 00 5E 1B 19 42 are shown in Figure 9-7.

Figure 9-7   IP Multicast to Ethernet Address Mapping

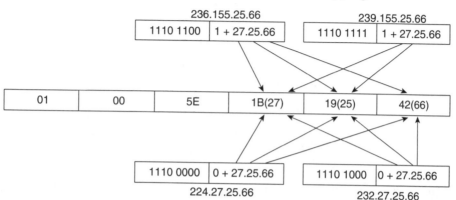

When a host receives a multicast Ethernet packet, the host must inspect the multicast IP group address to determine if the packet is for the multicast group from which it wants to receive traffic.

A switch learns the Ethernet address of connecting hosts by watching packets sent by hosts. When a switch receives an Ethernet message from a host, the message is received on a specific port. The switch looks at the source Ethernet address and learns the Ethernet address of the host attached to the port. Over time, the switch learns all the unicast Ethernet addresses of all the attached hosts. Multicast is different because the hosts are receiving multicast packets but not transmitting them. How does a switch learn which hosts want to receive multicast traffic from a particular source? The answer is by using the Internet Group Management Protocol (IGMP).

IGMP

The *Internet Group Management Protocol (IGMP)* is used between hosts and their local router to inform the router of the multicast groups that should be forwarded onto the local network. In Figure 9-8, a host uses an IGMP join message to inform the router it wants to receive traffic for multicast group 231.155.25.66.

Figure 9-8   IGMP Join Message

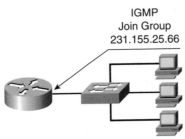

The router adds the multicast group to the list of groups that need to be forwarded onto the local network. Routers do not keep track of all the hosts wanting to receive traffic from multicast groups. It is sufficient for the router to know that at least one host wants to receive traffic. When a host no longer wants to receive the multicast traffic, an IGMP leave message is sent to the router. The router queries the hosts on the local network to determine if any other hosts still want to receive the traffic. If no other hosts respond saying they still want to receive the multicast traffic, the router removes the group from the list of groups needing to be forwarded.

As shown in Figure 9-8, IGMP is used between hosts and routers. The switch is used to enable only traffic between hosts and routers. When a router receives a multicast packet, the router forwards the packet to the switch if hosts have joined that particular multicast group. The switch treats the multicast packet as a broadcast packet and sends it to all hosts attached to the switch. (See Figure 9-9.)

Figure 9-9   Switches Normally Treat Multicast Traffic as Broadcast
                      Traffic

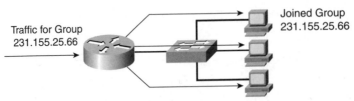

The broadcasting of multicast traffic is not an efficient use of available bandwidth. Two protocols are used so a switch only forwards multicast traffic to hosts that have joined the multicast group:

- Cisco Group Management Protocol (CGMP)

- IGMP snooping

CGMP

CGMP is a Cisco proprietary protocol used between Cisco routers and switches. (See Figure 9-10.)

Figure 9-10   Cisco Group Management Protocol

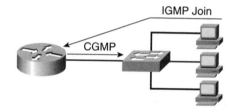

If CGMP has been configured on the router and the switch, the router informs the switch when a host has joined a particular multicast group using CGMP. The router knows the unicast Ethernet address of the host because the address is in the IGMP packet sent to the router. The router informs the switch of the host's unicast Ethernet address and the multicast group the host has joined. The multicast Ethernet address is added to the switching table. When the router forwards a multicast packet to the switch, the switch forwards the packet to the hosts having the multicast Ethernet address in the switching table. This prevents the multicast packets from being forwarded to hosts that have not joined the group. When a host no longer wants to receive packets for a particular group, an IGMP leave message is sent to the router. Using CGMP, the router informs the switch to remove this multicast group from the switching table for that host.

IGMP Snooping

IGMP snooping is a standards-based protocol used to perform the same function as CGMP. When IGMP snooping is enabled on the switch, the switch monitors for IGMP packets sent to the local router. (See Figure 9-11.) When a host joins a multicast group using IGMP, the switch adds the multicast Ethernet address to the switching table for the host. When the host leaves the group, the switch removes the multicast entry from the switching table.

Figure 9-11   IGMP Snooping

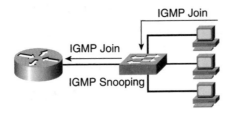

Multicast Forwarding

Unicast IP packets are routed based on the destination IP address. A multicast packet cannot be routed using the destination IP address because there can be multiple destinations. This depends on how many hosts want to receive the multicast traffic. Multicast forwarding is based on the source IP address using a technique called *Reverse Path Forwarding (RPF)*.

In Figure 9-12, the multicast source has an IP address of 172.16.1.1 and is sending to the multicast group 231.155.25.66. When Router A receives the multicast packet, the source IP address is checked to see if this is the interface the router would use to send a unicast packet back to the source. If it is, the packet is forwarded to multicast neighbor Routers B, C, and D. If the multicast packet is not received on the RPF interface, the packet is dropped.

Figure 9-12   RPF Interface

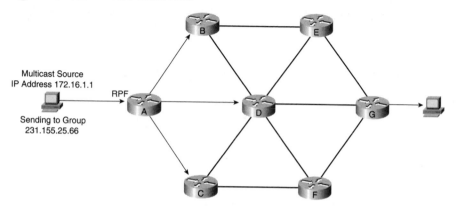

When Routers B, C, and D receive the multicast packet from Router A, the routers determine if the packet was received on their RPF interface. (See Figure 9-13.)

Figure 9-13   Multicast Packet Forwarding—Part 1

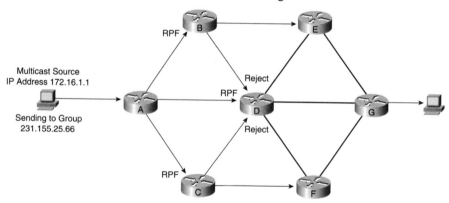

Routers B, C, and D receive the multicast packet from Router A on their RPF interface. The packet is accepted and forwarded to their multicast neighbors. Router D is receiving a multicast packet from Routers A, B, and C. The one from Router A is accepted and forwarded. The ones from Routers B and C are rejected. The RPF technique is a simple way of preventing multicast forwarding loops.

Routers D, E, and F forward the multicast traffic to Router G. Router G accepts the traffic from Router D while rejecting the traffic from Routers E and F. (See Figure 9-14.)

Figure 9-14   Multicast Packet Forwarding—Part 2

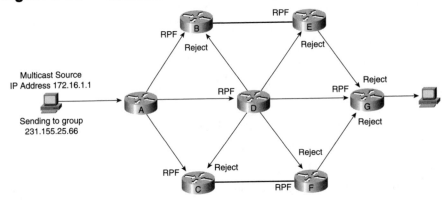

Using the RPF technique produces a loop-free, source-based, shortest-path delivery tree, as shown in Figure 9-15.

Figure 9-15   A Multicast Delivery Tree

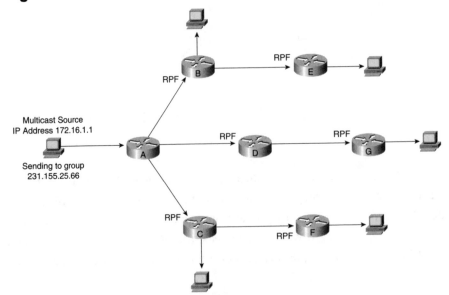

The source-based delivery tree is a loop-free topology from the multicast source to every leaf router. A *leaf router* is one with directly connected hosts that have joined the multicast group. The topology of the tree might be different depending on which unicast IP routing protocol is used in the network. Recall that because IP routing protocols use different metrics, the path back to the source might change. For example, RIP uses a hop count while OSPF uses a metric based on the interface speed—proving you can have a different delivery tree for different IP routing protocols.

Protocol Independent Multicast Routing Protocol

Cisco uses Protocol Independent Multicast (PIM) as the multicast routing protocol. Protocol independence means you are free to choose any unicast IP routing protocol such as RIP, IGRP, EIGRP, OSPF, or IS-IS as your interior gateway routing protocol. The RPF interface is determined from the unicast IP routing table and the IP routing table is derived from the IP routing protocol.

There are two types of PIM—dense mode and sparse mode—as described in the next sections.

PIM Dense Mode

Protocol Independent Multicast Dense Mode (PIM DM) is a broadcast and prune multicast routing protocol, utilizing source-based delivery trees. PIM DM assumes all PIM neighbors want to receive any multicast received by a router. If a leaf router has no hosts wanting to receive multicast traffic for a particular group, the leaf router sends a prune message to the forwarding router requesting the router to no longer forward traffic for that group. The prune has a lifetime of approximately three minutes after which the multicast traffic will again be forwarded to the leaf routers. In Figure 9-16, when the source begins to send multicast packets, these packets are sent (broadcast) to all multicast neighbors.

Figure 9-16   PIM DM Broadcasts Multicast Traffic to All Neighbors

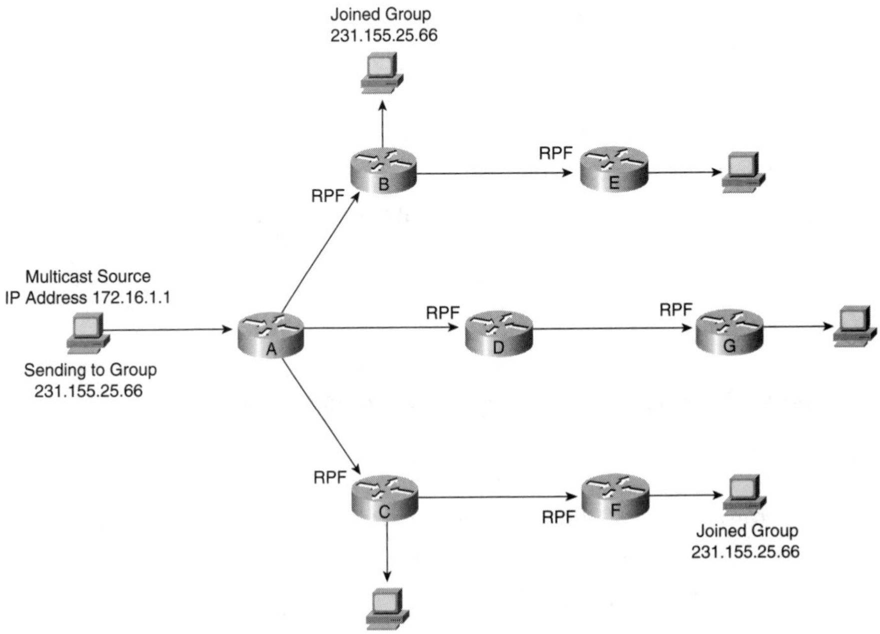

Joined Group
231.155.25.66

RPF

RPF   B

Multicast Source
IP Address 172.16.1.1

RPF   RPF

Sending to Group
231.155.25.66   A   D   G

RPF

RPF   C   RPF   F

Joined Group
231.155.25.66

The only leaf routers requiring the multicast traffic are Routers B, E, and F. Routers E and G have no attached hosts that have joined the multicast group, so they will send a prune message toward the source. Router C has no attached hosts requiring the traffic; but Router C has a multicast neighbor that does require the traffic, so C will not send a prune toward the source for this group. (See Figure 9-17.)

The network in Figure 9-18 demonstrates the configuration of PIM DM. The three steps for configuring a router for multicast routing are the following:

Step 1   Configure a unicast routing protocol.

Step 2   Enable multicast routing.

Step 3   Enable interfaces for multicast.

The first step configures an interior routing protocol to generate the unicast IP routing table used by the RPF process. The network in Figure 9-18 shows OSPF with a single area.

Figure 9-17   Multicast Traffic Pruning

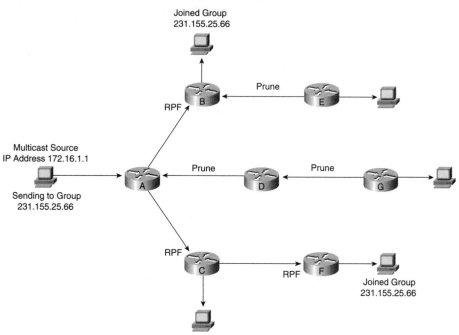

Figure 9-18   Network Demonstrating the Configuration and Operation of PIM DM

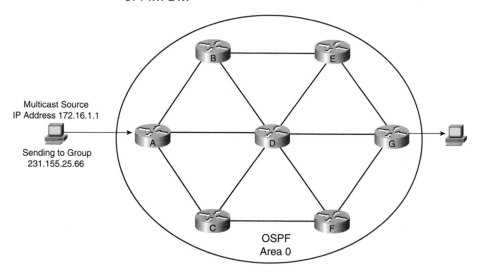

After OSPF is configured and the unicast IP routing table has been built, configuring PIM DM is easy. On every router, enable multicast routing using the **ip multicast-routing** command.

On every interface, enable PIM DM, as shown for one of the interfaces on Router A in Example 9-1.

Example 9-1 Enabling Router Interfaces for Multicast

```
Router A
interface Ethernet0/0
 ip address 172.16.4.1 255.255.255.0
 ip pim dense-mode
```

PIM DM is now configured in the network. When PIM DM is enabled on an interface, IGMP is automatically enabled for the interface and the router begins sending Hello messages to discover PIM DM neighbors. Neighbors are verified using the **show ip pim neighbor** command, as shown in Example 9-2.

Example 9-2 Verifying Neighbors with the **show ip pim neighbor** Command

```
G#show ip pim neighbor
PIM Neighbor Table
Neighbor Address  Interface        Uptime    Expires   Mode
172.16.15.97      FastEthernet0/0  00:14:42  00:01:32  Dense (DR)
172.16.10.1       Ethernet1/0      00:15:12  00:01:32  Dense
172.16.11.1       Serial2/0        00:15:12  00:01:33  Dense
172.16.12.1       Serial2/1        00:15:12  00:01:34  Dense
```

PIM DM uses a source-based delivery tree from every multicast source to every host that has joined the multicast group. Therefore, every PIM DM router maintains state for every source and group along the delivery tree. Source and group information is referred to as (S,G). In Figure 9-19, there are three sources sending to the same multicast group.

Figure 9-19   PIM DM Source-Based Delivery Tree

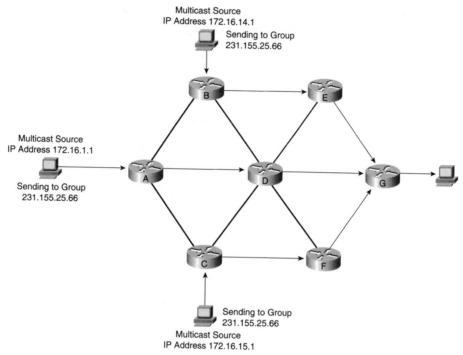

The PIM DM multicast routers maintain information for each multicast source and for each multicast group joined by a host. In addition, PIM DM routers forward multicast traffic to PIM DM neighbors whether the neighbor needs the traffic or not. The next section discusses a variation of PIM used to reduce the amount of information a multicast router has to maintain.

For more information regarding the configuration and operation of PIM DM, see the references at the end of the chapter.

PIM Sparse Mode

In *PIM Sparse Mode (PIM SM)*, shared delivery trees are used instead of source delivery trees. In a shared delivery tree, multicast traffic is sent to a common point called a *rendezvous point (RP)*. The RP forwards the traffic to hosts that have joined the group. (See Figure 9-20.) In this way, routers only maintain information about multicast groups and not the sources, thereby reducing the load on the routers.

Figure 9-20 PIM SM Shared Delivery Tree

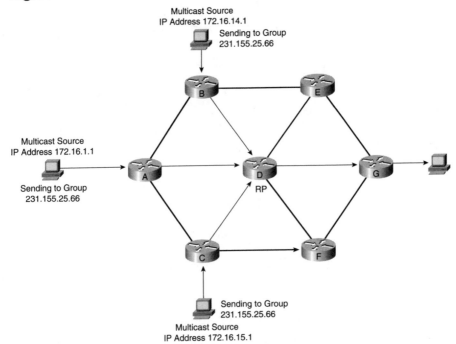

Using shared delivery trees means the shortest path from each source to each receiver is not taken because all traffic is sent to the RP first. The shortest path is taken from the RP to the receivers.

The four ways to configure PIM SM on Cisco routers are

- Static RP

- Auto RP

- PIM SM version 2

- Anycast RP

The next few sections examine each method.

Static RP

With *static RP*, a router is selected as the RP for the network and all multicast routers are configured with the IP address of the RP. When a leaf router receives an IGMP join message for a multicast group, the leaf router sends a join message to the RP to build a multicast path from the RP to the leaf router. When a router that is directly connected to a multicast source receives a multicast packet from the source, the multicast packet is sent in a register message to the RP. The register message is sent using IP unicast. The register message builds the multicast route from the router attached to the source to the RP. After the path is established, the RP sends a register stop message to the router. The router stops sending the packets using unicast and switches to sending them through multicast. In this way, every source has a shortest path to the RP, and the RP point has a shortest path to each receiver. (See Figure 9-21.)

Figure 9-21   Registering with the RP

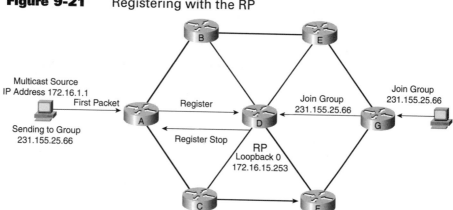

Every router must have IP multicasting enabled and an interior routing protocol configured. For sparse mode, each interface is configured using the **ip pim sparse-mode** command. (See Example 9-3.)

Example 9-3   Configuring PIM SM with a Static RP

```
All Routers
ip multicast-routing

ip pim rp-address 172.16.15.253

All interfaces
interface Ethernet0/0
 ip pim sparse-mode
```

The address of the RP is the IP address of the loopback interface on Router D. The loopback is used for availability. As long as there is an IP path to Router D, the loopback interface is reachable.

A drawback with using static RP is that there is only one RP. If the RP should fail, sparse mode will no longer be operational. The next methods for configuring sparse mode multicast—Auto-RP, PIM SM version 2, and Anycast RP—overcome this limitation.

Auto-RP

With *Auto-RP*, multiple RPs can be configured, and each RP can be the RP for the entire multicast address space, or a subset of the multicast address space. RPs advertise themselves as a candidate RP, and include the range of multicast addresses for which they are a candidate. Another entity called a Mapping Agent (MA) receives the candidate announcements from the candidate RPs, and the MA determines which RP will be the RP for the entire set—or subset— of multicast addresses. If there are multiple mapping agents, one of the mapping agents is elected as the active MA. Having multiple RPs and MAs in the network adds redundancy. (See Figure 9-22.)

Figure 9-22   PIM SM Using Auto-RP

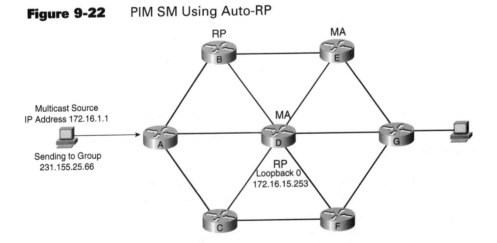

A router can be both a candidate RP and candidate MA, or the functions can be separated to different routers.

Every router must have IP multicasting enabled and an interior routing protocol configured. For sparse mode, each interface is configured using the **ip pim sparse-dense-mode** command. Sparse-dense allows the routers to revert to dense mode if the RP is unavailable. The basic configurations for Auto-RP are shown in Example 9-4.

Example 9-4   Configuring Auto-RP

```
All Routers
ip multicast-routing

On the Rendezvous Points
ip pim send-rp announce loopback0 scope 16

On the Mapping Agents
ip pim send-rp-discovery loopback0 scope 16

All interfaces
interface Ethernet0/0
 ip pim sparse-dense-mode
```

Loopback0 is used in the command to configure the RPs and MAs to provide redundancy. As long as there is an IP path to the RP, the other routers can contact the RP.

Scope 16 limits the range of the announcements sent by an MA or RP. The value used sets the hop count, or number of routers, an announcement can pass through before being dropped.

PIM SM Version 2

PIM SM version 2 is similar to Auto-RP. A set of one or more candidate RPs is configured. Each candidate RP can be configured to support the entire multicast address space or a subset of the multicast address space. Bootstrap routers (BSRs) serve the same function as MAs in Auto-RP. (See Figure 9-23.) One or more BSRs are configured as candidate BSRs. The priority of a BSR determines the router elected as the active BSR. If the candidate BSRs have the same priority, the candidate BSR with the highest IP address is elected as the active BSR. Usually, the candidate RPs and BSRs use the IP address of their loopback interface for identification.

Figure 9-23   PIM SM Version 2

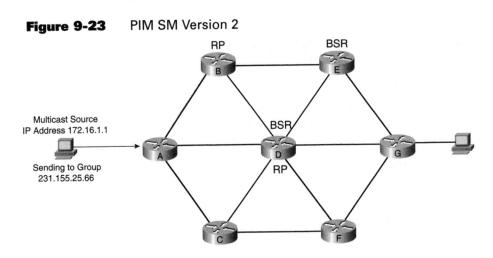

The active BSR collects candidate RP advertisements from the RPs and announces the set of RPs to the multicast routers in the network. The multicast routers select the RP they use by using the RP priority for the selection.

Every router must have IP multicasting enabled and an interior routing protocol configured. For sparse mode, each interface is configured using the **ip pim sparse-dense-mode** command. Sparse-dense allows the routers to revert to dense mode if the RP is unavailable. Example 9-5 contains the basic configurations for PIM-SM version 2.

Example 9-5   Configuring PIM SM Version 2

```
All Routers
ip multicast-routing

On the Rendezvous Points
ip pim rp-candidate loopback0

On the bootstrap routers
ip pim bsr-candidate loopback0

All interfaces
interface Ethernet0/0
 ip pim sparse-dense-mode
```

Anycast RP

A limitation of using Static RP is the address of the RP is static, and if the RP fails, the multicast network fails. Because the RP is static, the multicast routers cannot switch to dense mode as they have no way of knowing the RP has failed.

With Anycast RP, multiple RPs are configured with the same loopback IP address, and all multicast routers are statically configured with this loopback address. (See Figure 9-24.) This loopback address is advertised by the unicast interior routing protocol, and each multicast router chooses the nearest RP.

If one of the RPs fails, the unicast routing protocol no longer advertises the address of the RP. Routers using the failed RP switch to another RP after the interior routing protocol converges.

Figure 9-24 shows two multicast sources and two multicast receivers. The source directly connected to Router A is sending traffic to the multicast group 231.155.25.66. When Router A receives this traffic, it is sent to the nearest RP, Router B. The source directly connected to Router G is sending traffic to the multicast group 229.155.09.55. When Router G receives this traffic, it is sent to the nearest RP, Router F.

The receiver attached to Router E has joined the multicast group 229.155.9.55. Router G then builds a multicast path to the nearest RP, Router B. The receiver attached to Router C has joined group 231.155.25.66. Router C then builds a multicast path to the nearest RP, Router F. Do you see a problem?

Figure 9-24   Anycast RP

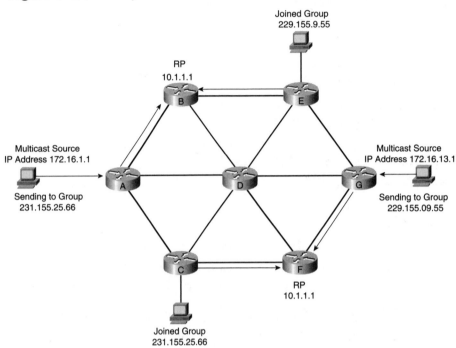

Router B is receiving traffic for the multicast group 231.155.25.66, and Router F is receiving traffic for the multicast group 229.155.9.55. Router E has a path to Router B, but needs the traffic from Router F. Router G has a path to Router F, but needs the traffic from Router B. You need a method to transfer the multicast traffic between the RPs. The protocol used to accomplish this is called the *Multicast Source Discovery Protocol (MSDP)*. In Figure 9-25, MSDP is configured between the RPs—Routers B and F—for the exchange of multicast source information.

Every router must have IP multicasting enabled and an interior routing protocol configured. For sparse mode, each interface is configured using the **ip pim sparse-mode** command. Sparse-dense mode cannot be used because the RPs are statically defined, and the routers have no way of knowing the RPs have failed. Example 9-6 shows the basic configurations for Anycast.

Figure 9-25   MSDP

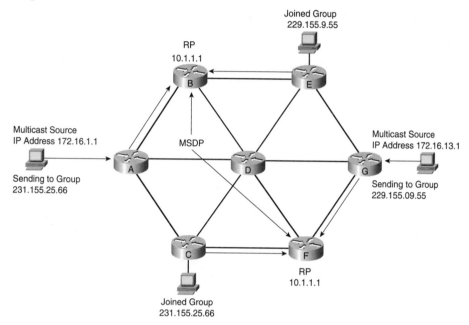

Example 9-6   Configuring PIM SM with Anycast

```
All Routers
ip multicast-routing

Router B
interface loopback0
 ip address 10.1.1.2 255.255.255.255 (whatever IP address you are using for
  loopback0)
interface loopback1
 ip add 10.1.1.1 255.255.255.255 (whatever IP address is used for the RP)
ip msdp peer 10.1.1.3 connect-source loopback0 (Address of router F)

Router F
interface loopback0
 ip address 10.1.1.3 255.255.255.255 (whatever IP address you are using for
  loopback0)
interface loopback1
 ip add 10.1.1.1 255.255.255.255 (whatever IP address is used for the RP)
ip msdp peer 10.1.1.2 connect-source loopback0 (Address of router B)

On all routers
ip pim rp-address 10.1.1.1

All interfaces
interface Ethernet0/0
 ip pim sparse-mode
```

Reserved Multicast Addresses

Table 9-1 lists some of the multicast addresses reserved for specific purposes. These should not be used by multicast applications. For example, the multicast address 224.0.0.5 is used by OSPF for the exchange of protocol information between OSPF routers.

Table 9-1   Reserved Multicast Addresses

Multicast Address	Description
224.0.0.1	All systems on a subnet
224.0.0.2	All routers on a subnet
224.0.0.5	All OSPF routers
224.0.0.6	OSPF designated routers
224.0.0.9	RIP version 2 routers
224.0.0.10	EIGRP routers
224.0.0.13	PIM routers

Summary

Multicast routing forwards class D IP packets from a source to one or more destinations. With unicast IP routing, an IP packet is forwarded based on the destination address. For multicast routing, a multicast packet is forwarded only if it is received on the RPF interface. The RPF interface is the interface that would be used to send a unicast packet back to the multicast source.

IGMP is the protocol used by multicast hosts to signal their group membership to their directly connected routers. IGMP group membership builds a multicast delivery tree between the multicast sources and receivers. PIM-DM uses source based delivery trees while PIM-SM uses shared delivery trees.

The two protocols used for multicast routing are PIM DM and PIM SM. PIM DM assumes all neighboring multicast routers want to receive all multicast traffic unless told otherwise. PIM SM routers assume multicast neighbors do not want to receive multicast traffic unless requested.

PIM SM can be configured one of four ways: static RP, Auto-RP, version 2, or Anycast RP. Static RP uses a fixed RP. If the RP fails, multicast routing fails. Auto-RP and version 2 use one or more dynamic RPs, allowing one RP to assume the duties of a failed RP. Anycast is a method of using more than one static RP, allowing a RP to assume the duties of a failed RP.

Chapter Review Questions

You can find the answers to these questions in Appendix A.

1. Explain the difference between the forwarding of a unicast IP packet and the forwarding of a multicast IP packet.

2. Explain the difference between dense mode and sparse mode multicast.

3. What is the multicast Ethernet address for IP address 227.128.64.12?

4. Determine at least four IP multicast groups that have the multicast Ethernet address of 01 00 5E 00 40 0C?

5. Why are the Cisco multicast routing protocols referred to as *protocol independent*?

6. What protocols do switches use to prevent the broadcasting of multicast traffic?

7. Describe the operation of Anycast RP.

8. What is the range of IP multicast addresses?

9. What is the purpose of the interface command **ip multicast spares-dense-mode**?

10. Explain the function of a rendezvous point?

References

Use the following references to learn more about the concepts described in this chapter:

- Cain, B., S. Deering, I. Kouvelas, B. Fenner, and A. Thyagarajan. October 2002. RFC 3376, Internet Group Management Protocol, Version 3.

- Cisco Documentation, Cisco.com.

- Cisco Systems, Inc. *Interdomain Multicast Solutions Guide*. 2002. Indianapolis: Cisco Press.

- Williamson, Beau. *Developing IP Multicast Networks*, Volume 1. 1999. Indianapolis: Cisco Press.

Answers to Chapter Review Questions

Chapter 1

1. Describe why postal addresses and telephone numbers are routable.

   Answer: A postal address has three components that can be used to deliver mail: state, city, and street. A phone number has an area code and exchange. At the core layer, mail can be delivered to the next post office based on only the state or city and state information. A phone number is delivered at the core layer based on the area code.

2. What is the purpose of a default route?

   Answer: A default route is used if there is not a specific entry in the routing table for the destination.

3. Describe the difference between routing and switching.

   Answer: Routing moves a letter or telephone call to the access layer (as in a street or telephone exchange). Switching makes the final delivery. A switching decision is made on the part of the address that is not used in routing (as in the street number or last four digits of a phone number).

4. What does the term information hiding mean in relation to route summarization?

   Answer: At the core layer in the postal system, the only information that is needed to make a routing decision is the state or city/state information. The specific street names and street numbers are hidden, the core layer does not need this information. At the core layer in the telephone system, the area code is used to make a routing decision. The specific exchange or last four digits of the phone number are not needed, or hidden, from the core layer.

5. How does the use of a hierarchical routing structure (access, distribution, and core) enable a scalable delivery system?

Answer: If a delivery system is not divided into access, distribution, and core layers, every point in the system needs to maintain every possible destination address to make a delivery decision. The use of a layered system means each layer needs only the information necessary to deliver to the next layer, either above or below.

6. Why are multiple protocols used, such as a package, addressing, delivery, and transportation instead of using one protocol defining everything?

Answer: Using multiple protocols is modular and allows changes to one protocol without affecting the others. For example, if the addressing protocol is dependent on the delivery protocol, changes to one would imply changes need to be made to the other.

7. Can you think of another familiar system that routes using a hierarchical delivery system?

Answer: The airport system. At the core routing level, there are major hub airports such as Denver, Chicago, New York, and Atlanta. The core airports are responsible for routing people and cargo to major geographical areas. Core airports connect with regional airports that serve a specific area; regional airports are at the distribution layer. Finally, to reach your final destination, you can take a bus, a cab, a train, or rent a car. This can be considered the access layer.

8. Explain how a letter from New York City to San Diego is routed using the address information.

Answer: The source address is not used unless the letter needs to be returned to the sender. Using the destination address, the access level post office in New York examines the state, city, and street information to determine if it is directly connected to the destination. If not, the letter is sent to the distribution layer post office using a default route. The distribution layer post office also examines the state, city, and street information to determine if it is directly connected to an access layer post office servicing the particular street. If it isn't, the letter is routed to the core level using a default route. The core level post office examines the state name, and if the state name does not equal New York, the letter is delivered to the core post office for the state of California. The California core post office delivers the letter to the distribution post office that handles the city of San Diego. The San Diego distribution post office delivers the letter to the access post office that handles the destination street. Finally, the access level switch delivers the letter to the proper destination.

9. What are the access, distribution, and core components of a postal address?

   Answer: The street name and number are the access layer components. The city name is the distribution layer component. The state name is the core layer component.

10. What are the access, distribution, and core components of a North American phone number?

   Answer: The last four digits are the used at the access layer to identify a particular telephone. The next three numbers are used at the distribution layer to identify an exchange that services several phone numbers. The area code is used at the core level for routing between different regions.

Chapter 2

1. This is a speed drill. Using only your head, convert the following binary numbers to decimal.

   11100000

   11111100

   10000000

   11110000

   00111111

   Answer: 224, 252, 128, 240, and 63 (64 − 1)

2. Convert $FACE1234_{16}$ to dotted decimal.

   Answer: $FA_{16} = 250_{10}$, $CE_{16} = 206_{10}$, $12_{16} = 18_{10}$, and $34_{16} = 52_{10}$

   $FACE1234_{16} = 250.206.18.52$ dotted decimal

3. Convert $10100010111101011001110110001011_2$ to hexadecimal.

   Answer: A2F59D8B

4. Convert $10100010111101011001110110001011_2$ to dotted decimal.

   Answer: Convert to dotted hexadecimal first, and then convert each hexadecimal number pair to decimal.

   A2.F5.9D.8B then 162.245.157.139

5. Convert $10100010111101011001110110001011_2$ to octal.

   Answer: 24275316613_8

6. True or False. Converting between number bases is fun.

   Answer: True.

7. Convert 12345670_8 to hexadecimal.

   Answer: Convert each octal digit into three binary digits, and then convert the binary result to hexadecimal.

   001 010 011 100 101 110 111 000

   0010 1001 1100 1011 1011 1000

   29CBB8

8. Convert 734215_8 to binary.

   Answer: 111 011 100 010 001 101

9. Convert 734215_{16} to binary.

   Answer: 0111 0011 0100 0010 0001 0101$_2$

10. Convert 262988031_{10} to hexadecimal.

Chapter 3

1. What is the broadcast address for network 142.16.72.0/23?

   Answer: 142.16.73.255

2. Subnet 198.4.81.0/24 into the maximum number of networks that can support 28 hosts each.

   Answer: 198.4.81.0/27 and the subnets are:

   198.4.81.0/27

   198.4.81.32/27

   198.4.81.64/27

   198.4.81.96/27

   198.4.81.128/27

   198.4.81.160/27

   198.4.81.192/27

   198.4.81.224/27

3. What is the broadcast address for network 198.4.81.96/27?

   Answer: 198.4.81.127

4. What is the prefix and subnet mask that summarizes the following networks:

   162.8.0.0/22

   162.8.4.0/22

   162.8.8.0/22

   162.8.12.0/22

   Answer: 162.8.0.0/20

5. Using the following routing table determine the best route to reach the host at address 132.19.237.5.

   NetworkOutput Interface

   132.0.0.0/8Serial 0

132.16.0.0/11Ethernet 1

132.16.233.0/22Ethernet 2

Answer: 132.16.0.0/11 because it matches more network bits than 132.0.0.0/8. Network 132.16.233.0/22 and 132.19.237.5/22 do not match on the network address.

6. What is the range of host addresses for network 172.16.53.96/27?

Answer: 172.16.53.97 through 172.16.53.126

7. How many two-host subnets can be made from a /24 network?

Answer: 64 because 2 bits are needed for the hosts on the network, leaving 6 bits for the subnet.

8. What is the full IPv6 address represented by FF02::130F:5?

Answer: FF02:0000:0000:0000:0000:0000:130F:0005

Chapter 4

1. For the network in Figure 4-15 and the configurations given, determine the contents of the routing table on Router B.

```
Router A
router rip
 version 1
 passive-interface Ethernet0
 passive-interface Ethernet1
 passive-interface Ethernet2
 network 172.16.0.0
 network 64.0.0.0

Router B
router rip
```

```
version 1
passive-interface Ethernet0
passive-interface Ethernet1
network 172.16.0.0
```

Figure 4-15   Review Questions 1 – 3

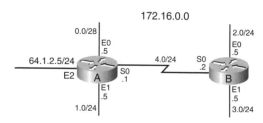

Answer: Router B routing table:

```
R    64.0.0.0/8 [120/1] via 172.16.4.1, 00:00:01, Serial0
     172.16.0.0/24 is subnetted, 4 subnets
C       172.16.4.0 is directly connected, Serial0
R       172.16.1.0 [120/1] via 172.16.4.1, 00:00:01, Serial0
C       172.16.2.0 is directly connected, Ethernet0
C       172.16.3.0 is directly connected, Ethernet1
```

172.16.1.0/24 is advertised by Router A, the same subnet mask and same major network number as the serial interface.

172.16.0.0/24 is not advertised; the subnet mask does not match the subnet mask on the serial interface.

Network 64.1.2.5/24 is autosummarized to a classful boundary (/8).

2. For the network in Figure 4-15 and the given configurations, determine the contents of the routing table on Router B.

```
Router A
router rip
```

```
version 2
passive-interface Ethernet0
passive-interface Ethernet1
passive-interface Ethernet2
network 172.16.0.0
network 64.0.0.0
Router B
router rip
 version 2
 passive-interface Ethernet0
 passive-interface Ethernet1
 network 172.16.0.0
```

Answer: Router B routing table:

```
R     64.0.0.0/8 [120/1] via 172.16.4.1, 00:00:02, Serial0
      172.16.0.0/16 is variably subnetted, 5 subnets, 2 masks
C        172.16.4.0/24 is directly connected, Serial0
R        172.16.0.0/28 [120/1] via 172.16.4.1, 00:00:02, Serial0
R        172.16.1.0/24 [120/1] via 172.16.4.1, 00:00:02, Serial0
C        172.16.2.0/24 is directly connected, Ethernet0
C        172.16.3.0/24 is directly connected, Ethernet1
```

All 172.16.0.0 networks are advertised along with their subnet masks.

Network 64.1.2.0/24 is autosummarized to a classful boundary (/8).

3. For the network in Figure 4-15, and the given configurations, determine the contents of the routing tables on Routers A and B.

```
Router A
router rip
 version 2
 passive-interface Ethernet0
 passive-interface Ethernet1
 passive-interface Ethernet2
```

```
network 172.16.0.0
network 64.0.0.0
no auto-summary


Router B
router rip
 version 2
 passive-interface Ethernet0
 passive-interface Ethernet1
 network 172.16.0.0
```

Answer: Router B routing table:

```
Router B
     64.0.0.0/24 is subnetted, 1 subnets
R       64.1.2.0 [120/1] via 172.16.4.1, 00:00:02, Serial0
     172.16.0.0/16 is variably subnetted, 5 subnets, 2 masks
C       172.16.4.0/24 is directly connected, Serial0
R       172.16.0.0/28 [120/1] via 172.16.4.1, 00:00:02, Serial0
R       172.16.1.0/24 [120/1] via 172.16.4.1, 00:00:02, Serial0
C       172.16.2.0/24 is directly connected, Ethernet0
C       172.16.3.0/24 is directly connected, Ethernet1
```

Network 64.1.2.0/24 is advertised by Router A because autosummary is disabled:

```
Router A
     64.0.0.0/8 is variably subnetted, 2 subnets, 2 masks
R       64.0.0.0/8 [120/2] via 172.16.4.2, 00:00:06, Serial0
C       64.1.2.0/24 is directly connected, Ethernet2
     172.16.0.0/16 is variably subnetted, 5 subnets, 2 masks
C       172.16.4.0/24 is directly connected, Serial0
C       172.16.0.0/28 is directly connected, Ethernet0
C       172.16.1.0/24 is directly connected, Ethernet1
R       172.16.2.0/24 [120/1] via 172.16.4.2, 00:00:06, Serial0
R       172.16.3.0/24 [120/1] via 172.16.4.2, 00:00:08, Serial0
```

Autosummarization is enabled on Router B, so Router B autosummarizes the 64.0.0.0/8 network and advertises to Router A. Router A accepts this prefix because it is not in the routing table.

4. For the network in Figure 4-16, determine the interface summary address commands on Routers B, C, D, E, F, and G to summarize the RIP routes. Assume RIP version 2 is being used.

Figure 4-16   Review Question 4

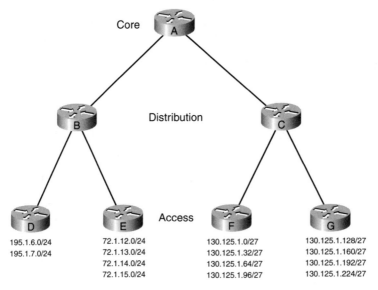

195.1.6.0/24	
195.1.7.0/24	

72.1.12.0/24	130.125.1.0/27	130.125.1.128/27	
72.1.13.0/24	130.125.1.32/27	130.125.1.160/27	
72.1.14.0/24	130.125.1.64/27	130.125.1.192/27	
72.1.15.0/24	130.125.1.96/27	130.125.1.224/27	

Answer:

Router D:

```
ip summary-address rip 195.1.6.0 255.255.254.0
```

Router E:

```
ip summary-address rip 72.1.12.0 255.255.252.0
```

Router F:

```
ip summary-address 130.125.1.0 255.255.255.128
```

Router G:

```
ip summary-address 130.125.1.128 255.255.255.128
```

Router B:

none—195.1.6.0/23 and 72.1.12/22 cannot be combined

Router C:

```
ip summary-address 130.125.1.0 255.255.255.0
```

Chapter 5

1. Determine the successor and any feasible successors for Network 1 in Figure 5-14 for each router in the network.

Figure 5-14   Network for Review Question 1

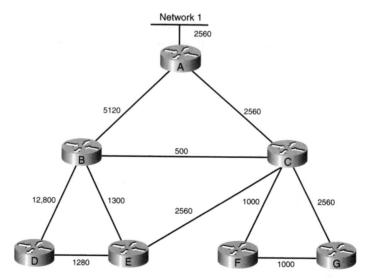

Answer:

Routers B and C receive a reported distance from Router A of 2560. The feasible distance (FD) on Router B is 2560 + 5120 = 7680 and will be advertised to C. The FD on Router C is 2560 + 2560 = 5120 and will be advertised to B.

Router B

From	RD	FD
A	2560	7680
C	5120	5620

Router C

From	RD	FD
A	2560	5120
B	7680	8180

The successor on B is Router C and the feasible successor is Router A (RD < FD). The successor on C is Router A and there is no feasible successor (Reported Distance > FD).

Router D

From	RD	FD
B	5620	18420
E	6920	8300

Router E

From	RD	FD
B	5620	6920
C	5120	7680

The successor on D is Router E and the feasible successor is Router B. The successor on E is Router B and the feasible successor is Router C.

Router F

From	RD	FD
C	5120	6120
G	7680	8680

Router G

From	RD	FD
C	5120	7680
F	6120	7120

The successor on F is Router C and there is no feasible successor. The successor on G is Router F and Router C is the feasible successor.

2. Explain the difference between a classful and a classless routing protocol.

Answer: Classless routing protocols advertise subnet mask information along with the network prefixes. Classful routing protocols do not. Therefore, for a classful protocol, all subnets for the major network number being used must be the same length. Also, classful protocol cannot support discontiguous networks prefixes.

3. What are the states that an EIGRP route can be in and what do these states mean?

Answer: The *passive state* means that a router has a successor for a route. The *active state* means that a router does not have a successor or feasible successor for a route and is actively sending queries to neighbors to get information about the route.

4. Explain the relationship between reported distance and feasible distance and how they determine successors and feasible successors.

Answer: The reported distance to a route that is sent to another router is the feasible distance on the reporting router. Feasible distance is the reported distance plus the metric between the receiving and reporting routers. The route with the lowest feasible distance is the successor. Any routes with a reported distance that is less than the feasible distance are feasible successors.

5. For the router in Figure 5-15, configure EIGRP so that it is active on all interfaces. Use a minimum number of network commands.

Figure 5-15   Network for Review Question 5

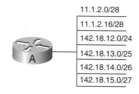

11.1.2.0/28
11.1.2.16/28
142.18.12.0/24
142.18.13.0/25
142.18.14.0/26
142.18.15.0/27

Answer: Don't make this difficult. Just use classful network statements.

```
router eigrp 1
 network 11.0.0.0
 network 142.18.0.0
```

6. Determine the EIGRP command to summarize the following networks:

10.1.0.0/19

10.1.32.0/19

10.1.64.0/19

10.1.96.0/19

Answer: You need to examine the third byte because that is the byte where the four prefixes differ:

0 = 0 0 0 0 0 0 0 0

32 = 0 0 1 0 0 0 0 0

64 = 0 1 0 0 0 0 0 0

96 = 0 1 1 0 0 0 0 0

The last 7 bits are irrelevant, so the mask is 1 0 0 0 0 0 0 0 and the EIGRP command is **ip summary-address eigrp 1 10.1.0.0 255.255.128.0**

Chapter 6

1. What are the purposes of areas in an OSPF network?

Answer: Areas allow the design of a hierarchical network. Routes can be summarized or blocked in an area to reduce the amount of routing information on internal OSPF routers.

2. Why are intra-area summary routes not allowed?

Answer: OSPF databases on routers in the same area must be identical. If route summarization was allowed within an area, some routers would have specific routes and some routers would have summary routes for routes in the area. If this were allowed, the databases for the area would never agree.

3. What types of routes are allowed into a stub area?

Answer: OSPF intra-area and interarea routes, and a default route. External routes are not advertised into a stub area.

4. What types of routes are allowed into a totally stubby area?

Answer: OSPF intra-area routes and a default route. OSPF interarea and external routes are not advertised into a totally stubby area.

5. What types of routes are allowed into a NSSA?

Answer: OSPF intra-area and interarea routes, and possibly a default route. External routes from ABRs are blocked, and external routes from ASBRs are converted to N1 or N2 routes.

6. What types of routes are allowed into a totally NSSA?

Answer: OSPF intra-area routes and a default route. External routes from ABRs are blocked, and external routes from ASBRs are converted to N1 or N2 routes.

7. What is the difference between an E1 and E2 OSPF route?

Answer: An E1 route contains the OSPF cost to reach the ASBR plus the cost from the ASBR to the external route. An E2 route contains only the cost from the ASBR to the external route.

8. What are the three types of OSPF routers?

Answer: ABR, internal router, and ASBR.

9. What are the six OSPF route types?

Answer: Intra-area, interarea, E1, E2, N1, and N2.

10. Where can routes be summarized in an OSPF network?

Answer: OSPF routes are summarized on an ABR. External routes are summarized on an ASBR.

11. How is the OSPF router ID determined?

Answer: If physical interfaces are only used, the OSPF router ID is the highest IP address assigned to an active physical interface. If loopback interfaces are used, the OSPF router ID is the highest IP address assigned to a loopback interface. If the **router-id**command is used with the OSPF configuration, the address used with this command will be the router ID.

12. How does OSPF determine the DR on a multi-access network?

Answer: The router with the highest interface priority will be the router ID. If all the interface priorities on the multi-access network are the same, the router with the highest router ID will be the DR.

13. How does OSPF determine an interarea shortest path?

Answer: First, calculate the shortest path to an ABR.

Second, calculate the shortest path across area 0 to an ABR that is attached to the destination area.

Third, calculate the shortest path across the destination area from the ABR to the destination network.

14. What is the purpose of an OSPF virtual link?

Answer: To connect a nonzero area to the backbone if the nonzero area becomes disconnected from the backbone. A virtual link can also be used if the backbone, or area 0, becomes discontiguous.

15. How is the OSPF cost of an interface calculated?

Answer: By default, the cost of an OSPF interface is 100,000,000/(Interface Bandwidth). The constant 100,000,000 can be changed using the **auto-cost reference-bandwidth** command.

16. The following OSPF routes originate in OSPF area 1:

188.14.19.0/28

188.14.19.16/28

188.14.19.32/28

188.14.19.48/28

What is the command to summarize these routes on the ABR between area 1 and the backbone?

Answer: Area 1 range 188.14.19.0 255.255.255.192

17. How many OSPF databases are on an OSPF router?

Answer: The number of OSPF databases on a router is equal to the number of OSPF areas configured on the router.

18. What is the administrative distance of OSPF routes?

Answer: 110

19. If a router learns about the same network prefix through RIP, IGRP, EIGRP, and OSPF, which route will be preferred?

Answer: EIGRP has an administrative distance of 90.

IGRP has an administrative distance of 100.

OSPF has an administrative distance of 110.

RIP has an administrative distance of 120.

Therefore, the EIGRP route is preferred.

Chapter 7

1. Describe the structure and format of an NSAP address.

Answer: An NSAP address has a length of 8 to 20 bytes and consists of three components:

- One to 13 byte area ID

- Six byte system ID

- One byte NSAP selector that is always equal to zero for a router

2. Assume a router has a loopback address of 135.77.9.254. Convert the loopback address to an IS-IS system ID.

Answer: The loopback address written in dotted decimal and using three digits for each byte has a value of 135.077.009.254. The system ID is 13.50.77.00.92.54.

3. Describe the difference between an OSPF and IS-IS backbone.

Answer: OSPF has a backbone area or area 0. All nonzero areas must be connected to the backbone through a router or a virtual link. IS-IS has a backbone area made up of a contiguous chain of Level 2 capable routers.

4. In IS-IS, what does Level 1 routing mean?

Answer: Level 1 routing is routing between destinations in the same IS-IS area.

5. What is the OSPF counterpart to Level 1 routing?

Answer: Intra-area routing.

6. In IS-IS, what is the function of a Level 1-2 router?

Answer: A Level 1-2 router has two IS-IS databases. The Level 1 database is used for routing to destinations within the router's configured area. The Level 2 database is used to route between destinations in different areas.

7. What is the OSPF counterpart to a Level 1-2 IS-IS router?

Answer: An Area Border Router (ABR).

8. What is the difference between the types of routes allowed by default into IS-IS and OSPF areas?

Answer: By default, all routes are advertised into all OSPF areas. This includes interarea OSPF routes and external routes that have been injected into OSPF. By default, IS-IS does not advertise interarea or external routes into an area, but injects a default route.

9. What is route leaking?

Answer: Redistribution of Level 2 routes into an area as Level 1 routes.

10. Compare IS-IS metrics with OSPF metrics.

Answer: An OSPF interface metric is determined from the interface bandwidth. By default, all IS-IS interface metrics are equal to 10.

11. What is the difference between an IS-IS narrow and wide metric?

Answer: A narrow metric uses 6 bits for the interface metric and 10 bits for the path metric. A wide metric uses 24 bits for the interface metric and 32 bits for the path metric.

Chapter 8

1. Describe four differences between the operation of IBGP and EBGP.

    Answer:

    A. IBGP is the protocol used between routers in the same autonomous system. EBGP is the protocol used between routers in different autonomous systems.

    B. IBGP routes must be synchronized before they can be transferred to the IP routing table (unless synchronization is disabled).

    C. EBGP sets the next hop attribute to the IP address of the interface used to communicate with the EBGP peer. The next hop attribute is not modified when an IBGP router advertises a prefix to an IBGP peer if the prefix was learned from an EBGP neighbor.

    D. EBGP advertises all prefixes learned from an EBGP neighbor to all other EBGP neighbors. IBGP routers do not advertise prefixes learned from one IBGP neighbor to another IBGP neighbor.

2. What is the purpose of the AS_PATH attribute?

    Answer: If a router has more than one route to the same IP prefix, the best path is the one with the shortest AS_PATH (assuming other BGP attributes are equal).

3. What is the purpose of the WEIGHT attribute?

    Answer: If a router has more than one route to the same IP prefix, the best path is the one with the highest WEIGHT value.

4. What is the scope of the WEIGHT attribute?

    Answer: WEIGHT has only local significance and is not advertised to BGP peers.

5. What is the purpose of the LOCAL_PREF attribute?

    Answer: If a router has more than one route to the same IP prefix, the best path is the one with the highest LOCAL_PREF (assuming the WEIGHT attribute for the routes is equal).

6. What is the scope of the LOCAL_PREF attribute?

Answer: The LOCAL_PREF attribute is advertised throughout the autonomous system.

7. What is the purpose of the metric or MULTI_EXIT_DISC attribute?

Answer: MED is used to prefer a path into an autonomous system. A lower MED value is preferred.

8. What is the order of preference for the BGP attributes AS_PATH, LOCAL_PREF, MED, and WEIGHT?

Answer: WEIGHT, LOACL_PREF, AS_PATH, MED

9. Name all the ways for installing a prefix in the BGP routing table.

Answer:

A. Using the **network**command to transfer a router from the IP routing table to the BGP routing table

B. Redistributing routes from the IP routing table to the BGP routing table

C. Learned from a BGP neighbor

10. What is the first thing that BGP checks to determine if a prefix is accessible?

Answer: BGP checks the NEXT_HOP attribute to determine if the NEXT_HOP is accessible or in the IP routing table.

11. What is synchronization?

Answer: Synchronization is a property of IBGP. An IBGP router will not accept a prefix received from an IBGP neighbor if the prefix is not already in the IP routing table.

12. Name two methods for reducing the number of IBGP connections.

Answer: Route reflector and confederation.

13. Why does IBGP require a full mesh?

Answer: BGP uses the AS_PATH attribute for loop detection. If a router sees its own AS number in a BGP advertisement, the advertisement is dropped. IBGP routers have the same AS number so the AS number cannot be used for loop detection. IBGP neighbors will not advertise prefixes learned from one IBGP neighbor to another IBGP neighbor; therefore, a full mesh is required.

14. What is the major difference between BGP and IGP route summarization?

Answer: When a summary address is created with an IGP (EIGRP, OSPF, and IS-IS), the specific routes of the summary are not advertised. BGP advertises the summary, and all the specific routes of the summary unless they are specifically suppressed.

15. Why is BGP a better choice for Internet routing than the IGPs?

Answer: RIP version 1 and IGRP are classful protocols and do not advertise subnet mask information. RIP version 2 has a limited network diameter of 15 hops. EIGRP, OSPF, and IS-IS use computational intensive algorithms for determining a shortest path. BGP relies on simple techniques for best path selection and loop detection, and can handle the number of network prefixes required for Internet routing.

16. What are the four general types of BGP attributes?

Answer: Well-known mandatory, well-known discretionary, optional transitive, and optional nontransitive.

Chapter 9

1. Explain the difference between the forwarding of a unicast IP packet and the forwarding of a multicast IP packet.

Answer: Unicast IP packets are forwarded based on the destination IP address. Multicast packets are forward based on the source IP address. If a multicast packet is received on the interface used to send a unicast packet back to the source, the multicast packet is forwarded to multicast neighbors. If the multicast packet is received on an interface that would not be used to send a unicast IP packet back to the source, the packet is discarded.

2. Explain the difference between dense mode and sparse mode multicast.

   Answer: Dense mode multicast assumes all multicast neighbors want to receive all multicast traffic unless the neighbors have specifically pruned the traffic. Sparse mode multicast assumes multicast neighbors do not want to receive multicast traffic unless they have asked for it. Dense mode uses source-based delivery trees while sparse mode uses shared delivery trees where traffic is first sent to an RP.

3. What is the multicast Ethernet address for IP address 227.128.64.12?

   Answer: The base Ethernet multicast address is 01 00 5E 00 00 00. The first byte of the IP multicast address is not used. If the second byte is greater than 127, subtract 128, giving a value of 0. The third and fourth bytes of the IP address are used as is after converting to hex. Their values, in hexadecimal, are 40 and 0C. So the Ethernet multicast address for the IP multicast address 227.128.64.12 is 01 00 5E 00 40 0C.

4. Determine at least four IP multicast groups that have the multicast Ethernet address of 01 00 5E 00 40 0C?

   Answer: The low order 32 bits of the IP address determine the multicast Ethernet address. The first four bits are always 1 1 1 0 and the next five bits can be anything. Therefore, the IP multicast addresses that map to the multicast Ethernet address of 01 00 5E 00 40 0C are

   1110 0000 0000 0000 0100 0000 1100 = 224.0.64.12

   1110 0000 1000 0000 0100 0000 1100 = 224.128.64.12

   1110 0001 0000 0000 0100 0000 1100 = 225.0.64.12

   1110 0001 1000 0000 0100 0000 1100 = 225.128.64.12

   1110 0010 0000 0000 0100 0000 1100 = 226.0.64.12

   1110 0010 1000 0000 0100 0000 1100 = 226.128.64.12

   1110 0011 0000 0000 0100 0000 1100 = 227.0.64.12

   1110 0011 1000 0000 0100 0000 1100 = 227.128.64.12

   1110 0100 0000 0000 0100 0000 1100 = 228.0.64.12

   1110 0100 1000 0000 0100 0000 1100 = 228.128.64.12

   1110 0101 0000 0000 0100 0000 1100 = 229.0.64.12

1110 0101 1000 0000 0100 0000 1100 = 229.128.64.12

1110 0110 0000 0000 0100 0000 1100 = 230.0.64.12

1110 0110 1000 0000 0100 0000 1100 = 230.128.64.12

1110 0111 0000 0000 0100 0000 1100 = 231.0.64.12

1110 0111 1000 0000 0100 0000 1100 = 231.128.64.12

1110 1000 0000 0000 0100 0000 1100 = 232.0.64.12

1110 1000 1000 0000 0100 0000 1100 = 232.128.64.12

1110 1001 0000 0000 0100 0000 1100 = 233.0.64.12

1110 1001 1000 0000 0100 0000 1100 = 233.128.64.12

1110 1010 0000 0000 0100 0000 1100 = 234.0.64.12

1110 1010 1000 0000 0100 0000 1100 = 234.128.64.12

1110 1011 0000 0000 0100 0000 1100 = 235.0.64.12

1110 1011 1000 0000 0100 0000 1100 = 235.128.64.12

1110 1100 0000 0000 0100 0000 1100 = 236.0.64.12

1110 1100 1000 0000 0100 0000 1100 = 236.128.64.12

1110 1101 0000 0000 0100 0000 1100 = 237.0.64.12

1110 1101 1000 0000 0100 0000 1100 = 237.128.64.12

1110 1110 0000 0000 0100 0000 1100 = 238.0.64.12

1110 1110 1000 0000 0100 0000 1100 = 238.128.64.12

1110 1111 0000 0000 0100 0000 1100 = 239.0.64.12

1110 1111 1000 0000 0100 0000 1100 = 239.128.64.12

5. Why are the Cisco multicast routing protocols referred to as *protocol independent*?

Answer: Multicast forwarding decisions are based on the entries in the unicast IP routing table. Multicast is not dependent on how the unicast IP routing table was built; you can use any dynamic interior routing protocol, static routes, or a combination of the two.

6. What protocols do switches use to prevent the broadcasting of multicast traffic?

Answer: CGMP and IGMP Snooping

7. Describe the operation of Anycast RP.

Answer: Two or more RPs are configured with the same IP address. The IP addresses of the RPs are advertised using a unicast IP routing protocol. Each multicast router chooses the closest RP. If an RP fails, the routers switch to the next nearest RP after the unicast IP routing protocol converges. The MSDP is used between RPs to exchange active multicast source information.

8. What is the range of IP multicast addresses?

Answer: 224.0.0.0–239.255.255.255

9. What is the purpose of the interface command **ip multicast spares-dense-mode**?

Answer: Used with PIMSM Auto-RP and version 2. If the RPs fail, the router reverts to dense mode.

10. Explain the function of a rendezvous point?

Answer: A RP is the focal point for multicast traffic. Traffic is forwarded to the RP from multicast sources. The RP then forwards traffic to multicast receivers.

Glossary

access layer   The routing layer containing the access routers.

access router   A router that is directly connected to the switches used for final delivery of packets.

Address Resolution Protocol (ARP)   Used to determine the Ethernet address associated with a specific IP address on a LAN.

administrative or admin distance   A number assigned to every IP routing protocol used to determine the best route to a destination when the route is learned from more than one routing protocol. The route with the lowest administrative distance is considered to be the best route.

aggregation   Grouping multiple destinations into one address. Also referred to as information hiding or summarization.

area border router (ABR)   In OSPF, a router that has at least one interface configured in area 0 and at least one interface configured in a nonzero area.

ARP request   A message sent by a host requesting the Ethernet address associated with a particular IP address.

asymmetrical routing   When the path taken from the source to the destination is different than the path taken from the destination to the source.

autonomous system   A set of routers under a single technical administration.

autonomous system boundary router (ASBR)   Any router that has been configured for OSPF and is injecting or redistributing static, connected, or routes learned from another dynamic routing protocol.

Auto-RP   A dynamic Cisco proprietary method of selecting RPs in a multicast network.

Backup Designated Router (BDR) The OSPF router that assumes the duties of the designated router if the designated router fails.

bandwidth The number of bits per second that can be sent or received on an interface.

bit or binary digit Symbol used in the binary number system having a value of 0 or 1.

Border Gateway Protocol (BGP) An exterior routing protocol (EGP) used for Internet routing between autonomous systems.

broadcast address The address used to send an IP packet to every host on a local network.

byte A group of eight bits. Can also be called an octet.

Cisco Group Management Protocol (CGMP) A Cisco proprietary protocol used between Cisco routers and switches to exchange multicast group membership information.

classful routing protocol Subnet mask information is not advertised in the routing updates.

classless routing protocol Subnet mask information is advertised in the routing updates.

community attribute A number used by BGP to group prefixes for the application of one or more routing policies.

confederation Technique that reduces the number of IBGP connections by dividing the autonomous system into two or more subautonomous systems.

convergence time The time it takes to advertise a change in the network to all routers.

core post office Routes mail between distribution and other core post offices.

dead time The amount of time that must elapse between hello packets before a neighbor is declared down.

default route The route of last resort or the route used when a destination is not known.

Designated Router (DR) The OSPF router on a multi-access network that receives router link-state advertisements from the other OSPF routers attached to the network.

destination address Where the mail is going.

diffusing update algorithm (DUAL) EIGRP algorithm that determines a loop-free path to every destination network.

discontiguous subnets Subnets from the same major network number separated by one or more subnets from another major network number.

distance vector Each router does not need to know the topology for the entire network.

distance-vector routing protocol A protocol that uses hop count as its metric.

distribution post office Routes mail between access post offices.

DROTHER Any OSPF router on a multiaccess network that is neither the designated nor the backup designated router.

EIGRP topology table The table containing destinations for which a feasible successor exists.

end system An IS-IS host.

Enhanced Interior Gateway Routing Protocol (EIGRP) A Cisco proprietary, classless, interior routing protocol.

External BGP (EBGP) A connection between BGP routers in different autonomous systems.

feasible distance (FD) The lowest EIGRP metric or distance to a route.

feasible successor   An EIGRP neighbor is a feasible successor to a route if the neighbor's advertised distance to the route is lower than the router's distance to the same route.

flapping   *See* route flap.

flooding   The advertisement of network prefixes throughout an area in a link-state routing protocol.

full mesh   IBGP requires every IBGP router to have a BGP connection to every other IBGP router unless route reflectors or confederations are used.

hello packet   A packet used for neighbor discovery. The packet is periodically sent to let the neighbor know the router is still functioning.

hop   Each router between an IP source network and an IP destination network is considered a hop.

hop count   The number of routers or hops between an IP source network and an IP destination network.

host address   The part of an IP address identifying a specific host on a network.

IGMP snooping   Used by switches to inspect IGMP messages between hosts and routers to learn IGMP group membership information.

incremental update   A routing update that only contains those routes that have changed.

information hiding   Grouping multiple destinations into one address. Also referred to as aggregation or summarization.

Integrated IS-IS   The form of IS-IS that routes both Connectionless Network Protocol (CLNP) and Internet Protocol (IP).

Interior Gateway Routing Protocol (IGRP)   A Cisco proprietary, classful, distance vector interior routing protocol.

interior routing protocol A routing protocol used for the routing of IP packets within a single organization such as a company, university, or organization.

intermediate system An IS-IS router.

Internal BGP (IBGP)   A connection between BGP routers in the same autonomous system.

internal router In OSPF, a router that has all its OSPF interfaces configured for the same area.

Internet Group Management Protocol (IGMP) Protocol used by IP hosts to report their multicast group memberships to their attached routers.

IP prefix   The part of an IP address that identifies the network.

IS-IS narrow metric   A narrow metric uses 6 bits for the interface metric and 10 bits for the path metric.

IS-IS wide metric   A wide metric uses 24 bits for the interface metric and 32 bits for the path metric.

leaf router   A multicast router that has directly attached multicast hosts.

Level 1 routing   Routing within the same IS-IS area.

Level 2 routing   Routing between IS-IS areas.

link-state advertisement (LSA) A router LSA is a packet that describes the local state of a router's interfaces. A network LSA is a packet that describes the state of all routers attached to a common network.

link-state database A database containing link-state advertisements.

link-state packet (LSP) Use by IS-IS to advertise Level 1 and Level 2 link-state information.

link-state routing protocol A protocol that uses information in the link-state database to construct a graph of the links in the network and then determine an optimal route to each destination using a shortest path algorithm.

loopback interface A nonphysical, or virtual, interface configured on a router.

metric A number associated with a route indicating the goodness of the route. If a router has learned more than one route to a destination using the same routing protocol, the route with the lowest metric is considered the best route.

multicast address An IP address in the range 224.0.0.0–239.255.255.255.

Multicast Source Discovery Protocol (MSDP) The protocol used between two or more static RPs for the exchange of multicast source and group information.

multicasting Sending one packet to multiple recipients.

network address The part of an IP address identifying a specific IP network.

next hop The next IP address where an IP packet is sent on the way to the final destination.

nibble A group of four bits (half a byte/bite).

not-so-stubby area (OSPF) External routes are advertised by an OSPF ASBR into the area as NSSA routes. These routes are converted to external routes on the ABR. The ABR does not advertise external routes into the NSSA.

OSPF interarea route If an OSPF router does not have an interface configured in the area where the route originates, the router sees the route as an interarea route.

OSPF intra-area route If an OSPF router has at least one interface in an area where the route originates, the router sees the route as an intra-area route.

packet The package of data in the Internet.

passive state When an EIGRP route has a successor and a computation is not being performed for the route.

peer A BGP neighbor.

PIM SM Version 2   A standards-based method of dynamically selecting the RP in a multicast network.

PIM Sparse Mode (PIM SM)   A multicast routing protocol that assumes routers do not want to forward multicast packets for a group, unless there is an explicit request for the traffic. PIM SM uses shared delivery trees.

poison reverse   Allows the readvertising of routes out the interface on which they were learned, but the hop count is set to 16, or infinity.

process ID   A number used to identify a particular instance of a routing protocol.

Protocol Independent Multicast Dense Mode (PIM DM)   A broadcast and prune multicast routing protocol that utilizes source based delivery trees.

protocol   A set of conventions or rules.

rendezvous point (RP)   A PIM SM router that receives multicast packets from multicast sources and forwards the packets to multicast hosts.

reported distance (RD)   The distance or metric of a route advertised by an EIGRP neighbor.

Reverse Path Forwarding (RPF)   Multicasting technique in which a multicast packet is forwarded to multicast neighbors if the multicast packet is received on the interface used to send a unicast IP packet back to the multicast source.

RIP flush time   The amount of time in seconds before an inaccessible route is removed from the routing table. Default value is 240 seconds.

RIP holddown time   A route enters holddown when an advertisement is received, declaring the route as inaccessible or the invalid timer has expired. During the holddown time, routing information regarding a better path is ignored. The value must be at least three times the update time. Default value is 180 seconds.

RIP invalid time   Time in seconds before a route is declared inaccessible in the absence of a periodic route update. Default value is 180 seconds.

RIP update time   Time in seconds between periodic advertisements of a route. Default value is 30 seconds.

route flap   When an interface is continually going from an up state to a down state.

route leaking   In IS-IS, the process of redistributing selected Level 2 routes into an area as Level 1 routes.

route redistribution   The process of taking routes from one routing protocol and turning them into routes in another protocol.

route reflector   In BGP, a technique used to reduce the number of IBGP connections. Client IBGP routers require only an IBGP connection to the route reflector.

router ID   A 32-bit number used to identify a router.

Routing Information Protocol (RIP)   A dynamic distance vector IP routing protocol.

scalable protocol   A protocol that continues to function well as the size of the system grows.

socket   The combination of a port number and an IP address is sufficient to identify a particular application on a specific host.

source address   Where the mail is from.

split horizon   A rule that states that a router will not advertise a route out an interface if the route was originally learned on that interface.

static route   A route that is manually configured on a router and does not change.

static RP   A PIM SM implementation using predefined RPs.

stub area (OSPF)   External routes are not advertised into the area. Instead, a default route is advertised.

stuck in active (SIA)   The position an EIGRP route is in when there is not a feasible successor, and replies from neighbors regarding the route have not been received in a specified amount of time.

subnet mask   A 32-bit number used to identify the network or prefix of an IP address. The 1s in a subnet mask identify the network prefix and the 0s identify the IP host address on the indicated network.

subnetting   When more bits are used for the network address portion of an IP address than are used with the Class A, B, and C address types.

successor   The next-hop EIGRP router with the lowest feasible distance to the destination.

summarization   Grouping multiple destinations into one address. Also referred to as aggregation or information hiding.

supernetting   When fewer bits are used for the network address portion of an IP address than are used with the Class A, B, and C address types.

totally not-so-stubby area (OSPF)   External routes are advertised by an OSPF ASBR into a not-so-stubby area as NSSA routes along with a default route. OSPF interarea routes are not advertised into a totally not-so-stubby area. These routes are converted to external routes on the ABR. The ABR does not advertise external routes into the NSSA.

totally stubby area (OSPF)   External and OSPF interarea routes are not advertised into the area. Instead, a default route is advertised.

triggered update   An update that is sent immediately whenever a change occurs to a route.

update time   *See* RIP update time.

variable-length subnet mask (VLSM)   Capability to use different subnet mask lengths for subnets of the same major network number.

virtual interface   *See* loopback interface.

wildcard bits   The inverse of the subnet mask used with IGRP, EIGRP, and network interfaces.

INDEX

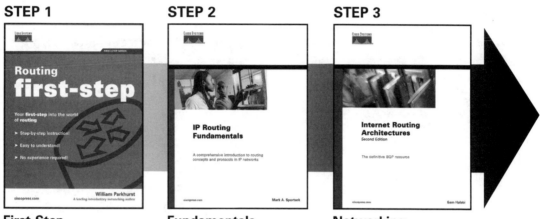

IF YOU'RE USING

CISCO PRODUCTS,

YOU'RE QUALIFIED

TO RECEIVE A

FREE SUBSCRIPTION

TO CISCO'S

PREMIER PUBLICATION,

PACKET™ MAGAZINE.

Packet delivers complete coverage of
cutting-edge networking trends and
innovations, as well as current product
updates. A magazine for technical, hands-on
Cisco users, it delivers valuable information
for enterprises, service providers, and
small and midsized businesses.

Packet is a quarterly publication. To
start your free subscription, click on the
URL and follow the prompts:
www.cisco.com/go/packet/subscribe

YES! I'm requesting a **free** subscription to *Packet*™ magazine.

❏ No. I'm not interested at this time.

❏ Mr.
❏ Ms.

First Name (Please Print) _____ Last Name _____

Title/Position (Required) _____

Company (Required) _____

Address _____

City _____ State/Province _____

Zip/Postal Code _____ Country _____

Telephone (Include country and area codes) _____ Fax _____

E-mail _____

Signature (Required) _____ Date _____

❏ I would like to receive additional information on Cisco's services and products by e-mail.

1. Do you or your company:
A ❏ Use Cisco products   C ❏ Both
B ❏ Resell Cisco products   D ❏ Neither

2. Your organization's relationship to Cisco Systems:
A ❏ Customer/End User   E ❏ Integrator   J ❏ Consultant
B ❏ Prospective Customer   F ❏ Non-Authorized Reseller   K ❏ Other (specify):
C ❏ Cisco Reseller   G ❏ Cisco Training Partner
D ❏ Cisco Distributor   I ❏ Cisco OEM _____

3. How many people does your entire company employ?
A ❏ More than 10,000   D ❏ 500 to 999   G ❏ Fewer than 100
B ❏ 5,000 to 9,999   E ❏ 250 to 499
C ❏ 1,000 to 4,999   F ❏ 100 to 249

4. Is your company a Service Provider?
A ❏ Yes   B ❏ No

5. Your involvement in network equipment purchases:
A ❏ Recommend   B ❏ Approve   C ❏ Neither

6. Your personal involvement in networking:
A ❏ Entire enterprise at all sites   F ❏ Public network
B ❏ Departments or network segments at more than one site   D ❏ No involvement
C ❏ Single department or network segment   E ❏ Other (specify): _____

7. Your Industry:
A ❏ Aerospace   G ❏ Education (K–12)   K ❏ Health Care
B ❏ Agriculture/Mining/Construction   U ❏ Education (College/Univ.)   L ❏ Telecommunications
C ❏ Banking/Finance   H ❏ Government—Federal   M ❏ Utilities/Transportation
D ❏ Chemical/Pharmaceutical   I ❏ Government—State   N ❏ Other (specify):
E ❏ Consultant   J ❏ Government—Local _____
F ❏ Computer/Systems/Electronics

CPRESS

PACKET

Packet magazine serves as the premier publication linking customers to Cisco Systems, Inc. Delivering complete coverage of cutting-edge networking trends and innovations, *Packet* is a magazine for technical, hands-on users. It delivers industry-specific information for enterprise, service provider, and small and midsized business market segments. A toolchest for planners and decision makers, *Packet* contains a vast array of practical information, boasting sample configurations, real-life customer examples, and tips on getting the most from your Cisco Systems' investments. Simply put, *Packet* magazine is straight talk straight from the worldwide leader in networking for the Internet, Cisco Systems, Inc.

We hope you'll take advantage of this useful resource. I look forward to hearing from you!

Cecelia Glover
Packet Circulation Manager
packet@external.cisco.com
www.cisco.com/go/packet

PACKET